iGen

Also by Jean M. Twenge

Generation Me

The Impatient Woman's Guide to Getting Pregnant

The Narcissism Epidemic (coauthor)

iGen

Why Today's Super-Connected Kids Are Growing
Up Less Rebellious, More Tolerant, Less Happy—
and Completely Unprepared for Adulthood*

* And what that means for the rest of us

Jean M. Twenge, PhD

ATRIA BOOKS

New York   London   Toronto   Sydney   New Delhi

ATRIA
BOOKS

An Imprint of Simon & Schuster, Inc.
1230 Avenue of the Americas
New York, NY 10020

First Atria Books hardcover edition August 2017

ATRIA BOOKS and colophon are trademarks of Simon & Schuster, Inc.

For information about special discounts for bulk purchases, please contact Simon & Schuster
Special Sales at 1-866-506-1949 or business@simonandschuster.com.

The Simon & Schuster Speakers Bureau can bring authors to your live event. For more information
or to book an event, contact the Simon & Schuster Speakers Bureau at 1-866-248-3049 or visit our
website at www.simonspeakers.com.

Interior design by Kris Tobiassen of Matchbook Digital

Manufactured in the United States of America

10 9 8 7 6 5 4 3 2 1

Library of Congress Cataloging-in-Publication Data has been applied for.

ISBN 978-1-5011-5198-9
ISBN 978-1-5011-5202-3 (ebook)

For Julia, the last of iGen

Contents

Introduction — 1
WHO IS IGEN, AND HOW DO WE KNOW?

Chapter 1 — 17
IN NO HURRY: GROWING UP SLOWLY

Chapter 2 — 49
INTERNET: ONLINE TIME—OH, AND OTHER MEDIA, TOO

Chapter 3 — 69
IN PERSON NO MORE: I'M WITH YOU, BUT ONLY VIRTUALLY

Chapter 4 — 93
INSECURE: THE NEW MENTAL HEALTH CRISIS

Chapter 5 — 119
IRRELIGIOUS: LOSING MY RELIGION (AND SPIRITUALITY)

Chapter 6 — 143
INSULATED BUT NOT INTRINSIC:
MORE SAFETY AND LESS COMMUNITY

Chapter 7 — 179

**INCOME INSECURITY:
WORKING TO EARN—BUT NOT TO SHOP**

Chapter 8 — 203

INDEFINITE: SEX, MARRIAGE, AND CHILDREN

Chapter 9 — 227

**INCLUSIVE: LGBT, GENDER,
AND RACE ISSUES IN THE NEW AGE**

Chapter 10 — 259

INDEPENDENT: POLITICS

Conclusion — 289

UNDERSTANDING—AND SAVING—IGEN

Acknowledgments — 315
Notes — 317
Index — 335

Who Is iGen, and How Do We Know?

When I reach 13-year-old Athena around noon on a summer day, she sounds as if she just woke up. We chat a little about her favorite songs and TV shows, and I ask her what she likes to do with her friends. "We go to the mall," she says. "Do your parents drop you off?" I ask, remembering my own middle school days in the 1980s when I'd enjoy a few parent-free hours with my friends. "No—I go with my family," she says. "We'll go with my mom and brothers and walk a little behind them. I just have to tell my mom where we're going. I have to check in every hour or every thirty minutes."

Hanging out at the mall with your mom around isn't the only difference in teens' social lives these days. Athena and her friends at her middle school in Houston, Texas, communicate using their phones more than they see each other in person. Their favorite medium is Snapchat, a smartphone app that allows users to send pictures that quickly disappear. They particularly like Snapchat's "dog filter," which inserts a cartoonish dog nose and ears on people's heads as they snap photos. "It's awesome—it's the cutest filter ever," she says. They make sure they keep up their Snapstreaks, which show how many days in a row they have Snapchatted with each other. Sometimes they screenshot particularly ridiculous pictures of friends so they can keep them—"it's good blackmail."

Athena says she spent most of the summer hanging out by herself in her room with her phone. "I would rather be on my phone in my room watching Netflix than spending time with my family. That's what I've been doing most of the summer. I've been on my phone more than I've been with actual people." That's just the way her generation is, she says. "We didn't have a choice to know any life without iPads or iPhones. I think we like our phones more than we like actual people."

iGen has arrived.

Born in 1995 and later, they grew up with cell phones, had an Instagram page before they started high school, and do not remember a time before the Internet.

The oldest members of iGen were early adolescents when the iPhone was introduced in 2007 and high school students when the iPad entered the scene in 2010. The *i* in the names of these devices stands for *Internet*, and the Internet was commercialized in 1995. If this generation is going to be named after anything, the iPhone just might be it: according to a fall 2015 marketing survey, two out of three US teens owned an iPhone, about as complete a market saturation as possible for a product. "You have to have an iPhone," said a 17-year-old interviewed in the social media exposé *American Girls*. "It's like Apple has a monopoly on adolescence."

The complete dominance of the smartphone among teens has had ripple effects across every area of iGen'ers' lives, from their social interactions to their mental health. They are the first generation for whom Internet access has been constantly available, right there in their hands. Even if their smartphone is a Samsung and their tablet is a Kindle, these young people are all iGen'ers. (And yes, even if they are lower income: teens from disadvantaged backgrounds now spend just as much time online as those with more resources—another effect of smartphones.) The average teen checks her phone more than eighty times a day.

But technology is not the only change shaping this generation. The *i* in iGen represents the *individualism* its members take for granted, a broad trend that grounds their bedrock sense of equality as well as their rejection of traditional social rules. It also captures the *income inequality* that is creating a deep insecurity among iGen'ers, who worry about doing the right things to become financially successful, to become a "have" rather than a "have not." Due to these influences and many others, iGen is distinct from every previous generation in how its members spend their time, how they behave, and their attitudes toward religion, sexuality, and politics. They socialize in completely new ways, reject once sacred social taboos, and want different things from their lives and careers. They are obsessed with safety and fearful of their economic futures, and they have no patience for inequality based on gender, race, or sexual orientation. They are at the forefront of the worst mental health crisis in decades, with rates of teen depression and suicide skyrocketing since 2011. Contrary to the prevalent idea that children are growing up faster than previous generations did, iGen'ers are growing up more slowly: 18-year-olds now act like 15-year-olds used to, and 13-year-olds like 10-year-olds. Teens are physically safer than ever, yet they are more mentally vulnerable.

Drawing from four large, nationally representative surveys of 11 million Americans since the 1960s, I've identified ten important trends shaping iGen'ers and, ultimately, all of us: *In No Hurry* (the extension of childhood into adolescence), *Internet* (how much time they are really spending on their phones—and what that has replaced), *In person no more* (the decline in in-person social interaction), *Insecure* (the sharp rise in mental health issues), *Irreligious* (the decline in religion), *Insulated but not intrinsic* (the interest in safety and the decline in civic involvement), *Income insecurity* (new attitudes toward work), *Indefinite* (new attitudes toward sex, relationships, and children), *Inclusive* (acceptance, equality, and free speech debates), and *Independent* (their political views). iGen is the ideal place to look for trends that will shape our culture in the years to come, as its members are very young but still old enough to express their views and report on their experiences.

I've been researching generational differences for nearly twenty-five years, starting when I was a 22-year-old PhD student in personality psychology at the University of Michigan. Back then I focused on how my own generation, Generation X, differed from Boomers (more gender equality and more anxiety, among other things). As time went on, I found a broad array of generational differences in behaviors, attitudes, and personality traits that distinguished the Millennials, the generation born in the 1980s and early 1990s. That research culminated in my 2006 book *Generation Me*, updated in 2014, a look at how the Millennials differed from their predecessors. Most of the generational differences that defined GenX and the Millennials came along gradually, building to a crescendo only after a decade or two of steady change. I had grown accustomed to line graphs of trends that looked like hills slowly growing into peaks, with cultural change making its mark after a measured rollout that started with a few young people and swelled to many.

But around 2012, I started seeing large, abrupt shifts in teens' behaviors and emotional states. All of a sudden, the line graphs looked like steep mountains—rapid drop-offs erased the gains of decades in just a few years; after years of gradual inclines or hollows, sheer cliffs suddenly brought traits to all-time highs. In all of my analyses of generational data—some of it reaching back to the 1930s—I had never seen anything like it.

At first I wondered if these were random blips that would disappear after a year or two. But they didn't—the trends kept going, creating sustained, and often unprecedented, trends. As I dug into the data, a pattern emerged: many of the large changes began around 2011 or 2012. That was too late to be caused by the Great Recession, which officially lasted from 2007 to 2009.

Then it occurred to me: 2011–12 was exactly when the majority of Americans started to own cell phones that could access the Internet, popularly known as smartphones. The product of this sudden shift is iGen.

Such broad generational shifts have big implications. A whole new group of young people who act and think differently—even differently from their neighbors the Millennials—is emerging into young adulthood. We all need to understand them, including friends and family looking out for them, businesses searching for new recruits, colleges and universities educating and guiding students, and marketers figuring out how to sell to them. Members of iGen also need to understand themselves as they explain to their elders and their slightly older peers how they approach the world and what makes them different.

Generational differences are larger and more broadly influential than ever. The biggest difference between the Millennials and their predecessors was in worldview, with more focus on the self and less on social rules (thus the term *Generation Me*). But with the popularity of the smartphone, iGen'ers differ most in how they spend their time. The life experiences they have every day are radically different from those of their predecessors. In some ways, this is an even more fundamental generational shift than that which created the Millennials; perhaps that's why the trends announcing the arrival of iGen were so sudden and large.

The Birth Year Cutoffs

The breakneck speed of technological change has created a surprisingly large gap between those born in the 1980s and those who started life in the 1990s. "I am not a true digital native," Juliet Lapidos, born in 1983, wrote in the *New York Times*. "The Internet wasn't a fact of nature. I had to learn what it was and how to use it. . . . I didn't have a mobile phone until I was 19." Lapidos was 19 in 2002, when texting required hitting the same key several times on your flip phone and surfing the Web meant sitting at a desktop computer. When the iPhone was introduced just five years later in 2007, all of that changed. iGen'ers are the first generation to enter adolescence with smartphones already in their hands—a stark difference with wide-ranging implications.

iGen got here faster than anyone anticipated. Until recently, most of the generational patter focused on Millennials, sometimes defined as Americans born between 1980 and 1999. Yet this is a long span for a recent generation: Generation X, immediately before the Millennials, lasted only fourteen years, from 1965 to 1979. If the Millennial generation lasts the same amount of time as GenX, the last Millennial birth year is instead 1994, meaning that iGen begins with those born in 1995—conveniently, that's also the year the Internet was born. Other milestones fall close to 1995 as well. In 2006, Facebook opened up to anyone over the age of 13—so those born since 1993 have been able to live their entire adolescence on social networking sites. A cut in the mid-1990s also makes sense based on the hard data: in 2011, the year when everything started to change in the survey data, the 13- to 18-year-olds answering the questions were born between 1993 and 1998.

It's anyone's guess when iGen will end; I'd put my money on fourteen to seventeen years after 1995. That would mean the last iGen'ers were born somewhere between 2009 and 2015, with 2012 right at the middle of that range. That makes the birth year span of iGen 1995–2012. As time goes on, those boundaries might be adjusted up or down, but 1995–2012 is a solid place to start. A lot is going to depend on the technology developed in the next ten years and whether it changes young people's lives as much as the smartphone did. With 1995–2012 as the range, the first iGen'ers graduated from high school in 2012 and the last will in 2030 (see Figure 0.1).

Any generational cutoff is arbitrary; there is no exact science or official consensus to determine which birth years belong to which generation. In addition, people born right before and right after the cutoff have experienced essentially the same culture, but those born ten years apart but technically within the same generation have experienced a different culture. Nevertheless, generational labels with specific cutoffs are useful; just like city boundaries, the demarcation of 18 as legal adulthood, and personality types, they

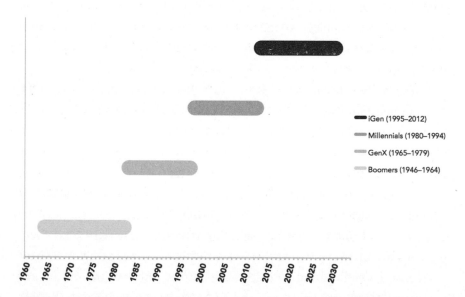

Figure 0.1: Time span when each generation dominated the population of high school seniors and entering college students, based on the generational birth-year cutoffs.

allow us to define and describe people despite the obvious limitations of using a bright line when a fuzzy one is closer to the truth. No matter where we set the cutoff, it's important to understand how those born after the mid-1990s differ from those born only a few years before.

The Name

As a label, *iGen* is concise, broad, and relatively neutral. At least one writer has described the *iGen* label as "bland," but that's actually a strength. A generational label needs to be inclusive enough to capture an extensive swath of people and neutral enough to be accepted by the generation itself and older generations. It also needs to capture something about the generation's experience, and for iGen'ers, the Internet and smartphones have defined many of their experiences thus far. The prominent magazine *AdvertisingAge* has backed *iGen* as the best name for the post-Millennials. "We think it's the name that best fits and will best lead to understanding of this generation," Matt Carmichael, *AdvertisingAge*'s director of data strategy, told *USA Today*.

Another name suggested for this group is *Generation Z*. However, that label works only if the generation before them is called *Generation Y*, and hardly anyone uses *Generation Y* now that the term *Millennials* has won out. That makes *Generation Z* dead on arrival. Not to mention that young people do not want to be named after the generation older than themselves. That's why *Baby Busters* never caught on for Generation X and why *Generation Y* never stuck for the Millennials. *Generation Z* is derivative, and the generational labels that stick are always original.

Neil Howe, who along with the late William Strauss coined the term *Millennials*, has suggested that the next generation be called the *Homelanders*, given their upbringing in the time of homeland security. I doubt that any generation wants to be named after the government agency that makes you take your shoes off at the airport. Howe also believes that the generation after the Millennials doesn't begin until those born in 2005, which seems unlikely given the fast pace of technological change and the sudden shifts in teens' time use and traits starting around 2011. Other labels have been suggested as well. In 2015, teens polled by MTV chose *the Founders* as their preferred generational label. But: founders of what?

As far as I know, I was the first to use the term *iGen*, introducing it in the first edition of my book *Generation Me* in April 2006. I've been using the term *iGen* to talk about the post-Millennial generation for a while; in 2010 I named my speaking and consulting business iGen Consulting.

The Data

What we know about iGen so far is just beginning to take shape. Polls will announce that 29% of young adults don't affiliate with a religion or that 86% of teens worry about finding a job. But these single-time polls could be capturing beliefs universal to young people across all generations. Boomer or GenX teens in the 1970s or 1990s may also have shunned religion and worried about employment. One-time polls with no comparison group tell us nothing about cultural change or iGen'ers distinctive experiences. You can't draw a generational conclusion with data from only one generation. Yet so far, nearly all the books and articles about iGen have relied on minimally useful polls like those.

Other one-time surveys include members of several generations. That's better, but even they have a major flaw: they can't separate the effects of age from those of generation. If a study finds (for example) that iGen'ers want to make friends at work more than GenX'ers do, that might be because iGen'ers are young and single and GenX'ers are older and married. In a one-time survey, there's no way to tell. That's unfortunate, because if you're capturing differences based on age, it doesn't tell you much about what has changed—whether what worked to motivate young employees or students ten years ago will work now.

To really understand what's unique about this generation—what is actually *new* about it—we need to compare iGen to previous generations when their members were young. We need data collected across time. That's what the large, over-time surveys I analyze in this book do: they ask young people the same questions year after year so their responses can be compared over several generations.

I draw primarily from four databases. One, called Monitoring the Future (MtF), has asked high school seniors (12th graders) more than a thousand questions every year since 1976 and queried 8th and 10th graders since 1991. The Youth Risk Behavior Surveillance System (YRBSS, administered by the Centers for Disease Control and Prevention) has surveyed high school students since 1991. The American Freshman (AF) Survey, administered by the Higher Education Research Institute, has questioned students entering four-year colleges and universities since 1966. Finally, the General Social Survey (GSS) has examined adults 18 and over since 1972. (For more details on these surveys and their methods, see Appendix A.) These surveys can show us how Boomers were grooving when they were in high school in the 1970s, how GenX'ers rocked it in the 1980s and 1990s, how Millennials bopped through the 2000s, and how iGen is making its own waves in the 2010s.

By comparing one generation to another at the same age, we can observe the views of young people about themselves, rather than relying on older people's reflections on a time gone by. We can see differences that are due to cultural changes and not to age. These differences can't be dismissed by saying that "young people have always been this way." In fact, these surveys show that young people are now quite different from young people in previous decades. The relative youth of these samples is also exciting—it allows us a peek at iGen'ers as they are forming their identities, starting to articulate their opinions, and finding their path toward adulthood.

These data sources have three other distinct advantages. First, they are large in sample size and scope, collecting data on thousands of people every year who have answered hundreds of questions anonymously. All told, they have surveyed 11 million people. Second, the survey administrators were careful to ensure that the people answering the questions were representative of the US population in terms of gender, race, location, and socioeconomic status. That means that the conclusions can be generalized to American young people as a whole (or, in the case of college students, to college students as a whole). Third, all of these data sets are publicly available online— they are not hiding behind paywalls or fees, so the data are transparent and open. These surveys are national treasures of Big Data, providing a glimpse of the lives and beliefs of Americans in decades gone by as well as an up-to-date look at young people in recent years. With this solid mass of generational data now emerging, we no longer need to rely on shaky one-time studies to understand iGen.

Because the survey samples are nationally representative, they represent American young people as a whole, not just an isolated group. Of course, the demographics of American youth have changed over time; for example, more are Hispanic than in previous decades. It's fair to ask whether the generational shifts are solely due to these demographic shifts—that's a question of cause rather than accuracy, but it's still worth asking. For that reason and others, I've also examined whether the trends appear across different groups (for example, black, white, and Hispanic; girls and boys; in the Northeast, Midwest, South, and West; in urban, rural, and suburban areas; lower socioeconomic status and higher socio-economic status—such as whether one's parents attended college or not). With only a few exceptions, the generational trends appear across all of these demographic groups. These sweeping changes appear among poor teens and rich ones, those of every ethnic background, and in cities, sub-urbs, and small towns. If you're curious about what the trends look like within these groups, I've put figures with some of these breakdowns in the appendices.

For a preview of some generational differences, take the quiz on the next page to find out how much your experiences overlap with those of iGen. Regardless of when you were born, how iGen are you?

The Demographics—and the World

Using the birth years 1995 to 2012, iGen includes 74 million Americans, about 24% of the population. That means one in four Americans is a member of iGen—all the more reason to understand them. iGen is the most ethnically diverse generation in American history: one in four is Hispanic, and nearly 5% are multiracial. Non-Hispanic whites are a bare majority, at 53%. The birth years at the end of iGen are the first to have a nonwhite majority: beginning with the iGen'ers born in late 2009, less than 50% are non-Hispanic whites.

**Take this 15-item quiz to find out how "iGen" you are.
Answer each question with "yes" or "no."**

_____ 1. In the past 24 hours, did you spend at least an hour total texting on a cell phone?

_____ 2. Do you have a Snapchat account?

_____ 3. Do you consider yourself a religious person?

_____ 4. Did you get your driver's license by the time you turned 17?

_____ 5. Do you think same-sex marriage should be legal?

_____ 6. Did you ever drink alcohol (more than a few sips) by the time you turned 16?

_____ 7. Did you fight with your parents a lot when you were a teen?

_____ 8. Were more than one-third of the other students at your high school a different race than you?

_____ 9. When you were in high school, did you spend nearly every weekend night out with your friends?

_____ 10. Did you have a job during the school year when you were in high school?

_____ 11. Do you agree that safe spaces and trigger warnings are good ideas and that efforts should be made to reduce microaggressions?

_____ 12. Are you a political independent?

_____ 13. Do you support the legalization of marijuana?

_____ 14. Is having sex without much emotion involved desirable?

_____ 15. When you were in high school, did you feel left out and lonely fairly often?

SCORING: Give yourself 1 point for answering "yes" to questions 1, 2, 5, 8, 11, 12, 13, 14, and 15. Give yourself 1 point for answering "no" to questions 3, 4, 6, 7, 9, and 10. The higher your score, the more iGen you are in your behaviors, attitudes, and beliefs.

That means no one group is in the majority, practically the definition of diversity. The generation after iGen—those born in 2013 and later—will be the first majority nonwhite generation.

The data here are from US samples, so the conclusions can't be directly generalized to other countries. However, many of the generational shifts that appear here are emerging in other cultures as well. Researchers around the world are documenting many of the same trends, with new studies constantly appearing. The Internet and smartphone boom hit other industrialized countries at about the same time as these technologies took hold in the United States, and the consequences are likely to be similar.

The Context

To flesh out my number crunching with a sense of real people, I have taken a deeper look at iGen in a number of ways. First, I interviewed twenty-three iGen'ers in person or on the phone for up to two hours, delving into their thoughts on pop culture, teen social life, current events, campus controversies, and their all-important smartphones. These young people ranged in age from 12 to 20; they were black, white, Asian American, Latino/a, and Middle Eastern American; from Virginia, Connecticut, Illinois, Ohio, Texas, Minnesota, Georgia, and California; and attending middle school, high school, community college, or four-year college, the vast majority at institutions that would not be considered particularly elite. I also posed written interview questions online on sites such as Amazon's MTurk Requester, conducted a survey of 250 introductory psychology students at San Diego State University, where I teach, and discussed various issues as they came up in classes with my undergraduate students. I also read a wide array of opinion pieces from college newspapers around the country. These sources are not nationally representative, so they are not a replacement for the survey data. These iGen'ers' individual experiences are just that and might not be representative of their generation. The survey data are always the gold standard; the interviews and essays illustrate that data and do not in any way replace it. They are, however, a path to humanizing the young people behind the data. As iGen'ers age and start to shape our world, they deserve to be heard in addition to being understood empirically.

When I wrote *Generation Me*, my book about the Millennials, I was just a little older than the cohort I was writing about and had experienced many of the same cultural phenomena. Hard data from surveys formed the core of that book, just as they do here, but as a GenX'er my own life mirrored much of what I wrote about. That's not as true in this book, where I'm twenty-five to thirty years older than iGen teens. (To my chagrin, one of the college students I interviewed told me I reminded him of his mother. As it turned out, I actually am the same age as his parents.) My role here is much more observer than participant. However, I now have another perspective: my three daughters were born in 2006, 2009, and 2012, in the later years of iGen. I have thus seen firsthand some of the quintessential iGen experiences such as a toddler, barely old enough to walk, confidently swiping her way through an iPad. I've also experienced having a 6-year-old ask for a cell phone and hearing a 9-year-old describe the latest app to sweep the 4th grade. Maybe if I name their generation, my kids will listen to me when I tell them to put on their shoes.

In this book, the voices of iGen'ers—whether the statistics from the large surveys or their own words in interviews—speak for themselves. The book also features more than a hundred graphs of the survey data spanning the generations so you can see the data for yourself—not just the data for iGen but the data for Millennials, GenX'ers, and Boomers as well. The graphs summarize a large amount of data in a small amount of space (a graph is worth a thousand words). You'll see firsthand how iGen stands out, with the abrupt drop-offs and sheer rock faces around 2011 for many traits and behaviors and more gradual changes in others.

The Caveats

As a generations researcher, I'm often asked questions such as "Why are you blaming the kids? Isn't it the parents' fault?" (Or "the Boomers' fault?" or "GenX'ers fault?") This question makes two false assumptions: first, it assumes that all generational changes are negative; second, it implies that a single cause (such as parenting) can be identified for each change. Neither is true. Some generational changes are positive, some are negative, and many are both. There's a natural human tendency to classify things as all good or all bad, but with cultural changes, it's better to see the gray areas and the trade-offs. Given that many generational differences are positive or at least neutral, using words such as *fault* and *blame* doesn't really make sense. It's also counterproductive, leaving us squabbling about whom to blame rather than understanding the trends, both good and bad. Cultural change also has many causes, not just one—it's not just parents, but technology, media, business, and education working together to create an entire culture that is radically different from the one our parents and grandparents experienced. It's nobody's fault or everybody's fault. Cultures change, and generations change with them; that's the important point. It's not a contest to see which generation is worse (or better); the culture has changed, and we're all in this together.

Once we know that a generational change has occurred, the natural next question is "Why?" This can be a difficult question to answer. The gold standard in science for showing that one thing causes another is an experiment, in which people are randomly assigned to have different experiences. For generational differences, that would mean randomly assigning people to grow up at different times—a true mission impossible. The next best way to identify possible causes is a two-step process. First, the two things must be correlated with each other. For example, we can see whether teens who spend more time on social media are more depressed. Second, the two things must change at the same time and in the correct direction. If social media use and depression both increase during the same years, one might cause the other. If they don't (say, one goes up while the other stays about the same), one is likely not causing the other. This approach can, at the very least, rule out possible causes. It can't fully rule causes in, but it can provide evidence that points toward something as the culprit.

Another caveat: the numbers here are averages. For example, the average iGen teen spends more time online than the average Millennial did in 2005. Of course, some iGen teens spend little time online, and some Millennials spent a lot of time—there is considerable overlap between the two groups.

Just because there is an average difference doesn't mean that everyone in the generation is exactly the same. So why not treat everyone as an individual? If you're going to analyze data, that's just not possible. Statistics rely on averages, so you can't compare groups of people without them. That's why virtually every scientific study of people relies on averages. This isn't stereotyping; it's comparing groups using a scientific method. Stereotyping occurs when someone assumes that any individual person must be representative of his or her group. It's not a valid criticism of generational studies to say that they describe "everyone" in a generation in one way or to say that they "overgeneralize." Any overgeneralizing that occurs is due to a mistaken interpretation by individual people, not to the data themselves.

What if the cultural changes are affecting everyone and not just iGen? In many cases, they are. This is known as a time-period difference, or a cultural change that has an equal effect on people of all ages. Pure time-period effects are fairly rare, because age usually affects how people experience events. Cultural change often affects the young first, and then spreads to older people. Smartphones and social media are a perfect example of that. However, much of this book is about how iGen'ers' adolescence is markedly different from their predecessors', which is naturally a generational difference as the teen years of Boomers, GenX'ers, and Millennials are already past.

The Way Forward

Where iGen goes, the country goes. Parents of adolescents wonder how their teens' constant smartphone use will affect their brains, their emotions, and their relationships. The majority of college students are already iGen, bringing their values, viewpoints, and ever-present smartphones to campuses around the country. Young recruits to businesses will soon be dominated by iGen'ers, not Millennials, which may catch some companies unprepared for iGen'ers' different perspective. iGen'ers' product preferences are already shaping the marketplace with their teen and young adult influences, and they will soon dominate the lucrative 18-to-29-year-old market. iGen'ers' political preferences will shape elections far into the future, and their attitudes will dictate policy and laws. Their marriage rates and birthrates will affect the demographic balance of the country, determining whether there will be enough young workers to support Millennials and GenX'ers in their retirement. iGen is at the forefront of the enormous changes under way in the United States today, driven by the Internet, individualism, income inequality, and other forces of cultural change. Understanding iGen means understanding the future—for all of us.

So what's really different about iGen?

Chapter 1

In No Hurry: Growing Up Slowly

It's a bright fall afternoon when I arrive at a high school just outside San Diego and make my way to the psychology classroom. The teacher reminds the students that they have an exam coming up on Monday and tells them it's a "work day" for them to organize their notes and study. We move two desks into the breezeway outside the classroom, and the teacher rifles through the permission slips. "Azar," he says, and a girl with long dark hair fist-pumps the air and says, "Yes!"

Azar exudes unbridled enthusiasm for just about everything, talking at the rapid, singsong pace favored by many southern California teens. "Have you seen *Spy*? It's sooo good," she gushes. When I ask her if she has a favorite song on the radio right now, she says, "Yes. 'Wildest Dreams' by Taylor Swift, 'Blank Space' by Taylor Swift, and 'Bad Blood' by Taylor Swift." "So you like Taylor Swift?" I tease. "Well, I wouldn't say that—I've only memorized all of her songs," she replies. When I ask her what she likes to read, she says, "Harry Potter is my life—I *love* him." She tells me she doesn't have her driver's license yet, so her mom drops her off at school.

With her fixation on Taylor Swift, her love of Harry Potter, and the rides she's getting from her mom, you might guess that Azar is 14. But she's not—she's 17.

Azar is growing up slowly, taking longer to embrace the responsibilities and pleasures of adulthood. It's tempting to think she's the exception: with porn on the Internet, sexy Halloween costumes for young girls, 7th-grade boys requesting nude pictures of their classmates, and other adults-too-soon trends gaining attention, many people believe that children and teens are instead growing up more quickly than in the past. "Childhood is gone. They have access to this world of adults they feel they have to participate in," lamented a Brooklyn middle school principal recently. Many believe that teens are barreling toward adulthood faster than ever. But are they?

(Not) Going Out and (Not) Getting It On

When I knock on the door of the neat suburban house on a Friday evening, 14-year-old Priya answers. She's a pretty Indian American with long hair and braces who is a few months into her freshman year of high school in a suburban neighborhood at the far northern edge of the city limits of San Diego. Her mother offers me a glass of ice water as we sit at their dining room table next to Priya's study books and her pink calculator; Priya is already carrying a heavy academic load of honors classes. I ask her what she does for fun with her friends. "Sometimes we make plans and go see a movie or something . . . or go out to dinner sometimes," she says. But those are not parent-free outings. "Usually, like, one parent comes along, or two, depending on how many want to go," she says. "It's kind of fun—with parents and kids." They find a movie everyone will like, she says, and the parents and children go together—just as they did when the kids were in elementary school.

I reach Jack, 15, after his busy day of school and track practice at his high school in suburban Minneapolis, where he's a sophomore. We've met in person a few times before when I've visited Minnesota—he's white, a serious young man with dark hair and a shy smile who is very close to his equally athletic family. When I ask what movies he's seen recently, he mentions two he saw with his parents and sister. That made me curious about whether he ever sees movies with his friends. "Where do you like to hang out with your friends, and what do you normally do together?" I ask. "Most of the time we go on a run or something," he says. "We have a pool at our house, and we go swimming, or I go over to their house." I ask if he's gone to any parties, and he mentions a summer party at a friend's house where they played volleyball; his friend's parents were there the whole time. His typical weekend usually involves a running event and doing something with his family. "Do you ever go places without your parents?" I ask. "Well, football games . . . but not really," he says.

Priya and Jack are increasingly typical: iGen teens are less likely to go out without their parents. The trend began with Millennials and then accelerated at a rapid clip with iGen'ers (see Figure 1.1). The numbers are stunning: 12th graders in 2015 are going out less often than 8th graders did as recently as 2009. So 18-year-olds are now going out less often than 14-year-olds did just six years prior.

These declines are not due to shifts in racial demographics: the trend is the same for white teens (see Appendix B). They also look the same for students

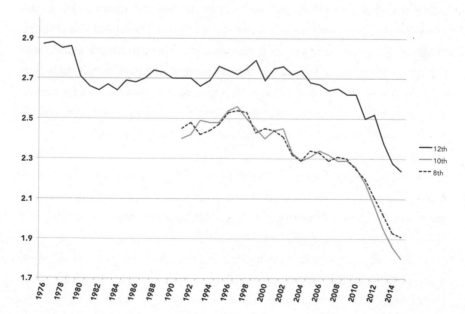

Figure 1.1. Times per week 8th, 10th, and 12th graders go out without their parents. Monitoring the Future, 1976–2015.

from working-class and middle-class homes. Nor is the trend caused by the recession: even after the economy rebounded around 2012, the number of teens' independent forays continued to slide. The more likely candidate is smartphones, used by the majority of teens since around 2011–12.

No matter what the cause, the result is the same: iGen teens are less likely to experience the freedom of being out of the house without their parents—those first tantalizing tastes of the independence of being an adult, those times when teens make their own decisions, good or bad.

Contrast this to the 1970s, when Boomer teens were growing up. Bill Yates recently published a book of his photographs of teens taken at a roller-skating rink outside Tampa, Florida, in the early 1970s. In one, a shirtless teen stands with a large bottle of peppermint schnapps stuck in the waistband of his jeans. In another, a boy who looks about 12 poses with a lit cigarette in his mouth. Several shots show couples kissing. As Yates describes it, the rink was a place where kids could get away from their parents and create a world of their own where they could drink, smoke, and make out in the backs of their cars. The photos feature the usual 1970s panoply of plaid pants, wide belts, and long hair, but what struck me the most was how adult even the youngest teens look—not physically but in their bold and insouciant independence. They gaze at the camera with the self-confidence born of making your own choices—even if your parents wouldn't think they were the right ones, and even if, objectively speaking, they are not. These are the Boomers, raised in a time when their parents were happy for them to leave the house and economic success didn't require a graduate degree.

Those kisses at the rink are also less common: iGen teens are less likely to date (see Figure 1.2, next page). Only about half as many iGen high school seniors vs. Boomers and GenX'ers at the same age) ever go out on dates. In the early 1990s, nearly three out of four 10th graders sometimes dated, but by the 2010s only about half did.

The students I interviewed assured me that they still call it "dating," so a change in wording is probably not the primary cause of the decline. The initial stage, what GenX'ers called "liking" ("Oooh, he likes you!"), iGen'ers now call "talking"—an ironic choice for a generation who prefer texting to talking on the phone. After a couple has "talked" for a while, they might

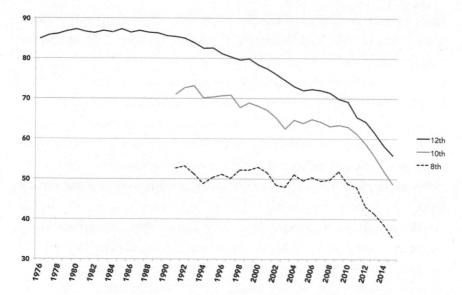

Figure 1.2. Percentage of 8th, 10th, and 12th graders who ever go out on dates. Monitoring the Future, 1976–2015.

start dating. Emily, 14 and from Minnesota, says some of her friends have gone on dates. I asked her what they usually did. "Maybe go to each other's houses. Or they might go shopping together," she said. "Normally it's the girl that's shopping and the boy is, like, following." I laughed and told her that it's about the same when you're older.

Chloe, 18 and from Ohio, has had two romantic relationships. In both, she says that about a third of their "getting to know you" conversations were done via texting and social media (that was the "talking" part) and the other two-thirds in person. So it could be that young people are still pairing up but don't see each other in person as often—with that in-person interaction necessary for it to count as a date. In other cases, parents may be more protective than they once were. "My dad always said that high school relationships were dumb, and that no one should date in high school," wrote Lauren, 19. "I always thought that it was interesting he said this, because my mom and dad started dating their sophomore year of high school and have been together ever since. When I would mention this to them they said, 'I know, we were stupid.'" Other teens, especially some boys, said they just didn't have the courage to date. Mike, 18, wrote, "Nope. I ain't got no game. It was a lack of confidence in myself which brought upon a female famine during high school."

The lack of dating leads to the next surprising fact about iGen: they are less likely to have sex than teens in previous decades (see Figure 1.3).

The drop is the largest for 9th graders, where the number of sexually active teens has almost been cut in half since the 1990s. The average teen now has sex around the spring of 11th grade, while most GenX'ers in the 1990s got started a year earlier, by the spring of 10th grade. Fifteen percent fewer 12th graders in 2015 (vs. 1991) have had sex.

Fewer teens having sex is one of the reasons behind what many see as one of the most positive youth trends in recent years: the teen birthrate hit an all-time low in 2015, cut by more than half since its modern peak in the early 1990s (see Figure 1.4, next page). Only 2.4% of girls aged 15 to 19 had a baby in 2015, down from 6% in 1992. So with fewer teens having sex, fewer are getting pregnant and fewer are giving birth at a young age. Parenthood,

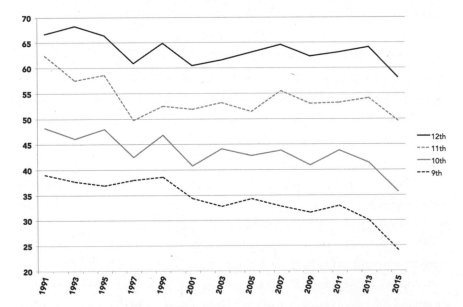

Figure 1.3. Percentage of high school students who have ever had sex, by grade. Youth Risk Behavior Surveillance System, 1991–2015.

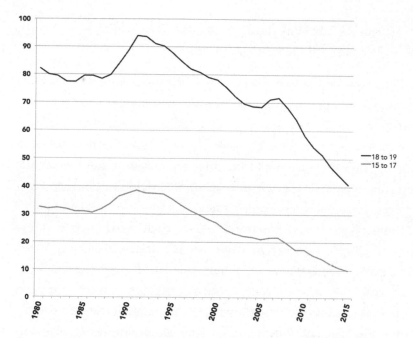

Figure 1.4. Teen birthrate per 1,000 population among 18- to 19-year olds in the United States. Centers for Disease Control, National Center for Health Statistics, 1980–2015.

one of the more irrevocable milestones of adulthood, is less likely to be reached by today's teens.

The low teen birthrate is also an interesting contrast to the post–World War II era—in 1960, for example, 9% of teen girls had babies. Back then, though, most of them were married; the median age at first marriage for women in 1960 was 20. Thus, half of the women getting married for the first time in 1960 were teenagers—unthinkable today but completely accepted then. These days, marriage and children are many years off for the average teen, something we'll explore more in chapter 8 (along with another intriguing question: Does the trend toward less sexual activity continue into adulthood?). Overall, the decline in teen sex and teen pregnancy is another sign of the slowed developmental speed of iGen: teens are waiting longer to have sex and have babies just as they are waiting longer to go out without their parents and date.

An Interlude About Why Teens Act Less like Adults— and Why It's Not All Good or All Bad

You might be wondering *why* teens are less likely to do adult things such as go out without their parents and have sex, and whether this trend of growing up more slowly is a good thing or a bad thing. An approach called *life history theory* provides some insights. Life history theory argues that how fast teens grow up depends on where and when they are raised. In more academic parlance, developmental speed is an adaptation to a cultural context.

Today's teens follow a slow life strategy, common in times and places where families have fewer children and cultivate each child longer and more intensely. That's a good description of our current culture in the United States, when the average family has two children, kids can start playing organized sports at 3, and preparing for college seems to begin in elementary school. Compare that to a fast life strategy, where families are larger and parents focus on subsistence rather than quality. This fast life strategy involves less preparation for the future and more focus on just getting through the day. The fast strategy was a more common approach in the Boomer era, when fewer labor-saving devices were available and the average woman had four children—and, as a result, some of them ended up playing in the street. When my uncle told me about going skinny-dipping in the river when he was 8, I wondered why his parents had let him do that and why they hadn't been with him. Then I remembered: his parents had seven other children and ran a farm, and it was 1946. The goal was survival, not violin lessons by age 5.

Life history theory explicitly notes that slow or fast life strategies are not necessarily good or bad; they just are. Keep this in mind as we explore the trends; just because something has changed from previous generations does not make it bad (or good), and I do not mean to imply that it does. For example, in some cultures, dating in early high school is considered good— it means a young person is popular with the opposite sex and will have no trouble producing the grandchildren the parents want, and quickly. In other cultures, early dating is considered bad—if she dates too soon, the thinking goes, she might focus too much on relationships and won't finish college. So the "bad"-vs.-"good" question depends a lot on one's cultural perspective. I suggest the same caution about seeing behaviors as "mature" or "immature." Is going out with your friends mature or immature? What about having sex? They are really neither—or both. Such labels also miss the more complete, and more accurate, explanation that teens are now on a different developmental path. The key is not bad or good, mature or immature, but that these milestones of adulthood are now passed later.

Another crucial point: nearly all of the generational shifts in this chapter and the rest appear across different demographic groups. The samples we're drawing from here are nationally representative, meaning the teens reflect the demographics of the United States. Every group is included. Even within specific groups, the trends consistently appear; they are present in working-class homes as well as upper-middle-class ones, among minorities as well as whites, among girls as well as boys, in big cities, suburbs, and small towns, and all across the country. That means they are not isolated to the white, upper-middle-class teens whom journalists often wring their hands over. Youths of every racial group, region, and class are growing up more slowly.

License to Drive

I reach Matthew, 19, by phone in his room at a small college in Pennsylvania. He's originally from New England and wants to be a high school history teacher. In online pictures from his high school tennis matches, he's a lanky young man with a graceful swing. His playlist on YouTube features videos by the band Imagine Dragons and a College Humor video called "Gluten Free Duck" (featuring a duck that won't eat bread crumbs and asks for "a brown rice tortilla or maybe some quinoa crackers?"). When we talk, he is articulate and thoughtful, discussing the history books he likes and his views on social issues. He didn't get his driver's license until he was 18, two years later than he legally could have. For most of his senior year, he took the bus to school, or his parents would pick him up. "Why did you wait?" I ask. "I was too lazy to get around to it," he says. "I was actually pretty nervous as well, because I have an older sister and she failed the [driver's] test one or two times—and she's really smart, so I thought if she failed it there's no way I'm going to pass it. I guess I was nervous and afraid of failing." Teens have always been nervous about passing their driving tests, of course, but the lure of adult freedom was usually strong enough to overcome it.

Matthew typifies an iGen trend: though nearly all Boomer high school students had their driver's license by spring of their senior year, by 2015 only 72% did. That means more than one out of four iGen'ers do not have a driver's license by the time they graduate from high school (see Figure 1.5).

For some, Mom is such a good chauffeur that there's no urgent need to drive. "My parents drove me everywhere and never complained so I always had rides," wrote Hannah, 21. "By 18 most of my friends had a license and cars but I was still not in a hurry. I didn't get my license until my mom told me I had to because she could not keep driving me to school." She finally got her license six months past her eighteenth birthday. Other iGen'ers said similar things, seeing getting a license as something to be nagged into by one's parents—a notion that would have seemed nonsensical to previous generations of teens, who were chomping at the bit to get their license. Juan, 19, said he didn't get his license right away "because my parents didn't 'push' me to get my license."

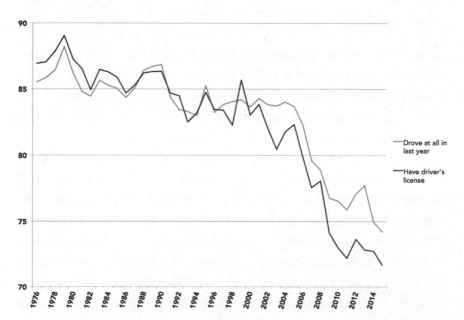

Figure 1.5. Percentage of 12th graders who drove at all in the last year and who have a driver's license. Monitoring the Future, 1976–2015.

As a GenX'er, that sentence makes my jaw drop every time I read it. It used to be the other way around: you wanted to get your license, and your parents wanted you to wait. In the 1988 Corey Haim and Corey Feldman vehicle *License to Drive*, Haim's character fails his driving test but takes his dad's car out for the night anyway (his parents don't notice because his mother is just about to give birth to their fourth child—a nice manifestation of life history theory). Feldman's character delivers a rousing speech about the greater meaning of getting a driver's license and what it means for one's dating life and independence. "You've had to stand and watch as all of the pretty girls drove off in some older jerk's car. Humiliation—I know, I've been through it," he says. "But that's all over now. That thing in your wallet—that's no ordinary piece of paper. That is a driver's license! . . . It's a license to live, a license to be free, to go wherever, whenever, and with whomever you choose!" As he talks, patriotic music plays in the background, and he stands tall with pride.

iGen'ers, on the other hand, think about getting their license and say, "Meh."

Are fewer teens driving because of ride-sharing services such as Uber and Lyft? Not likely. First, these services usually require that riders be 18 years old or older, so most high school students can't use them alone. In addition, Uber debuted in 2009 and Lyft in 2012, and the decline in getting a driver's license began long before that. The decline appears in suburbs and rural areas, where Uber is often unavailable. The most consistent decline appears among suburban teens—suggesting that the downslide has more to do with Mom and Dad driving Junior around (see Appendix B).

It's true that some states changed their laws on teen driving during the 2000s. That might account for shifts for younger teens, but it's unlikely to explain the trends for high school seniors: they fill out the survey in the spring, when virtually all are at least 17 and most are 18. (And in fact, *more* are 18 than in previous decades—57% in 2015, up from 53% in 1992.) As of 2016, forty-nine states (all but New Jersey) allowed teens to drive alone after age 16½ (sometimes with restrictions such as on night driving or passengers, but still driving alone). Another way to get around the influence of the new laws is by examining trends in the western region, where the highest percentage of states (eleven out of thirteen, or 85%, including

California) allow full, unrestricted driving privileges by age 17. There the decline in having a driver's license was just as large or larger (see Appendix B).

Even apart from getting their license, fewer teens are driving at all. All states allow teens to get learner's permits that let them drive with a licensed adult driver in the car, at minimum ages ranging from 14 to 16. That means virtually all 12th graders have been eligible to drive for at least a year by the time they fill out the survey, yet by 2015 one in four did not drive at all. The vast majority (84%) of states allow 15-year-olds to get learner's permits, and all states allow permits by 16; with most students turning 16 before the spring of 10th grade, the vast majority of 10th graders are able to start driving. But in 2015, for the first time, the majority of 10th graders did not drive at all—not even on a learner's permit. The decline in driving appears across all regions, ethnic groups, and socioeconomic classes (see Appendix B).

The Retreat of the Latchkey Kids

In 2015, a Maryland couple allowed their 10- and 6-year-old children to walk by themselves about a mile from a local park to their home. Someone saw the children walking alone and called the police, and the couple was investigated for child neglect by Child Protective Services. The story made national news, partially because many Boomers and GenX'ers can remember having free rein around their neighborhoods at what would now be considered young ages. In a 2015 poll, 71% of adults said they would not allow a child to go to the park alone, but 59% of adults over age 30 said they did so when they were kids themselves. One GenX friend of mine remembers walking to kindergarten by herself on a route that included crossing train tracks. Now when her 6-year-old daughter walks to the end of the block by herself, neighbors often accompany her back, worried that she is lost.

Another GenX memory is being a latchkey kid: walking home from school and using your key to enter an empty house, since your parents were still at work. Some kids did so as early as 2nd grade, and by middle school and especially high school it was taken for granted. Fewer iGen teens now have this experience (see Figure 1.6, next page).

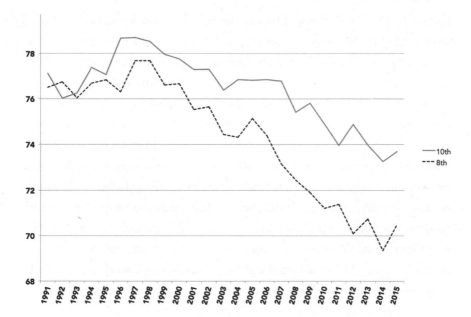

Figure 1.6. Percentage of 8th and 10th graders who spend time at home after school with no adult present. Monitoring the Future, 1991–2015.

These aren't large shifts, but the direction of the trend is surprising because more mothers in the 2010s worked full-time than in the 1990s. Given that, more teens—not fewer—should be spending time alone after school. (And it can't be because more teens are working or doing extracurricular activities in the afternoon; as we'll explore later, fewer of them work and time spent on activities has stayed the same.) Whether through after-school programs or some other mechanism, parents have arranged for fewer 14-, 15-, and 16-year-old teens to be at home by themselves in the afternoon. Thus teens are not just less likely to go out without their parents; they are also less likely to be at home without their parents.

The Decline of the Teen Job

Many Boomers and GenX'ers can remember the first time they bought something with their own money—maybe from mowing the lawn or babysitting. Or they might remember cashing their first paycheck from their job at the mall, using it to buy cool clothes or a music album they'd been saving up to buy.

iGen is less likely to have that experience. The decline in the percentage of teens working is considerable: in the late 1970s, only 22% of high school seniors didn't work for pay at all during the school year, but by the early 2010s, twice as many (44%) didn't (see Figure 1.7). The number of 8th graders who work for pay has been cut in half. These declines accelerated during the years of the Great Recession (2007–2009), but working did not bounce back in the postrecession years, when unemployment reached very low levels and jobs were easier to find. Among the youngest teens, the number working continued to decline even as the economy boomed. Teens also work fewer hours a week on average—for example, 12th graders headed to college in 2016 (vs. in 1987) worked about five fewer hours a week—about forty minutes a day less (see Appendix B).

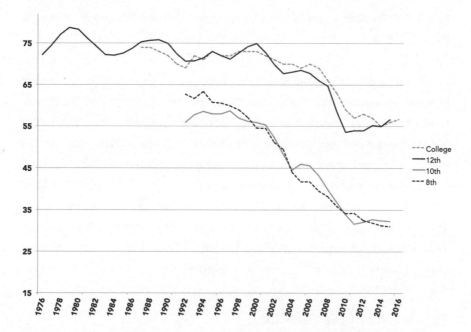

Figure 1.7. Percentage of 8th, 10th, and 12th graders and entering college students who earned any money from paid work in an average week. Monitoring the Future and American Freshman Survey, 1976–2016.

Fewer teens work during the summer as well: in 1980, 70% had a summer job, which sank to 43% in the 2010s (see Appendix B). The decline in the summer job doesn't seem to be due to the inability to find a job; according to Bureau of Labor Statistics data, the number of teens who want a summer job but can't find one has stayed about the same, but the number who don't want a job has doubled.

Maybe teens don't have jobs anymore—and don't go out as much anymore—because they are devoting more time to homework and extracurricular activities. Article after article declares that American students, especially young teens, are spending more and more time studying as schools become more academically demanding. There's also a lot of talk about students piling on more and more activities in their drive to polish those ever-more-competitive college applications.

Except they're not. Let's look first at extracurricular activities. The most comprehensive measure is in the entering college student survey, exactly the group you'd expect to show the most pronounced upswing in extracurricular time. However, that didn't happen. Time spent on student clubs and on sports/exercise as 12th graders changed little over time (see Appendix B). The one rise was in volunteer work, which is now often required for high school graduation; recent students did about ten minutes a day more volunteer work than those in the late 1980s. However, the rise in volunteering took place between the 1980s and the 1990s, well before the large drop in working for pay. So although volunteering has ticked up a little, the timing is wrong and the change is too small for it to account for the large drop in working for pay.

What about time spent on homework? As it turns out, iGen 8th, 10th, and 12th graders actually spent *less* time on homework than GenX teens did in the early 1990s, and high school seniors headed for four-year colleges spent about the same amount of time (see Appendix B). Between 2005 and 2015—the period when working for pay decreased the most—homework time was a mixed bag: 8th graders spent eight minutes fewer a day in 2015 than in 2005, and 10th and 12th graders spent about ten more minutes a day. These shifts are too small to account for the much larger drop in time spent working for pay—and for 8th graders they are in the wrong direction, with both homework time and paid work time decreasing.

We can also consider the total amount of time teens spend on paid work, homework, volunteering, and extracurricular activities. If that total has gone up or stayed the same, teens have shifted the time they used to work for pay into homework and extracurricular time. If that total has gone down, homework time has not filled in the hours teens used to spend at a job.

The trends in this total are clear: iGen teens are spending *less* time on homework, paid work, volunteering, and extracurriculars combined, not more (see Figure 1.8). For example, high school seniors heading to college in 2015 spent four fewer hours a week on homework, paid work, volunteer work, and extracurricular activities during their last year in high school than

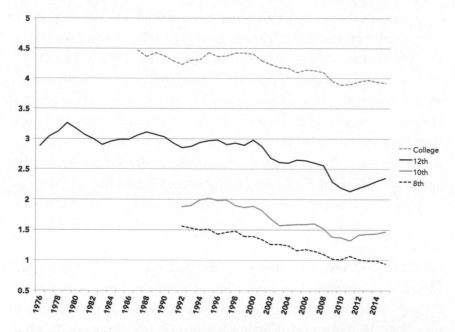

Figure 1.8. Total hours per day spent on work and activities, 8th, 10th, and 12th graders and entering college students reporting on their last year in high school. Monitoring the Future and American Freshman Survey, 1976–2015. (For entering college students, total includes homework, paid work, volunteer work, sports/exercise, and student clubs. For 12th graders, total includes homework, paid work, and volunteer work. For 8th and 10th graders, total includes homework and paid work.)

those entering college in 1987. That means iGen teens—even those heading for college—had thirty-three minutes *more* leisure time per day than GenX'ers did. Thus, time spent on homework and activities doesn't seem to be the reason teens are now less likely to work during the school year.

So is it good or bad that fewer teens are working? It's likely some of both. Most teen jobs are low-skilled work that don't necessarily prepare young people for the higher-level jobs they will have later. My students at SDSU tell me they have worked folding clothes at the Gap, stocking shelves at Target, and cleaning the bathroom at Bath & Body Works. Although they learned some customer service skills, such jobs are very different from the white-collar professions most will pursue once they graduate from college. Jobs can also keep teens from getting the sleep they need, especially if they are at work late at night and have to start school early in the morning. And although homework time doesn't seem to be preventing the average teen from working at a job, teens who work long hours often find it difficult to complete their schoolwork.

However, even if teens don't learn high-level skills from their jobs, they often learn the value of responsibility and money. Vicki, 22, was a student in my personality psychology class at SDSU. She says her parents didn't want her to work in high school, so looking for a job when she entered college was a rude shock. "No one would hire me due to my lack of experience, and even when I finally did get a job, I wasn't acting in a professional manner on the job and I ended up getting fired a few months later," she wrote. "If I had worked in high school, regardless of where, I would have known how to behave on the job. In fact, if I had had a job I probably would have learned a discipline and work ethic that would have helped me in many areas of my life. I would have learned the importance of attendance, which is something I have a huge struggle with when it comes to school and appointments. I never learned what it was like to earn something."

Jobs can also confer benefits on specific populations. One study found that disadvantaged teens randomly assigned to a summer jobs program were 43% less likely to be involved in violence. Most of the effect occurred after the eight-week job period was over, suggesting that employment had a longer-term beneficial effect than simply filling time. For teens bound for college, a part-time job can provide badly needed funds, especially in the current era of rising tuition costs and the large debt burden many students find themselves with after college graduation. Whether it's good or bad, working is yet another adult activity teens are putting off until later.

Taking Out Loans from the Bank of Mom and Dad

I meet Ellie, 16, at her high school; we sit outside her classroom and talk on a sunny fall day just before lunch. She's a pretty junior with long light brown hair who tells me all about using geotagging to post to Instagram. She has put off getting her driver's license but hopes to take care of that soon, since her parents still have to drop her off at the mall when she wants to hang out with her friends. I ask her if she has a job, and she says no; she also doesn't get an allowance. "So do your parents buy you the things that you want—is that how it works?" I ask. "Yeah," she says. "Like, usually if I need money they will, like, give it to me or something. Usually I just ask them. They don't always, but sometimes."

With fewer teens working, you might think that more would get an allowance to buy the things they want. However, *fewer* iGen'ers get an allowance. When teen employment began to drop in the 1980s, parents at first responded by giving more teens an allowance. But after 2000, fewer teens got an allowance and many fewer had money from a job, leaving 20% of these 17- and 18-year-olds without any money of their own to manage (see Figure 1.9, next page; see Appendix B for the equivalent for 10th graders). When they need money, they must, like Ellie, ask for it from their parents. It's yet another example of 18-year-olds now being like 15-year-olds: just like children and young adolescents, one out of five iGen high school seniors asks their parents for what they want instead of managing their own cash flow.

It's hard to say whether this parental control of funds is the parents' or the teens' idea. If it's the parents', it suggests that parents think high school seniors aren't ready to manage their own money. Or maybe teens have realized they'll get more money out of their parents by asking rather than having a set allowance. Either way, the result is more young people graduating from high school without even the introductory money-managing

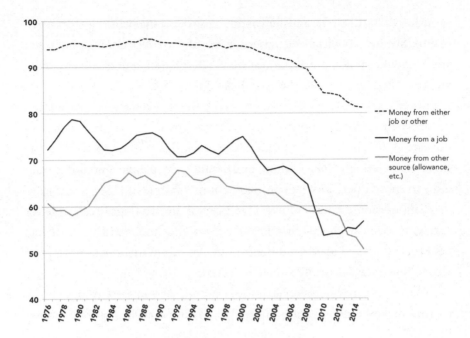

Figure 1.9. Percentage of 12th graders with money from jobs, allowances, or either. Monitoring the Future, 1976–2015.

experience of figuring out how much to spend on movies, gas, and meals out—a kind of training ground for the larger adult job of paying for rent, utilities, and food.

You Booze, You Lose

I reach Chloe, 18, on her cell phone just as school lets out on a mild spring Wednesday. She's a senior at a high school in a suburb of Cleveland, Ohio, and has just decided that she'll go to college at Ohio State ("I'm sooo excited," she says). When she was younger, she thought she might pursue a career in fashion, but she now thinks she'll major in psychology. When I ask her about her favorite TV shows, she admits with a tinge of embarrassment that she likes *Keeping Up with the Kardashians*—not for the drama, she clarifies, but because of the glimpse it provides into a posh California lifestyle. She also loves watching funny animal videos online.

Most of the time, she and her friends hang out at the mall or go for frozen yogurt. She has a boyfriend, a part-time job, and a driver's license, but other adult activities hold little appeal for her. When I ask about going to parties and drinking, for example, she's skeptical of the whole scene. "People I work with will say, 'I went down to the university this weekend and I got messed up or whatever and I hooked up with some guy'—it's just, like, drunken mistake stuff," she says. "And that doesn't sound appealing to you?" I ask, somewhat teasingly. "No—I don't understand why people would not want to be in control of themselves or their actions," she says.

Chloe is more typical of her iGen peers than you might realize; fewer and fewer drink alcohol. Nearly 40% of iGen high school seniors in 2016 had never tried alcohol at all, and the number of 8th graders who have tried alcohol has been cut nearly in half (see Figure 1.10).

The decline in trying alcohol is the largest in the youngest groups and by far the smallest among young adults. The decline is a steep black diamond

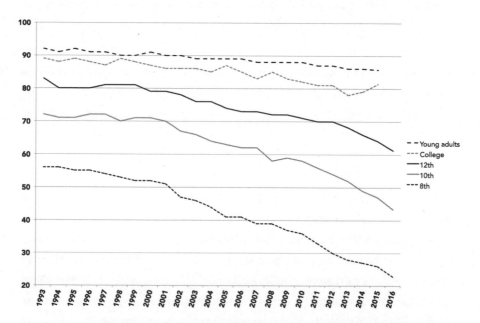

Figure 1.10. Percentage who have ever tried alcohol (more than just a few sips), 8th, 10th, and 12th graders, college students, and young adults (ages 19–30). Monitoring the Future, 1993–2016.

mountain for 8th graders, a bunny hill for 12th graders, and a gently slop-ing cross-country ski course for young adults. Nearly all young adults have tried alcohol, and that has declined only slightly over the decades. What's changed is the age when they first start drinking. In the early 1990s, the average 8th grader had already tried alcohol, but by 2014 the average 10th grader had not. That means most iGen teens are putting off trying alcohol until the spring of 10th grade or later; they are growing more slowly into the adult activity of drinking alcohol. Similar trends show up for alcohol use in the last month and in other surveys such as the CDC's Youth Risk Behavior Surveillance Survey of teens (see Appendix B).

The steep decline in alcohol use for the youngest teens is especially encouraging; most people would agree that 13- and 14-year-olds drinking is not a good idea. When they get to 10th and 12th grade and drinking can be combined with driving, it's also a big public health benefit that fewer young people are imbibing. These are huge, and encouraging, changes.

There is one downside to these trends: more young people arrive on college campuses or enter adult life without much experience drinking. Since drinking among college students and young adults hasn't changed much, iGen is ramping up their drinking over a much shorter period of time than did previous generations. Many are going from zero to sixty in their alcohol experience in a short time.

That's especially true for binge drinking, usually defined as having five or more drinks in a row. Binge drinking is the most dangerous kind of alcohol use, as it is the most likely to lead to alcohol poisoning, poor judgment, and drunk driving. The number of 18-year-olds who binge drink has been cut in half since the early 1980s, but binge drinking among 21- to-22-year-olds has stayed about the same (see Figure 1.11, next page).

The rapid increase in binge drinking from age 18 to age 21 can be risky. A study of this trend by the National Institutes of Health concluded, "Any increase in heavy drinking from age 18 to 21/22 increases the risk of negative consequences; it is likely that the faster the increase, the less experience one has with heavy drinking situations and the more risk is involved."

This phenomenon is especially acute for those who attend college. High school students bound for college are less likely to drink alcohol than those

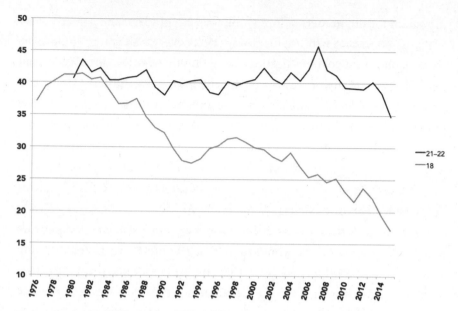

Figure 1.11. Percentage of 18-year-olds and 21- to 22-year-olds reporting binge drinking in the past two weeks. Monitoring the Future, 1976–2015.

who don't plan on attending college, but once they get there they are more likely to binge drink than those who are not in college. For college students, the experience curve is very steep. As one college student put it, "I'm 21 and in my prime drinking years, and I intend to take full advantage of it!" This can be a challenge for student affairs professionals and others helping young people navigate their college years, as students are arriving on campus fairly naive about drinking but are quickly immersed in a culture of heavy alcohol consumption.

What about drug use? The heyday of illicit drug use among teens—the vast majority of which is marijuana—was in the late 1970s and early 1980s. Use then plummeted in the early 1990s before going back up again through the 2000s and 2010s (see Figure 1.12, next page). With drug use, there's very little difference between 18-year-olds and 21- to 22-year-olds, and drug use ticks up a little in the transition to iGen in the early 2010s.

Why the different patterns for alcohol and drug use? Drug use, at least in most states, is illegal at any age. Any rule breaking is roughly equal for drug use whether you are over or under 21. Buying alcohol, however, becomes legal at 21—perhaps why this cautious generation is more likely to avoid it as teens yet still indulges after they turn 21. As more states legalize recreational marijuana for adults, this pattern may change. (We'll explore more about these trends in chapter 6, on safety.) For now iGen drinks less but smokes pot more than the Millennials who preceded them.

Growing Up Slowly

So: compared to their predecessors, iGen teens are less likely to go out without their parents, date, have sex, drive, work, or drink alcohol. These are all things adults do that children do not. Most people try them for the first time as teens—the transitional time between childhood and adulthood. As high school students, iGen'ers are strikingly less likely to experience these once nearly universal adolescent milestones, those breathtaking first experiences

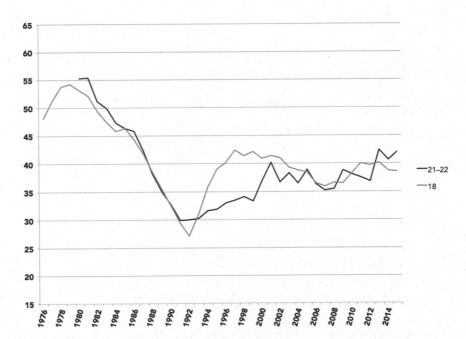

Figure 1.12. Percentage of 18-year-olds and 21- to 22-year-olds using any illicit drug in the past twelve months. Monitoring the Future, 1976–2015.

of independence from your parents that leave you feeling, for the first time, that you're an adult (see Figure 1.13). Even iGen'ers who do reach these milestones during high school are doing so at older ages than in previous generations. That includes both the pleasures of adulthood, such as sex and alcohol, and the responsibilities of adulthood, such as working and driving. For good or for ill, iGen teens are not in a hurry to grow up. Eighteen-year-olds now look like 14-year-olds once did and 14-year-olds like 10- or 12-year-olds.

The full story of growing up slowly began long before iGen. The first changes in developmental speed appeared not among teens but among young adult GenX'ers in the 1990s, who began to postpone the traditional milestones of adulthood such as settling into a career, getting married, and having children. The average Boomer woman in 1975 married at 21; the average GenX'er in 1995 married at 25. Working at a full-time career was also postponed until later as more young people went to college.

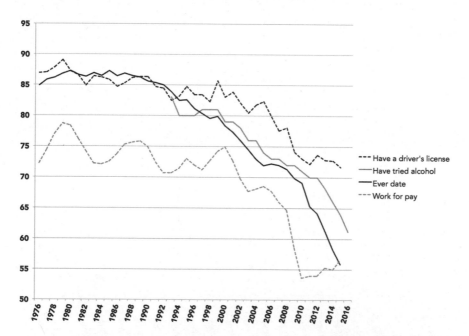

Figure 1.13. Percentage of 12th graders who have a driver's license, have ever tried alcohol, who ever go out on dates, and who worked for pay at all during the school year. Monitoring the Future, 1976–2016.

Yet GenX'er *teens* didn't slow down—they were just as likely to drive, drink alcohol, and date as their Boomer peers and more likely to have sex and get pregnant as teens. But then they waited longer to reach full adulthood with careers and children. So GenX'ers managed to lengthen adolescence beyond all previous limits: they started becoming adults earlier and finished becoming adults later.

Beginning with Millennials and then going full speed with iGen, adolescence is becoming shortened again—at the lower end. Childhood has lengthened, with teens treated more like children, less independent and more protected by parents than they once were. The entire developmental trajectory, from childhood to adolescence to adulthood, has slowed. Adolescence—the time when teens begin to do things adults do—now happens later. Thirteen-year-olds—and even 18-year-olds—are less likely to act like adults and spend their time like adults. They are more likely, instead, to act like children—not by being immature, necessarily, but by postponing the usual activities of adults. Adolescence is now an extension of childhood rather than the beginning of adulthood.

Is This Because Teens Are More Responsible?

In a 2014 op-ed for the *Washington Post*, the sociologist David Finkelhor argued that iGen teens, with their lowered alcohol use, reduced crime rates, and more limited sexuality, are "showing virtues their elders lacked." He concluded, "We may look back on today's youth as relatively virtuous, as the ones who turned the tide on impulsivity and indulgence." Today's teens, he believes, should be praised for being so responsible. A 2016 *Post* article continued with this theme, trumpeting "Today's Teens Are Way Better Behaved than You Were."

Other observers, such as the 20-year-old writer Jess Williams, have spun the same trends more negatively: Williams describes iGen as "boring." Teens just aren't any fun anymore, she says. One magazine agreed, headlining a recent article "Charting the Rise of Generation Yawn: 20 Is the New 40."

In my view, these characterizations miss the point. Terms such as *virtue*, *indulgence*, *better behaved*, and *boring* focus solely on whether the trends are "good" or "bad." This approach is incomplete, including only some of the generational differences while leaving others out entirely. For example, none of these articles mentions that iGen teens are also less likely to work at a job, have a driver's license, stay at home alone, or manage their own money, activities not necessarily associated with being more (or less) "virtuous," "responsible," "better behaved," or "boring." As a whole, the trends do not unequivocally support the idea that adolescents have become more responsible, virtuous, or boring (and thus perhaps are *more* like adults). But the trends do nearly unequivocally support the idea that teens are growing up more slowly (and are thus *less* like adults). Only growing up more slowly explains why working, driving, staying alone, and managing one's own money would also decline among teens. Neither "better behaved" nor "boring" captures what's really going on with iGen: they are simply taking longer to grow up.

Instead, it's more informative to employ the terms of life history theory, discussed earlier: teens have adopted a slow life strategy, perhaps due to smaller families and the demands wrought by increasing income inequality. Parents have the time to cultivate each child to succeed in the newly competitive economic environment, which might take twenty-one years when it once took sixteen. The cultural shift toward individualism may also play a role: childhood and adolescence are uniquely self-focused stages, so staying in them longer allows more cultivation of the individual self. With fewer children and more time spent with each, each child is noticed and celebrated. Sure enough, cultural individualism is connected to slower developmental speeds across both countries and time. Around the world, young adults grow up more slowly in individualistic countries than collectivistic ones. And as American culture has grown more individualistic from 1965 to the present, young adults have taken longer and longer to enter adult work and family roles (see Appendix B).

There's another factor, too—several well-publicized studies of brain development have shown that the frontal cortex, the brain area responsible for judgment and decision making, does not complete its development until age 25. This has spawned the idea that teens are not quite ready to grow up and thus need more protection for a longer time. These findings about underdeveloped teen brains have generated numerous books, articles, and online parenting advice. Interestingly, the interpretation of these studies seems to ignore a fundamental truth of brain research: that the brain changes based on experience. Maybe today's teens and young adults have an underdeveloped frontal cortex because they have not been given adult responsibilities. If brain scanners existed in 1950, I wonder what they would have shown of a generation that usually started work at 18, married at 21, and had children soon after. That interpretation of such studies is never offered, however, leaving parents believing that their teen and young adult children are biologically programmed to make poor choices. So, they think, it's better to protect them as long as possible.

Partners, Not Prisoners

Here's another key question: Are teens willing participants in growing up more slowly, or are parents strong-arming them into it? It would be easy to imagine teens chafing against being treated like children. But if growing up slowly is a natural adaptation to the culture, they might be more willing to go along with it.

Parents do keep a closer watch over teens these days. More teens say that their parents *always* know where they are and who they are with when they go out at night (see Figure 1.14, next page). This surveillance is probably facilitated by phone-tracking apps that allow parents to see where their teens are. Yet the apps can't tell parents whom their kids are with, and teens say their parents know that, too. It's another sign of growing up slowly: like the mother at the playground who knows whether her 5-year-old is about to run in front of the swings, the parents of teens are more likely to know where their kids are and whom they're with.

Most adults can remember being a teen and chafing against this kind of parental meddling: "Who's going to be at the party? I dunno—people?" Or upon your return from downtown, possibly but not definitely maybe having had a drink or two: "We went bowling. Yeah, bowling."

Given the teen tendency to resist restrictions, you'd think teens and their parents would get into more fights. The easiest way to get into a fight with a teen is to take her car keys away, right? (And that's effectively what's happened to iGen en masse.) If iGen teens don't like the restrictions, they should fight with their parents more than previous generations did. However, iGen teens fight *less* with their parents; the number who had a serious fight with their parents more than three times a year fell from 66% in 2005 to 56% in 2015 (see Appendix B). So iGen is not only kept on a tighter leash by their parents but also fight with them less, bucking the Boomer and GenX assumption that teens will automatically battle parental restrictions. iGen teens and parents are on the same page—the page of growing up more slowly.

In the most extreme cases of resistance to parents, teens might consider running away. Since running away is virtually never a parent's idea, it gives a view into what teens are thinking on their own—their deepest feelings unfettered by parental guidance. As it turns out, running away is less common among iGen: the number of teens who say they've tried to leave home plummeted in just the five years from 2010 to 2015 (see Figure 1.15, next page). Thankfully, teens are less likely to consider making a break for independence.

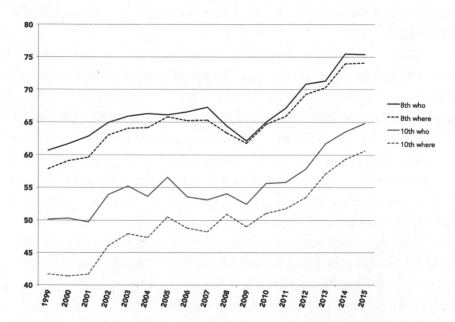

Figure 1.14. Percentage of 8th and 10th graders whose parents always know where they are and whom they are with when they go out at night. Monitoring the Future, 1999–2015.

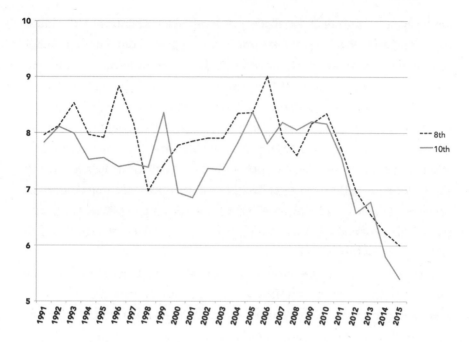

Figure 1.15. Percentage of 8th and 10th graders who have tried to run away from home in the last 12 months. Monitoring the Future, 1999–2015.

So apparently, teens are along for the ride of growing up more slowly; they are willingly staying children for longer. A recent study found that iGen college students (vs. students in the 1980s and 1990s) scored markedly higher on a measure of "maturity fears." iGen'ers were more likely to agree "I wish that I could return to the security of childhood" and "The happiest time in life is when you are a child." They were less likely to agree "I would rather be an adult than a child" and "I feel happy that I am not a child anymore." Instead of resenting being treated like children, iGen'ers wish they could stay children for longer.

Many people now seem to associate being a child (as opposed to being an adult) with less stress and more fun; witness the 2014 emergence of the neologism "adulting," which means taking care of one's responsibilities. The Adulting School in Maine now offers classes for young adults teaching them how to perform tasks such as managing finances and folding laundry. The Twitter hashtag #adulting features posts such as "One thing I hate about adulting . . . Paying bills," "I'm just gonna lay in bed . . . I don't feel like adulting today," and "Remember when you were a kid and counted the number of days until school was out? #adulting needs something like that." The word *adult* is now used as a verb, and it seems to mean the end of all fun: "When you're drunk at 4am and realize you have to get up and #adult in 5 hours" or "When everyone's all snuggled in bed and I'm walking out the door to go to work. I'm done adulting." Many echo the idea that growing up is no fun. Wrote one Twitter user, "HOW ARE PEOPLE EXCITED TO TURN 18???? IM VERY SCARED OF ADULTING!!!!" Another posted, "I miss the trivial and juvenile concerns I had as a child, things like crayon sets and cute play dates. Adulting sucks. I want to quit." How, exactly, can you quit being an adult? That's not explained.

Recent years have seen a boom in products such as "adult coloring books" that invite full-grown humans to color with crayons like elementary schoolers, touting the activity as "relaxing." A 2016 article in *Adweek* noted that brands are tapping "into millennials' anxiety about growing up." When I interviewed Josie, a 17-year-old high school senior in the midst of applying to college, I asked her what her favorite movies were. Her answer? *Tangled* and *Frozen*—both children's movies by Disney.

Instead of longing to be older as many previous generations did—remember Tom Hanks in the movie *Big* in the 1980s?—kids like being kids. In a 2013 poll, 85% of 8- to-14-year-olds agreed "I like being my age," up from 75% in 2003. When 7-year-old Hannah was asked, "Do you want to be older?" she replied, "No. I like being a kid. You get to do more things."

When I asked twenty iGen'ers why being a child was better than being an adult, almost all said that being an adult involved too much responsibility. When they were children, they said, their parents had taken care of everything and they'd just gotten to have fun. "I could take care of my own desires, more or less, without ever having to worry about the logistics or practicality of making them real," wrote Elizabeth, 22. "Nor was I ever really forced to encounter the consequences of having fun or taking a day off. It was just something I would do." In other words, as children they could live in a cocoon, with all of the fun but little of the work. Their parents made childhood a wonderful place with lots of praise, an emphasis on fun, and few responsibilities. No wonder they don't want to grow up.

Even once they get to college, students' parents continue to treat them like children. Parents register their adult children for classes, remind them of deadlines, and wake them up in time for class, observed Julie Lythcott-Haims, the former freshman dean at Stanford. Cell phones made that easy. "These students weren't mortified when their parents did all of this—as my generation and the ones before it would have been—they were grateful!" she notes. "Grateful to be able to communicate with a parent multiple times a day, in the dorm, in the dining halls, in the student union, going to class, going to another class, going somewhere after class, in the lobby of the advising office. Even in my office. Or they tried to. 'It's my mom,' they'd say, sheepishly, with a small shrug. 'Do you mind if I just . . . get this? I'll just . . . Mom?'" Over her decade in the job, Lythcott-Haims says, students began referring to themselves as "kids."

Thus the generational sweep is complete: never having known another parenting style, iGen doesn't rebel against their parents' overprotection—instead, they embrace it. "We want you to treat us like children, not adults," one college student told a startled faculty member. Some suggest that this cocoon mentality is behind recent campus trends such as "trigger warnings" to alert students that a reading or lecture material might be disturbing and "safe spaces" where students can go if they are upset by a campus speaker's message. One safe space, for example, featured coloring books and videos of frolicking puppies, neatly connecting the idea of safe spaces with that of childhood.

No matter what the reason, teens are growing up more slowly, eschewing adult activities until they are older. This creates a logical question: If teens are working less, spending less time on homework, going out less, and drinking less, what *are* they doing? For a generation called iGen, the answer is obvious: look no further than the smartphones in their hands.

Chapter 2

Internet: Online Time— Oh, and Other Media, Too

The New York Police Department's 33rd Precinct recently warned residents about a danger lurking in their beds: their phones. Several had caught fire when people kept them under their pillows while they slept, creating clickbait pictures of scorched phones and beds with large brown burn marks. A similar incident happened in Texas, where a 13-year-old girl woke to the smell of something burning. Her charging phone, tucked under her pillow, had overheated and melted into the sheets.

It turned out that some Samsung phones had a spectacular issue with spontaneously combusting batteries. But to me, the flaming cell phone wasn't the only surprising thing in these stories. Why would anyone have her phone under her pillow? my GenX self wondered. It's not as though you can surf the Web while you're sleeping. And who could slumber deeply inches from a buzzing phone? Curious, I asked my undergraduate students what I thought was a very simple question: "What do you do with your phone while you sleep? Why?"

Their answers were a profile in obsession. Nearly all slept with their phones, putting them under their pillows, on the mattress, or at the very least within arm's reach of the bed. They checked social media websites and watched videos right before they went to bed, and reached for their phones again as soon as they woke up in the morning (they had to—all of them used it as their alarm). Their phone was the last thing they saw before they went to sleep and the first thing they saw when they woke up. If they woke up in the middle of the night, they often ended up looking at their phones. They talked about their phones the way an addict would talk about crack: "I know I shouldn't, but I just can't help it," one said about looking at her phone while in bed. Some saw their phones as a lifeline or as an extension of their bodies or like a lover. "Having my phone closer to me while I'm sleeping is a comfort," wrote Molly, 20.

Smartphones are unlike any other previous form of media, infiltrating nearly every minute of our lives, even when we are unconscious with sleep. While we are awake, the phone entertains, communicates, glamourizes. Azar, the high school senior we met in chapter 1, is a good example. When I ask to take her picture, she sweeps her long dark hair to the front and chirps, "Have to look pret-ty!" I ask what her favorite apps are; she names Instagram, Snapchat, and one I hadn't heard of called iFunny. When I ask if she can show me how iFunny works, she gets visibly excited and says, "Really? I can take out my phone?" and proceeds to show me all of the areas of the site, keeping up a constant patter about all of the funny memes and videos. When the wireless signal starts to waver, she sighs in frustration. "Where is it? My Internet—noooo!" Her phone plan, she tells me, has unlimited data and texting but only one hundred minutes of talk time a month, "because I never call people." She keeps her phone out for the rest of the interview, showing me pictures and apps.

It seems obvious that teens (and the rest of us) spend a lot of time on phones—not talking but texting, on social media, online, and gaming (together, these are sometimes labeled "new media"). Sometime around 2011, we arrived at the day when we looked up, maybe from our own phones, and realized that everyone around us had a phone in his or her hands. But maybe what we see in the coffee line or at the dinner table isn't representative, and the endless parental and media hand-wringing over screen time isn't necessary. Maybe the smartphone obsession is pronounced only in middle-class and affluent communities, or maybe we just don't notice the teens who aren't always on their phones. Fortunately, we can turn to the large, nationally representative over-time surveys, since they ask teens how much time they spend online, gaming, and texting. So how much time is it?

The short answer is: a lot. iGen high school seniors spent an average of 2¼ hours a day texting on their cell phones, about 2 hours a day on the Internet, 1½ hours a day on electronic gaming, and about a half hour on video chat in the most recent survey. That totals to six hours a day with new media—and that's just during their leisure time (see Figure 2.1). Eighth graders, still in middle school, were not far behind, spending 1½ hours a day texting, 1½ hours a day online, 1½ hours a day gaming, and about half an hour on video chat—a total of 5 hours a day with new media. This varies little based on family background; disadvantaged teens spent just as much or more time online as those with more resources. The smartphone era has meant the effective end of the Internet access gap by social class (see Appendix C).

Considering that teens spend about seventeen hours a day in school, sleeping, and on homework and school activities, nearly all of their leisure hours are now spent with new media. The hour and a half that's left is used up by TV, which teens watch about two hours a day. Of course, this makes it look as if they have more than twenty-four hours in their days. But more than likely, they are multitasking—texting while web surfing, watching TV while posting to Instagram. (They might also be sleeping less, a possibility we'll return to in chapter 4.) Overall, teens spend much more time online

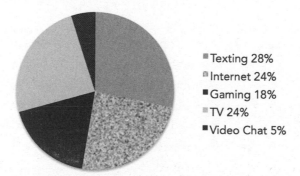

Figure 2.1. How 12th graders spend their screen time. Monitoring the Future, 2013–2015.

now than they did just a few years ago—12th graders in 2015 spent twice as much time online as 12th graders in 2006 (see Figure 2.2; see Appendix C for online time for 8th and 10th graders).

Even with multitasking included, six hours a day is a staggering amount of time. What are teens doing with that time? Lots of texting—the teens I talked to all said it's the primary way they communicate with their friends. About what? Many of the same things adults text about, but more often. "I am usually texting my girlfriend over random things, school items, and relationship issues. I also text my friends and just send jokes throughout the day," wrote Victor, 18. "I text my best friend or my boyfriend," said Eva, 19. "We are generally talking about something funny that happened during the day or just checking in to see how their day is going/anything new that's happened since we last talked." Texting has mostly replaced talking on the phone: in 2015, teens talked on the phone about forty-five minutes a day, about a third of the time they spent texting.

The surveys did not start asking about texting until 2010, when the practice was already well established, so we can't really see its popularity take off

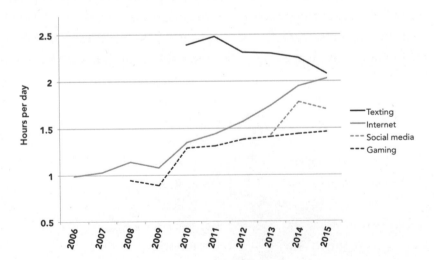

Figure 2.2. Hours per day spent by 12th graders on new media (texting, on the Internet, social media, and gaming). Monitoring the Future, 2006–2015.

from nonexistent in the 1990s to a two-hour-a-day activity by 2010. From 2010 to 2015, the time teens spent texting actually declined slightly—by about thirteen minutes a day. Why? Probably because they were spending more time on social media.

Everybody's Doing It: Social Media

As my rental car rumbles up the dirt road, I can see the barn in the distance against the green cornfields and blue sky of a summer day in rural Minnesota. Emily and her family are there when I pull up at the lake cabin where Emily's extended family has gathered for the July Fourth weekend. Emily is 14 and has just finished her freshman year in high school. A member of the track team, she's runner lean, with wavy blond hair in loose braids and a wide, happy smile that shows off her braces. She ends most sentences with a happy "So, yeah!"

Emily lives in the Twin Cities, two hours away, but her best friend lives at the farm next door to the lake cabin, and the two shuttle back and forth frequently. So the first order of the day is for me to meet Emily's cow, Liberty, born two years ago on the Fourth of July. Barefoot, Emily hops the fence at the barn door and brings Liberty over, smiling as we take her picture next to the huge black-and-white animal looking at us warily with dark brown eyes.

A girl on a farm, braids swinging, showing off her cow—it's a timeless scene, at home at any time in the last two hundred years. But it's not just any time, and Emily is like most iGen teens in the 2010s: she connects with her friends through social media, partially because it's virtually mandatory. "Everyone uses it," she says. "It's a good way to, like, make plans with people. If you don't, you might miss out on plans that you could have gone to." Emily got her first smartphone fairly late for an iGen'er, at the beginning of 9th grade, but already finds it indispensible. When I ask her what apps she uses, she says, "The main ones are Snapchat, Instagram, and Twitter. . . . I'll get updates from the track team and watch funny videos. I post pictures from my track meets and just if I'm doing a fun activity with my family or my friends. A lot of other people post a ton of selfies—like, every other post will be a selfie." She tells me how tagging photos on Instagram works; if someone doesn't tag you, that means "you're not really friends anymore, or they're mad at you." This is the new reality of teen social life: it's conducted online, for all to see, with clear messages about who's in and who's out.

How much time are teens spending on social media, and is it really any different from ten years ago? Social media sites are not new. The first social media sites appeared as early as 1997, MySpace debuted in 2003, and Facebook opened up to everyone over age 13 in 2006. (I'll use the terms *social networking sites* and *social media* interchangeably.) The Monitoring the Future survey first asked about social networking sites in 2008 (so sadly late that the otherwise diligent survey administrators must have been asleep at the wheel). The question about social media use is very general, asking whether teens use social networking sites "almost every day," "at least once a week," "once or twice a month," "a few times a year," or "never." Even with the survey late to the party and asking such a broad question, the growth in these sites' popularity is still very evident (see Figure 2.3).

In seven years, social media sites went from being a daily activity for half of teens to almost all of them. That's especially true for girls: 87% of 12th-grade girls used social media sites almost every day in 2015, com-

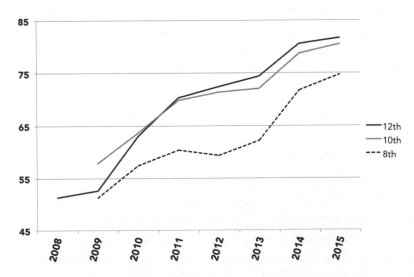

Figure 2.3. Percentage of 8th, 10th, and 12th graders using social networking sites almost every day. Monitoring the Future, 2008–2015.

pared to 77% of boys. The increases in use have been even larger for minority and lower-income teens—in 2008, white and higher-SES (social scientists call this socioeconomic status, or SES) teens were more likely to use social media sites every day, but by 2015 the race and class differences had disappeared. The daily use of social media sites is now an equal opportunity experience among teens. They have become almost required: in 2008, 14% of 12th graders said they never used the sites, enough to perhaps form a group; by 2015, those who never used them had dwindled to 3%. Only 2% of 12th-grade girls said they "never" use social media sites. So 97% of 12th graders and 98% of 12th-grade girls use social media sites at least sometimes—about as universal an experience as you can get.

Social media also requires a specific strategy of self-presentation. Harper, 12, was the youngest iGen'er I interviewed. She and her aunt arrived at our house on a sunny spring afternoon, and we chatted as her aunt played with my kids. Harper still looks more like a kid than a teen, although she's used to wearing lots of makeup for the cheerleading competitions she participates in nearly every weekend. She lives in a small town in the California mountains, sometimes staying with her grandparents due to her parents' divorce. She already has an iPhone and uses it frequently. Like many teens I talked with, she agreed that social media was mostly for posting positive things, requiring a certain cultivation of one's image. "Normally you don't want to look sad on there," she said. She uses social media mostly to follow her friends on Instagram: "If your friend is, like, out doing something, you can see all the cool things that they're doing," she says. "No one does anything bad on it—we just see what each other is doing."

The *Washington Post* recently profiled Katherine, a 13-year-old living in McLean, Virginia. The story described what she did on her iPhone during the twelve-minute drive home from school: "Her thumb [is] on Instagram. A Barbara Walters meme is on the screen. She scrolls, and another meme appears. Then another meme, and she closes the app. She opens BuzzFeed. There's a story about Florida Gov. Rick Scott, which she scrolls past to get to a story about Janet Jackson, then '28 Things You'll Understand If You're Both British and American.' She closes it. She opens Instagram. She opens the NBA app. She shuts the screen off. She turns it back on. She opens Spotify.

Opens Fitbit. She has 7,427 steps. Opens Instagram again. Opens Snapchat. She watches a sparkly rainbow flow from her friend's mouth. She watches a YouTube star make pouty faces at the camera. She watches a tutorial on nail art. She feels the bump of the driveway and looks up. They're home." Katherine has 604 followers on Instagram and keeps only the photos that get enough likes: "Over 100 likes is good, for me," she says. When she changed her Snapchat username, her Snapchat score went to zero (Snapchat users get a point for every snap they send or receive). So she sent 1,000 snaps in one day to up her score. She uses her phone so much that her father has had trouble finding a data plan to cover all of it.

For her book *American Girls: Social Media and the Secret Lives of Teenagers*, reporter Nancy Jo Sales interviewed hundreds of teen girls across the country about what they do on their phones and how it affects them. She described girls constantly in search of likes and positive comments on their pages, with persistent pressure to post sexy and revealing photos. Those, after all, get the most likes. One spring day she interviewed a group of 13-year-olds in Montclair, New Jersey. The girls, just like the teens I interviewed, had a love-hate relationship with their phones and social media. "I spend so much time on Instagram looking at people's pictures and sometimes I'll be like, Why am I spending my time on this? And yet I keep doing it," said Melinda. "If I go on my phone to look at Snapchat, I go on it like an hour, I lose track," noted Riley. "The minute I start my homework I have to have my phone by me to see what my friends are texting. . . . It's like someone is constantly tapping you on the shoulder, and you have to look," said Sophia. They'd like to stop, but they feel they can't. When Melinda's parents deleted her Instagram app for a week as a punishment, "By the end of the week I was stressing, like, What if I am losing followers?" "I've always wanted to delete my Instagram," said Sophia. "But then I think, I look so good in all my photos."

Eventually, many iGen'ers see through the veneer of chasing likes—but usually only once they are past their teen years. James, 20, is a college student in Georgia. "When you go on social media you post a status or you post a picture and all of a sudden you get all those likes, you get all those affirmations from people, and it can be addictive because you have the constant pats on the back that, like, 'You're smart, you're funny, you're attractive,'" he says. But, he acknowledges, "I feel like it's also kind of hollow."

This is, of course, a different world from the one GenX'ers and even Millennials grew up in. "You realize how insane things are today when you think about the relative rate of change," says Paul Roberts, the author of *The Impulse Society: America in the Age of Instant Gratification.* "When I was in high school, if I had gone around saying, 'Here's a picture of me, like me,' I would have gotten punched. If a girl went around passing out naked pictures of herself, people would have thought she needed therapy. Now, that's just Selfie Sunday."

So which sites are teens using? Social media sites go into and out of fashion, and by the time you read this book several new ones will probably be on the scene. In fall 2016, the management firm Piper Jaffray found that only 30% of 14-year-olds used Facebook at least once a month, compared to 80% using Instagram and 79% using Snapchat. Those platforms were also growing among young adults: by spring 2016, Pew Research Center found that 59% of 18- to 29-year-olds used Instagram and 56% used Snapchat, a big increase since 2015. The teens I talked to, in late 2015 and 2016, mentioned Instagram and Snapchat the most often. Most recently, group video chat apps such as Houseparty were catching on with iGen, allowing them to do what they call "live chilling."

Matthew, the 19-year-old Pennsylvania college student we met in chapter 1, uses a Snapchat feature called Snapstory. "If I'm at tennis practice or at one of the dining halls with some friends, I'll take a video or a picture and add it to my Snapstory and share it with friends. I'll also see other friends' Snapstories, and see what they're doing," he says. On Snapstory, photos stay for twenty-four hours and then disappear, forming a continuous, updated stream of photos that are sent to everyone you've tagged as a friend. It's easy, he says, because "The app is basically just a camera" and the pictures upload much faster than they do to Facebook. "It helps me stay in the loop and just know what's going on with everybody." Many teens use the regular version of Snapchat, in which pictures and messages automatically disappear (according to the company, Snapchat servers automatically delete "snaps" after they have been viewed). Teens see Snapchat as a "safe" way to talk to their friends, because there is no embarrassing permanent record that can be shared around. A relatively new feature alerts users when someone has tried to keep their message by using a screenshot—"and then they get mad at you," one teen told me.

As we saw earlier, girls usually spend more time on social media sites than boys do. So what are boys doing instead? Often, they're playing video games—and so are many of the girls. Teens spend more time playing games on their computers than they did just a few years ago—12th graders spend about 1½ hours a day, compared to less than an hour a day in 2008. Girls have caught up quickly in video game time, perhaps due to less violent, more girl-friendly games on phones such as *Candy Crush*.

Gaming has what statisticians call a "bimodal distribution": some teens don't do it at all, and others do it a lot. In 2015, 27% of teens said they played video games less than an hour a week, and 9% said they played more than forty hours a week—the time commitment of a full-time job.

When I interview Max, 16, at his San Diego high school and ask him about what he likes to do for fun, he says, "Play video games." He usually plays multiplayer games online in which he can talk to other players through his headset, he tells me. I've never played those games, so I ask him how they work, and he tries to explain. "You start at one point, and you're trying to capture or destroy the enemy's thing and you have minions and stuff that fight each other and take down towers along the way," he says. He and his group of four friends talk about things other than the game, but when I ask if he gets together with his friends in person, he says, "Sometimes, but not really that often." He doesn't do much on social media sites, either. When I ask him about other social activities, he says he doesn't go out much. That's when I begin to realize that playing video games is Max's only social activity.

Mark is a 20-year-old community college student in Texas who describes himself as "a big gamer." He met his best friend when he heard him say "Snapshot" (a reference to his favorite video game, *Halo*) in the high school hallway. They exchanged their Xbox gamer tags and have been playing together ever since. When I ask Mark what he most wants older people to understand about his generation, he surprises me by saying that the most important thing is for older people to understand how video games work.

"With Xbox whenever you play online with people, you can't pause your game. Well, when your parents want something of you, they demand it then and now. And when you try to explain to them, 'I'm playing online with other people,' I can't just pause and hop to it, they don't understand."

Some young men spend so much time playing video games they eventually have to cut themselves off. Twenty-year-old Darnell is majoring in business at a state university in Georgia. In high school, he says, "I had a problem where I would play and I really wouldn't do anything else. I'd get out of sports practice at eight thirty, nine, I'd come home and start playing video games and I'd probably play until three thirty, four o'clock in the morning. And I'd have to be ready for school at, like, six thirty," he says. Now he restricts his gaming to school breaks and doesn't play when classes are in session. "I didn't want that to be a problem in college. There's no one to say, 'Go to class,' so I just wouldn't go to class."

Overall, both boys and girls are spending much more time online and with electronic devices. Here's the thing: this time must come from somewhere—there must be something else that iGen teens are *not* doing that previous generations did. There are probably several, but one obvious candidate is all the other ways people used to communicate and entertain themselves. And I don't mean flip phones.

Are Books Dead?

The cool air inside the house is a welcome relief as we come in from a muggy late-spring day in suburban Virginia. Thirteen-year-old Sam opens the door to his room gingerly—his arm is encased in a black sling after he injured it tussling with a friend. His room is a mix of sports posters and school clutter, with wood furniture and navy blue curtains. He plans to play football in high school, and maybe wrestle as well: "I like physical sports where you take people to the ground," he tells me matter-of-factly. His favorite thing to do is hang out with his friends, and they tease each other in the easy, friendly way that only males can get away with. One friend's slight mustache inspired the nickname "Pube-stash," and another is dubbed the "Diabeto Torpedo." Although Sam prefers to see his friends in person, he also likes Snapchatting with them, especially the face swap feature, which switches the faces (but not the body or hair) of two people in a photo. "It usually ends up being super-funny," he says. If he has a half hour of downtime, he'll watch *SportsCenter* on ESPN or sports videos on YouTube. That made me wonder: Does he read *Sports Illustrated* or the sports section of a newspaper or books about sports? No, he says, "I only read what's assigned for an English project. I'm not a big fan of reading for fun."

Is Sam's aversion to print typical of iGen? They spend so much time on their phones, it would be an easy guess to say yes. Even if it is typical, maybe teens have never liked to read. As always, the best way to tell is to compare teens of the same age across time: are iGen teens less likely to read than teens in previous eras?

That appears to be the case. In the late 1970s, the clear majority of teens read a book or a magazine nearly every day, but by 2015, only 16% did. In other words, three times as many Boomers as iGen'ers read a book or maga-zine every day. Because the survey question was written in the 1970s, before e-readers existed, it does not specify the format of the book or magazine, so Millennials or iGen'ers who read on a Kindle or iPad would still be included.

Ebook readers did seem to briefly rescue books: the number who said they read two or more books for pleasure in the last year bounced back in the late 2000s—but then it sank again as iGen (and smartphones) entered the scene in the 2010s. By 2015, one out of three high school seniors admit-ted they had not read any books for pleasure in the past year, three times as many as in 1976. Even college students entering four-year universities, the young people presumably most likely to read books, are reading less (see Figure 2.4, next page).

This huge decline flatly contradicts a 2014 Pew Research Center study cheered by many in publishing, which found that 16- to 29-year-olds were *more* likely to read books than older people. Why the difference? The Pew study included books read for school assignments, which younger people are of course more likely to have. Thus it committed the classic mistake of a one-time study: confusing age and generation. In the data here, where everyone is the same age, iGen teens are much less likely to read books than their Millennial, GenX, and Boomer predecessors.

Why? Maybe because books just aren't fast enough. For a generation raised to click on the next link or scroll to the next page within seconds, books just don't hold their attention. Twelve-year-old Harper, whom we met earlier, makes all A's in school but says, "I'm not a really big reading person. It's hard for me to read the same book for such a long time. I just can't sit still and be superquiet. We have to read for twenty minutes a day, and if a book takes a while to get interesting, it's really hard for me to read."

Books are not the only print media in decline for iGen. The 8th- and 10th-grade surveys ask about reading magazines and newspapers, and the declines are steady, large, and breathtaking (see Figure 2.5, next page). Newspaper readership plummeted from nearly 70% in the early 1990s to only 10% in 2015 (and this is reading a newspaper once a week or more, a fairly low bar). Magazine readership fared little better.

Some of you might be thinking, yeah, no kidding. However, this is a surprising result according to many prominent theories of media use. Some

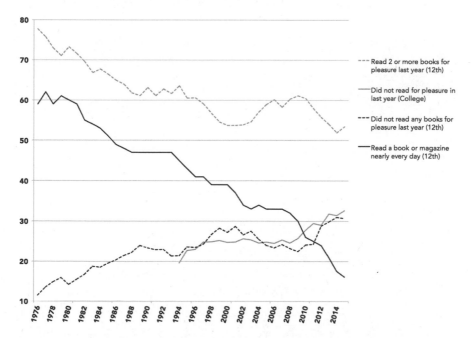

Figure 2.4. Percentage of 12th graders who read books and magazines, (Monitoring the Future), and entering college students (American Freshman Survey, 1976–2015).

researchers have argued that new technology doesn't replace older forms of media but instead supplements them. People who are interested in a topic often seek it out in many forms of media, they point out. In addition, technology makes reading books and magazines easier, since they can be delivered instantly to iPads and Kindles. But those factors were not enough to stem the tide of the decline of print. (As one librarian in a cartoon puts it as she hands a book to a teen, "Just think of it as a long text message.")

Are teens reading for pleasure less because they have more homework and more extracurricular activities? No—as we saw in chapter 1, teens are spending about the same or less time on these activities than in previous decades. (And recall that they also spend much less time working for pay.) 8th graders are the most clear-cut example: they spent two hours less on homework a week than they did in the early 1990s, but they are also much less likely to read magazines and newspapers. When NPR asked Washington, DC, 9th grader Jamahri Sydnor if she ever reads, she said, "I don't really read for pleasure. . . . I watch Netflix shows, or Hulu shows, mostly

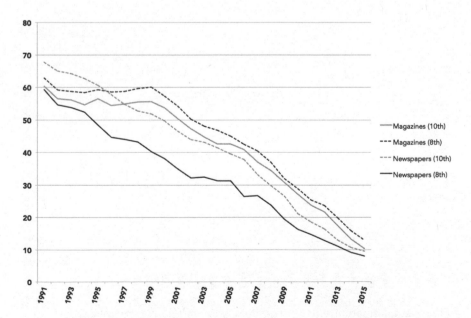

Figure 2.5. Percentage of 8th and 10th graders who read magazines and newspapers once a week or more. Monitoring the Future, 1991–2015.

TV. That's it," she said. Her friend Chiamaka Anosike said, "I don't read for pleasure either, unless it's for a school assignment. I'm usually on my phone or watching TV, too."

Of the two hundred San Diego State freshmen and sophomores I surveyed in 2015, most said they never read newspapers, and their magazine reading was restricted to celebrity gossip or fashion magazines. One was very specific: "I read magazines like *Cosmopolitan* when I'm flying on an airplane." A typical response mentioned required assignments for classes: "[I read] only if a school assignment requires it because I'd rather not spend my free time reading extensively."

Although many said they enjoyed reading books, those who did not were steadfast in their dislike. "I do not enjoy books," wrote one. "They put me to sleep and they are boring." Another noted, "I do not have the patience to read books that I do not have to read." One stated flatly, "I never read any books."

To paraphrase the cult classic movie *The Princess Bride*, print is not dead—it's just mostly dead. Or perhaps on life support. With smartphones taking up so much of teens' time, there is little left for other leisure pursuits. As one teen put it in a *Chronicle of Higher Education* interview, "My dad is still into the whole book thing. He has not realized that the Internet kind of took the place of that."

Perhaps this move away from print is innocuous, especially if teens are still keeping up their academic skills. But they are not: SAT scores have slid since the mid-2000s, especially in writing (a 13-point decline since 2006) and critical reading (a 13-point decline since 2005; see Figure 2.6, next page). Unfortunately, iGen'ers' academic skills lag behind their Millennial predecessors' by significant margins.

Declines in SAT scores are often attributed to more students choosing to go to college: if more high school students take the test, the population taking the test will be a less academically talented group over time. That's probably why SAT scores declined so much between the 1970s and the 1990s, when college enrollment soared. However, that's not the case for the shift from Millennials to iGen in the late 2000s and early 2010s, when college enrollment stayed fairly steady. It's interesting that the change in critical reading scores follows the same pattern as that of those reading two or more books for pleasure each year, which bumped up in the mid-2000s and then fell again.

Apparently, texting and posting to social media instead of reading books, magazines, and newspapers are not a boon for reading comprehension or academic writing. That might partially be due to the short attention span that new media seem to encourage. One study installed a program on college students' laptops that took a screenshot every five seconds. The researchers found that students switched between tasks every nineteen seconds on average. More than 75% of the students' computer windows were open less than one minute. This is a very different experience from sitting and reading a book for hours.

The decline in reading creates some distinct challenges for a wide swath of concerned elders, including parents, educators, and publishing companies. For example, how are students who rarely read books going to digest an eight-hundred-page college textbook? Most faculty report that their students simply don't read the textbook, even if it's required. Many

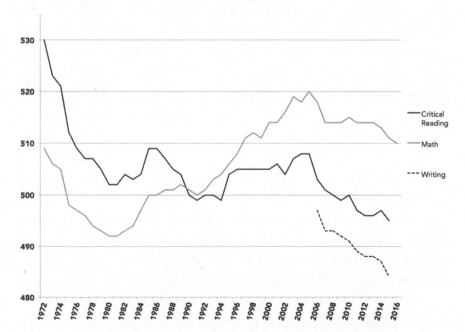

Figure 2.6. National average SAT scores, 1972–2016. College Board.

publishers are moving toward more interactive ebooks to try to keep students engaged. As a university faculty member and the author or coauthor of three college textbooks, I think this needs to go even further. iGen'ers need textbooks that include interactive activities such as video sharing and questionnaires, but they also need books that are shorter in length and more conversational in their writing style. They are coming to college with much less experience reading, so we have to meet them where they are, while still teaching them what they need to know. That might mean leaving behind some detail, but that's better than students' not cracking the book at all.

Regular books and magazines have already taken some of these steps, such as making their articles shorter and lowering their reading level. They may also eventually incorporate some of the same features as textbooks, imbedding quizzes and polls to keep readers interested or including images and videos just as web pages do. Perhaps then iGen—and the rest of us—will return to reading.

Funny Cats Big Compilation 2017!

"They have, like, a dog climbing a baby gate, and it, like, unhinges the baby gate, and you see the gate swing back with the dog on it, and you see the dog fall out of the frame—I just think it's really funny," says Chloe, the 18-year-old high school senior from Ohio we met in chapter 1. She and her friends watch video clips on Twitter, Buzzfeed, Facebook, and YouTube, with animal videos their usual faves. There's another one she likes on YouTube, she says: "The dog, like, got into something—have you ever seen when a dog is in trouble and they know they did something and they'll kind of, like, try to smile? The dog was, like, smiling, and [the video] had this weird, sympathetic music. I was in love with that video for two days in January—I couldn't, like, not watch it every five minutes."

These types of short video clips are very popular and have been since YouTube debuted in 2006. Although none of the over-time surveys specifically tracks the amount of time teens spend watching them, a good chunk of teens' online time is likely spent watching videos, either through social media or via sites such as YouTube. iGen'ers find videos through Twitter as well—20-year-old Darnell says he follows several people on Twitter who post nothing but dog photos, so, he says, "sometimes I look at puppies all day." The most popular videos seem to feature "fails," animals, or animal fails. Laughing babies, children drugged at the dentist, music videos, and dancing chickens have also been popular. We have the most complete and instant access to information in all of history, and we're using it to watch funny cat videos.

Online videos have replaced some TV time for teens, although the declines in TV watching are not as steep as those in reading. Teens watched about an hour a day less TV in 2015 than in the early 1990s (see Figure 2.7). Even with new TV options such as Netflix and Amazon Prime, funny cats are winning.

And when iGen'ers do watch TV, it's more likely to be on demand or streaming. "I don't even know how to turn on our TV at home and consume all of my 'television' content on my laptop," wrote 17-year-old Grace Masback in the Huffington Post.

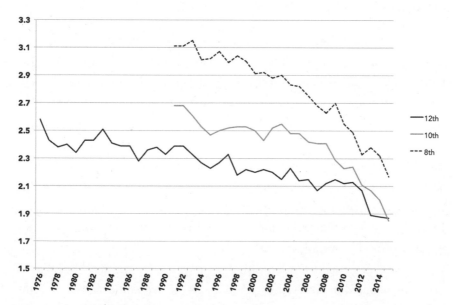

Figure 2.7. Hours 8th, 10th, and 12th graders spent watching TV on weekdays. Monitoring the Future, 1976–2015.

iGen teens also don't go out to see movies as often. Going to the movies stayed fairly steady through the video rental era of the 1980s and 1990s and remained robust until the mid-2000s, when it started to slide (see Figure 2.8). So at least among teens, Blockbuster Video (which opened in 1985) didn't kill going to the movies, nor did Netflix's mail service (which debuted in 1997). But streaming video and other online activities did (and of course they also killed Blockbuster).

When I asked my students if they preferred to see a movie in the theater or at home, most answered at home, citing convenience, cost, and being able to stay in their pajamas. Many iGen'ers prefer to personalize their movie experience in ways that can't be done at the theater. "I do not quite understand people who say that they enjoy paying to go watch a movie at the movie theater," wrote Carmen, 22. "With today's technology, you can stream the

Figure 2.8. Percentage of 8th, 10th, and 12th graders who go out to the movies once a month or more. Monitoring the Future, 1976–2015.

movie online, wear your most bum-like outfit (or don't wear pants at all), and eat snacks straight from your fridge and pantry. You can also pause, rewind and fast-forward the movie as you please, something that does not happen in a movie theatre. Ever."

So: iGen is spending much more time online and texting and much less time with more traditional media such as magazines, books, and TV. iGen'ers are spending so much time on their smartphones that they just aren't interested in or available to read magazines, go to movies, or watch TV (unless it's on their phones). Although TV presaged the screen revolution, the Internet has hastened the demise of print. The printing press was invented in 1440, so for more than five hundred years words printed on paper were the standard way to convey information. We are living, right now, in the time when that is changing.

iGen's future—and all of ours—will be shaped by this revolution. It could turn out well, with web pages supplemented by long passages of text in the form of ebooks, with all of the information we'll ever need contained in our laptops and on the Internet. No more recycling the newspaper, no more packing boxes of books when you move. Or it could turn out badly, with iGen and the next generations never learning the patience necessary to delve deeply into a topic and the US economy falling behind as a result.

There's another, more immediate question: If teens are spending more time communicating with their friends online, how much are they seeing their friends in person? Has electronic interaction replaced face-to-face interaction? Let's find out.

Chapter 3

In Person No More: I'm with You, but Only Virtually

Kevin and I sit down at two desks just outside his third period class at a high school in northern San Diego. He is 17 years old and Asian American, with spiky black hair, fashionable glasses, and a wan smile. He is the oldest of three children, with his parents expecting another child in a few months. Until recently, the family lived in an apartment, where the noise from his younger siblings was deafening. Perhaps as a result, he is unusually empathetic for a teenage boy. "Been doing this all day?" he asks as I take a drink of water before beginning our interview.

Kevin is not the most organized student: he initially neglects to have his dad sign the back of the permission slip, and when I talk to the class later, he forgets his question by the time I call on him. But when I ask him what makes his generation different, he doesn't hesitate: "I feel like we don't party as much. People stay in more often. My generation lost interest in socializing in person—they don't have physical get-togethers, they just text together, and they can just stay at home."

Kevin is onto something. For example, iGen teens spend less time at parties than any previous generation (see Figure 3.1). The trends are similar for college students, who are asked how many hours a week they spent at parties during their senior year in high school. In 2016, they said two hours a week—only a third of the time GenX students spent at parties in 1987. The decline in partying is not due to iGen'ers' studying more; as we saw in chapter 1, homework time is the same or lower. The trend is also not due to immigration or changes in ethnic composition; the decline is nearly identical among white teens.

Priya, the high school freshman we met in chapter 1, says she hasn't been to any parties and doesn't want to. "What you read in books is, like, oh my God, high school has all these football games and parties, and when you come there, eh, no one really does it. No one is really that interested—including me." In the SDSU freshman survey, several mentioned that the high school parties they had gone to had been adult-run affairs, not exactly the ragers memorialized in the 1980s John Hughes movies, where kids got

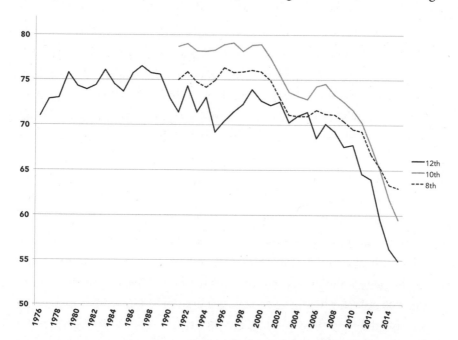

Figure 3.1. Percentage of 8th, 10th, and 12th graders who attend parties once a month or more. Monitoring the Future, 1976–2015.

drunk and wrecked their parents' houses. "The only parties I went to in high school were birthday parties, and they were almost always supervised or included an adult somewhere," noted Nick, 18.

Why are parties less popular? Kevin has an explanation for that: "People party because they're bored—they want something to do. Now we have Netflix—you can watch series nonstop. There's so many things to do on the Web." He might be right—with so much entertainment at home, why party? Teens also have other ways to connect and communicate, including the social media websites they spend so much time on. The party is constant, and it's on Snapchat.

Just Hangin'

Maybe parties aren't for this cautious, career-focused generation. Especially with the declining popularity of alcohol, perhaps iGen'ers are eschewing parties in favor of just hanging out with their friends.

Except they're not. The number of teens who get together with their friends every day has been cut in half in just fifteen years, with especially steep declines recently (see Figure 3.2, next page).

This might be the most definitive evidence that iGen'ers spend less time interacting with their peers face-to-face than any previous generation—it's not just parties or craziness but merely getting together with friends, spending time hanging out. That's something nearly everyone does: nerds and jocks, introverted teens and extroverted ones, poor kids and rich kids, C students and A students, stoners and clean-cut kids. It doesn't have to involve spending money or going someplace cool—it's just being with your friends. And teens are doing it much less.

The college student survey allows a more precise look at in-person social interaction, as it asks students how many hours a week they spend on those activities. College students in 2016 (vs. the late 1980s) spent four fewer hours a week socializing with their friends and three fewer hours a week partying—so seven hours a week less on in-person social interaction. That means iGen'ers were seeing their friends in person an *hour* less a day than GenX'ers and early Millennials did. An hour a day less spent with friends is an hour a day less spent building social skills, negotiating relationships, and navigating emotions. Some parents might see it as an hour a day saved for more productive activities, but, as we saw in the previous two chapters, the time has not been replaced with homework; it's been replaced with screen time.

Teens also go out with their friends less. Chapter 1 showed the steep decline in the number of times a week teens go out without their parents. The flip side of this is those who don't go out with their friends in a typical week—the ones who are at home on Friday and Saturday night on a regular basis. That used to be a very small percentage of 12th graders—less than 8%—but by 2015 nearly one out of five high school seniors did not go out with their friends during a typical week. The trend is even larger for 8th and 10th graders: in the 1990s, only one out of five rarely went out, but by 2015 that increased to one out of three.

The timing of the recent, severe drop in going out and getting together with friends is highly suspicious: it occured right when smartphones

Figure 3.2. Percentage of 8th, 10th, and 12th graders who get together with friends every day or nearly every day. Monitoring the Future, 1976–2015.

became popular and social media use really took off. Time spent with friends in person has been replaced by time spent with friends (and virtual friends) online. "Some kids are too addicted to social media and games to interact with other people that are actually next to them," explains Kevin. "They make, like, the fake online friends. Some people, like, help cheer you up online, but you don't really know them, so you can't really have a deep relationship."

Let's All Go Together (or Not)

If you were a teen in the 1980s or 1990s, you probably have memories of walking around the mall with your friends, checking out the gear at Sports Authority or the earrings at Claire's and then sitting at the tables in the food court. iGen'ers don't do that as much, either (see Figure 3.3); fewer and fewer teens are meeting their friends at the mall to hang out.

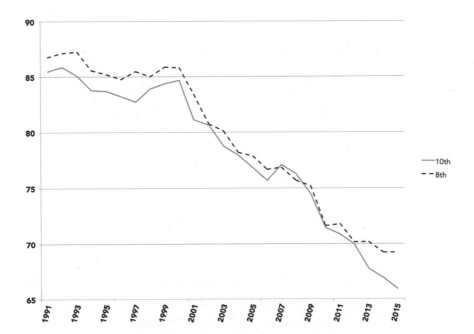

Figure 3.3. Percentage of 8th and 10th graders who go to a shopping mall once a month or more. Monitoring the Future, 1991–2015.

That is at least one reason why so many malls across the country have closed. There's even a Buzzfeed collection of photos of abandoned malls, capturing images such as the dying plants around a mirrored escalator at the Rolling Acres Mall in Akron, Ohio, shuttered in 2013. At the former Cloverleaf Mall in Chesterfield, Virginia, a popcorn cart sits abandoned, the neon "Food Court" sign over it no longer lit. Just down the hallway, dead palm trees are bent in half around an empty fountain in the floor, with broken store displays and other debris around it. Another photo, from the Randall Park Mall in Ohio, features a circular bank of pay phones. At the base, a phone book lies with its pages splayed, roadkill on the information superhighway.

Activity after activity, iGen'ers are less social than Millennials, GenX'ers, and Boomers were at the same age. As we saw in chapter 1, iGen'ers are less likely to go out or to go on dates. They are also less likely to "drive around in a car just for fun"—the activity at the center of teen movies of previous eras such as *Dazed and Confused* and *American Graffiti* (see Appendix D). A night at the movies has been a standard teen social activity for generations (what would adolescence be if it didn't involve some immature throwing of popcorn?), but, as we saw in chapter 2, iGen'ers are less likely to go to movies. iGen teens are less likely to go to bars and nightclubs—even since 1988, when the drinking age was raised to 21 nationwide, the number of high school seniors who went to bars or nightclubs has been cut in half. In 2006, the *New York Times* documented the new trend of nightclubs for teens (called "starter clubs"), with some for teens under 18. By 2016, however, the *Times* and other newspapers noted that many dance clubs were closing.

That doesn't mean teens are always staying at home having wholesome family time. Thirteen-year-old Athena, whom we met in the introduction, told me that she and her friends are often on their phones when they are at home. "I've seen my friends with their families—they don't talk to them," she says. "They just say, 'Okay, okay, whatever,' while they're on their phones. They don't pay attention to their family." Athena has spent a lot of time by herself lately: after her summer of Netflix, texting, and social media holed up in her room, "my bed has, like, an imprint of my body," she says. As her summer activities illustrate, there is one activity that iGen'ers do more than their predecessors: they spend more leisure time alone (see Appendix D).

Although we can't say for sure, it's a good guess that this alone time is being spent online, on social media, streaming video, and texting.

In short: iGen teens are less likely to take part in every single face-to-face social activity measured across four data sets of three different age groups. These fading interactions include everything from small-group or one-on-one activities such as getting together with friends to larger group activities such as parties. They include activities with no real aim, such as cruising in a car, and those that may have more of a goal in mind, such as going to see a movie. They include activities that might be replaced by online convenience, such as going to a shopping mall, and those that can't be easily replicated online, such as going out with friends.

Instead, they are communicating electronically. For example, see Figure 3.4. Its conclusion is inescapable: the Internet has taken over. Teens are Instagramming, Snapchatting, and texting with their friends more, and seeing them in person less. For iGen'ers, online friendship has replaced offline friendship.

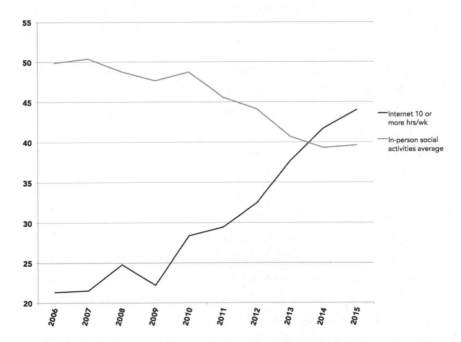

Figure 3.4. Percentage of 12th graders who spend ten or more hours a week online and the percentage average of four in-person social activities. Monitoring the Future, 2006–2015.

Some maintain that all of the uproar over screen time is misplaced; teens are just connecting with their friends online, and the rest of their lives have stayed the same. This graph strongly suggests that that is not true: with the advent of social media and smartphones, teens' social lives shifted decisively away from in-person interaction. They spend much less time with their friends in person than teens in previous decades did—about an hour a day less. The lives of teens—and the rest of us—may never be the same again as mobile Internet access puts down deeper and deeper roots in our lives.

Others have argued that social media has not replaced in-person interaction, because the same teens who spend more time on social media also spend more time with their friends in person. However, that says more about variations among teens (the highly social "popular" kids vs. the less social "nerds") than about shifts over time. It's not surprising that highly social teens are more social both on social media and in person. But on average, today's teens are spending less time with each other in person and more time online than teens did five years ago, fundamentally changing the lives of adolescents.

If you're not an iGen'er, think back to high school: What do you remember the most vividly? Maybe it's the after-prom party, your first kiss, or the time you and your friends got into trouble at the mall. Chances are it's something that happened with your friends when your parents weren't around. Such experiences are less and less common for today's teens. What will they remember—that funny text exchange they had with their friend? their best selfie? a meme that went viral? Or will they remember the few times they were actually with their friends in person?

Darnell, the 20-year-old college student in Georgia, explicitly connects iGen'ers' smartphone use with their disinclination to see people in person. "The last generation always wants us to be in person, and a lot of us are not like that," he says. "We're more of a technology-based generation. Without my phone I literally would be lost. I have my calendar, I have my email, I've researched different things, I'm always reading about something." Twenty-year-old James, a student at the same college, says it's just easier to use social media instead of meet up in person. "It's so tempting to just text someone or to just go on social media and like someone's photo and comment instead of calling and being, like, 'Hey, do you want to go and get something to eat?' That takes planning," he says.

Even when they do see their friends in person, technology, especially texting, allows iGen to avoid certain social interactions. Henry, 23, likes how texting can get him out of potentially awkward social exchanges. "When I arrive at a friend's house, instead of knocking on the door and coming face-to-face with his or her roommates or parents, I just text [my friend] saying I have arrived," he says. It's easy to imagine Henry pulling over to the curb on a suburban street, sending a quick text as his phone glows, and watching his friend walk across the lawn alone. He gets in, and Henry's car speeds into the darkness, all other social interactions avoided.

The Screens Go Dark: Mental Health and Happiness

Many people have argued that teens' communicating with their friends electronically is no big deal—they're connecting with their friends, so who cares how they do it? In this view, electronic communication is just as good as in-person communication. If so, it would be just as good for mental health and happiness: teens who communicate via social media and text should be just as happy, be just as likely to dodge loneliness, and be just as likely to avoid depression as teens who see their friends in person or engage in other activities that don't involve screens.

We can find out if that's true. Let's start with happiness. The MtF surveys ask teens how happy they are in general ("very happy," "pretty happy," or "not very happy") and also how much time they spend on various activities during their leisure time, including both screen activities such as social networking sites, texting, and Internet time and nonscreen activities such as in-person social interaction, exercise, and print media. Thus we can see which activities create joy and which are more likely to lead to misery.

The results could not be clearer: teens who spend more time on screen activities (the black bars in Figure 3.5, next page) are more likely to be unhappy, and those who spend more time on nonscreen activities (the gray bars) are more likely to be happy. There's not a single exception: all screen activities are linked to less happiness, and all nonscreen activities are linked to more happiness.

For example, 8th graders who spend ten or more hours a week on social media are 56% more likely to be unhappy than those who don't. Admittedly, ten hours a week is a lot—so what about those who spend merely six hours a week or more on social media? They are still 47% more likely to say they are unhappy. But the opposite is true of in-person social interaction: those who spend more time with their friends in person are 20% *less* likely to be unhappy (listed as –.20 on the chart; see Appendix A for more on relative risk). If you were going to give advice for a happy life based on this graph, it would be straightforward: put down the phone, turn off the computer or iPad, and do something—anything—that does not involve a screen.

These analyses can't unequivocally prove that screen time causes unhappiness; it's also possible that unhappy teens spend more time online. However, three recent studies suggest that screen time (particularly social media use) does indeed cause unhappiness. One study asked college students with Facebook pages to complete short surveys on their phones over the course of two weeks—they'd get a text message with a link five times a day and report on their mood and how much they'd used Facebook. The more they'd used

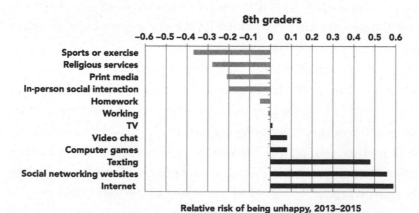

Figure 3.5. Relative risk of being unhappy based on time spent on screen (black bars) and nonscreen (gray bars) activities, 8th graders. Monitoring the Future, 2013–2015.

Facebook, the unhappier they later felt. However, feeling unhappy did not lead to more Facebook use. Facebook use caused unhappiness, but unhappiness did not cause Facebook use.

Another study of adults found the same thing: the more people used Facebook, the lower their mental health and life satisfaction at the next assessment. But after they interacted with their friends in person, their mental health and life satisfaction improved. A third study randomly assigned 1,095 Danish adults to stop using Facebook for a week (the experimental group) or to continue to use Facebook as usual (the control group). At the end of the week, those who had taken a break from Facebook were happier, less lonely, and less depressed than those who had used Facebook as usual (and by fairly substantial margins—36% fewer were lonely, 33% fewer were depressed, and 9% more were happy). Those who stayed off Facebook were also less likely to feel sad, angry, or worried. Because the participants were randomly assigned to conditions, that rules out the explanation that people who are already unhappy, lonely, or depressed use Facebook more—as a true experiment, it shows that Facebook use causes unhappiness, loneliness, and depression.

The risk of unhappiness due to social media use is the highest for the youngest teens. Eighth graders who spent ten or more hours a week on social networking sites were 56% more likely to be unhappy, compared to 47% for 10th graders and 20% for 12th graders (see Figure 3.6, next page). As vulnerable middle schoolers, 8th graders are still developing their identities and are often struggling with body image issues. Add in cyberbullying online, and it's a toxic mix. As teens get older, they are less likely to bully one another and more confident in themselves, protecting them somewhat from the slings and arrows of teen social media experience.

Perhaps there are still some benefits to social media. At least in theory, social media sites are about connecting with others. Maybe using social media doesn't lead to happiness, but it might still help teens feel more included, more surrounded by friends, and less alone. That's certainly what social networking sites promise. A recent commercial for Facebook Live advises, "If you have more to say, take out your phone and press this [Facebook icon], tap this [video camera icon] and go live. Now you're not alone. Your friends are here to listen." In other words, social media can help us feel less alone and surround us with friends at every moment. If that's true, teens who spend a lot of time on social media should be less lonely, and social media should be just as good as in-person social interaction when it comes to feeling less lonely.

Unfortunately for the always online iGen, that turns out not to be true. Teens who visit social networking sites every day are actually *more* likely to agree "I often feel lonely," "I often feel left out of things," and "I often wish I had more good friends" (see Figure 3.7, next page; there are fewer activities on this list than for happiness because the loneliness measure is asked on fewer versions of the questionnaire). In contrast, those who spend time with their friends in person or who play sports are less lonely.

Just as for happiness, the results are clear: screen activities are linked to more loneliness, and nonscreen activities are linked to less loneliness. Teens who spend a lot of time with their friends in person are much less likely to be lonely (with their risk cut nearly in half), and those who visit social networking sites every day or nearly every day are 11% more likely to be lonely. It's nonscreen activities that help teens feel less alone, not social media. The loneliest teens are those who spend more time on social media and less time with their

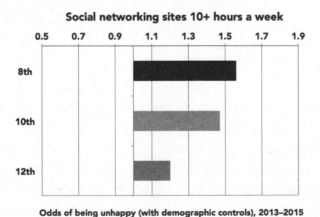

Figure 3.6. Relative risk of being unhappy from spending ten or more hours a week on social networking sites, 8th, 10th, and 12th graders. Monitoring the Future, 2013–2015.

friends in person. If social media time reduces in-person social interaction, it may lead to more loneliness through that less direct route as well.

Just as with happiness, it could be that lonely teens use social media more. However, two of the studies mentioned previously both showed that social media use caused loneliness to increase. In addition, the correlation between social media use and loneliness appears across all demographic groups: boys and girls, Hispanics, whites, and blacks, and those both lower and higher in socioeconomic status.

"At school, people are quieter," confides Olivia, an 18-year-old high school senior. "They all are on their technology ignoring each other. I am dissatisfied with my life because a lot of my friends are addicted to their phones—they seem like they do not want to talk to me because they are on their phones."

Olivia sounds not just lonely but sad, even depressed. Many parents and educators are concerned that teens who are constantly on their phones might be setting themselves up for depression and other mental health issues. They worry that spending that much time in front of a screen can't possibly be healthy.

We can find out if those worries are well founded or not. MtF measures symptoms of depression with six items: agreeing with "Life often seems

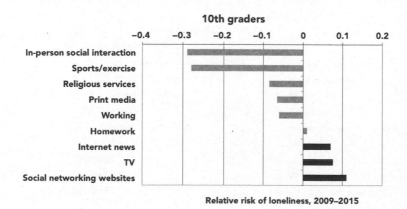

Figure 3.7. Relative risk of loneliness based on time spent on screen (black bars) and nonscreen (gray bars) activities, 10th graders. Monitoring the Future, 2009–2015.

meaningless," "The future often seems hopeless," "I feel that I can't do anything right," "I feel that my life is not very useful," and disagreeing with "I enjoy life as much as anyone" and "It feels good to be alive." A questionnaire like this can't diagnose clinical-level depression—that must be done by a professional using a structured interview—but it does measure classic symptoms of depression, including hopelessness, lack of meaning, and loss of interest in life.

Once again, the split between screen and nonscreen activities is unmistakable: teens who spend more time on screens are more likely to be depressed, and those who spend more time on nonscreen activities are less likely to be depressed (see Figure 3.8). Eighth graders who are heavy users of social media increase their risk of depression by 27%, while those who play sports, go to religious services, or even do homework cut their risk significantly. The teens who are the most active on social media are also those who are most in danger of developing depression, a mental health issue that devastates millions of US teens each year.

Younger teens are more at risk for depression connected to heavy social media use. For 10th graders, social media use carries about even odds for depression (see Appendix D). At the very least, social networking sites do not spark joy or protect against depression the way nonscreen activities do; they don't help and, especially among younger teens, actually hurt.

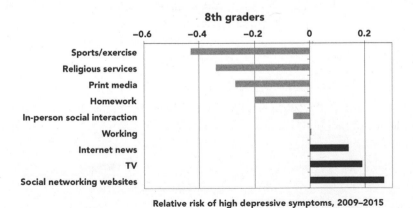

Figure 3.8. Relative risk of high depressive symptoms based on time spent on screen (black bars) and nonscreen (gray bars) activities, 8th graders, 2009–2015.

Ben, 18, lives in Champaign, Illinois, not far from the flagship campus of the University of Illinois. When I reach him one late-August morning, he's just four days away from beginning his freshman year at a private college in the Northeast. He's a bookworm who is happy to be heading to a place that takes academics seriously. We chat about the challenges of packing to go away to college and then turn to the topic of social media. "I got my first Facebook [page] at 13," he says—the minimum age set by the site. "Of course, everyone else already had one." At that age, he says, social media was a fraught experience. "When I posted stuff, I was always incredibly anxious. I would sit there refreshing to make sure there were likes and stuff," he says. "Now my relationship with social media is pretty different. I definitely have more self-confidence, and as a result I sort of care less what people think of my social media. And as a result I basically don't use it." He has hit on three truths about social media and teens: their effects on mental health seem to be strongest for the youngest teens, social media can inflame anxiety among those who are susceptible, and those who truly crave the "hit" of likes are often those who are the most vulnerable to mental health issues.

Googling "Facebook and depression" brings up a long list of pages, including a chat board titled "I think Facebook makes me depressed." MissingGirl, who gives her age as 16 to 17, writes, "Definitely it makes me depressed. All my friends share the fun details of their glamorous lives and it makes me feel like ****. Kinda hate FB." A poster on Reddit wrote, "Scrolling through my feed, seeing [my friends] being happy makes me sad. Also because . . . I get no messages. . . . The sight of a message box with no notifications gives me a really sad, gut wrenching feeling of loneliness. Facebook depresses me, so I'm going to stop using it."

Depression is not just a sad mood: if it leads someone to contemplate suicide, it can be physically dangerous as well. The YRBSS (the high school survey administered by the Centers for Disease Control and Prevention) assesses suicide risk, measured by answering "yes" to at least one of the following: feeling very sad and hopeless for two weeks, seriously considering committing suicide, making a plan to commit suicide, or having attempted to commit suicide. Once again, the link between screen time and mental health issues is distressingly clear: teens who spend more than three hours a day on electronic devices are 35% more likely to have at least one suicide risk factor (see Figure 3.9). That's much more than the risk related to TV watching, suggesting that it's not just screens but new media such as smartphones, games, and social media that are behind the link. Nonscreen activities such as exercise instead lower suicide risk factors. So teens who spend a lot of time looking at their phones aren't just at higher risk of depression—they are also at an alarmingly higher risk for suicide.

These analyses show that three hours of screen time a day increases the chance that a teen will be at risk for committing suicide. So how much screen time is too much? Risks start to increase with screen time of two hours or more a day and go up from there, with very high levels of use (five or more hours) linked to considerably higher risks of suicide and unhappiness (see Figure 3.10, next page). This suggests that moderation, not necessarily a complete elimination of electronic devices from teens' lives, is the key.

Why is electronic device use linked to such heightened odds of suicide risk? It's not demographics; the odds look virtually identical when gender, race, and grade are taken into account. It could be that teens at risk for suicide are drawn to electronic devices. Perhaps, but you'd think that those

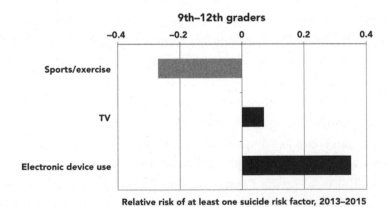

Figure 3.9. Relative risk of having at least one suicide risk factor based on time spent on screen (black bars) and nonscreen (gray bars) activities, 9th–12th graders. Youth Risk Behavior Surveillance System, 2013–2015. (Electronic devices include smartphones, tablets, video games, and computers.)

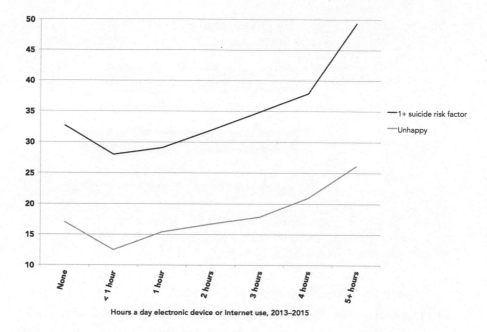

Figure 3.10. Percentage with at least one suicide risk factor and percentage unhappy by hours a day spent on electronic devices or online (exposure-response curve), 9th–12th graders (Youth Risk Behavior Surveillance System), and 8th, 10th, and 12th graders (Monitoring the Future), 2013–2015.

teens, who are often depressed, would be more drawn to passive activities such as TV rather than interactive ones such as social media and computer games. So what, specifically, is so bad about electronic devices that is so much worse than TV? One factor is cyberbullying.

Bullying has always been one of the biggest risk factors for suicide among teens, so it's not surprising that kids who are bullied at school are twice as likely to have at least one suicide risk factor such as considering suicide or making a suicide plan. However, cyberbullying—electronic bullying via texting, social media, or chat rooms—is even worse (see Figure 3.11, next page). Two-thirds (66%) of cyberbullied teens have at least one suicide risk factor, 9% more than those who were bullied offline at school. Teens who are cyberbullied often say that there's no way to get away from their tormentors—unlike with in-person bullies, they can't just avoid certain people. Unless they give up their phones entirely, the bullying continues.

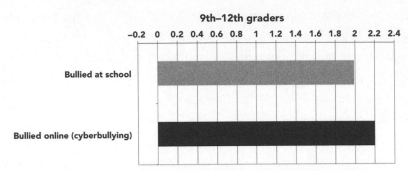

Figure 3.11. Risk of having at least one suicide risk factor based on cyberbullying (black bar) and school bullying (gray bar), 9th–12th graders. Youth Risk Behavior Surveillance System, 2011–2015.

"They said, 'Nobody likes you, go kill yourself,'" 15-year-old Sierra from Virginia said in *American Girls* about the girls who cyberbullied her. She received one Instagram comment that read, "You have no ass girl, stop trying to take pictures like you have one, it's not cute, you look like a ho. You look stupid . . . that outfit makes you look like a cheap prostitute that stands on the corner." The constant bullying sent Sierra into a tailspin. "I started eating ice cream all the time to not let it all get to me, but I don't want to get fat. So I just solved it by cutting," she said, referring to self-injury (which involves purposefully cutting yourself with a knife or razor blade, usually on the legs and arms). Eventually, she tried to kill herself, first by swallowing as many pills as she could find and later by jumping in front of an oncoming car. A friend grabbed her and pulled her back.

David Molak was a high school sophomore at Alamo Heights High School in San Antonio, Texas, when his classmates began relentlessly bullying him through text messages, denigrating his physical appearance and hurling other insults. On January 4, 2016, he committed suicide. "I saw the pain in David's eyes three nights ago as he was added to a group text only to be made fun of and kicked out two minutes later," his older brother Cliff wrote in a Facebook post. "He stared off into the distance for what seemed like an hour. I could feel his pain. . . . David had been enduring this sort of abuse for a very long time. In today's age, bullies don't push you into lockers

. . . they cower behind user names and fake profiles from miles away constantly berating and abusing good, innocent people."

Even when cyberbullying doesn't lead to suicide, it can certainly lead to unhappiness or depression. Even famous and successful iGen'ers are not immune. Gabby Douglas, the Olympic gymnast who won gold in the all-around competition at the 2012 Games, was cyberbullied after a disappointing performance in 2016. "I wonder how many times I cried. Probably enough to fill so many gallons of water. And it would be like, deep, emotional cries because I was so hurt," the 21-year-old told *People* magazine. One set of studies by the Cyberbullying Research Center suggests that cyberbullying has become more common, with 34% of teens in 2016 affected, compared to 19% in 2007. Teens' entire lives are online, and one out of three is being bullied right where he or she lives.

There's one last piece of data that indirectly but stunningly captures the move away from in-person activities and toward solo, online interaction. Since 2007, the homicide rate among teens has declined, but the suicide rate has increased. The steady decline in teen homicide from 2007 to 2014 looks very similar to the decline in in-person social interaction (see Figure 3.12, next page). As teens have spent less time with one another in person, they have also become less likely to kill each other. In contrast, teen suicide rates began to tick up after 2008. The rise looks small on the graph because of the scale, but it's not—46% more teens killed themselves in 2015 than in 2007. The rise occurred just as new-media screen time started to increase and in-person social activities began to wane. In 2011, for the first time in twenty-four years, the teen suicide rate was higher than the teen homicide rate. The gap grew larger from 2011 to 2014, with the suicide rate 32% higher than the homicide rate by 2014—the largest gap since records have been kept (the gap remained high, 30%, in 2015).

The astonishing, though tentative, possibility is that the rise of the smartphone has caused both the decline in homicide and the increase in suicide. With teens spending more hours with their phones and less with their friends, more are becoming depressed and committing suicide and fewer are committing homicide. To put it bluntly: teens have to be with each other in person to kill each other, but they can cyberbully each other into suicide

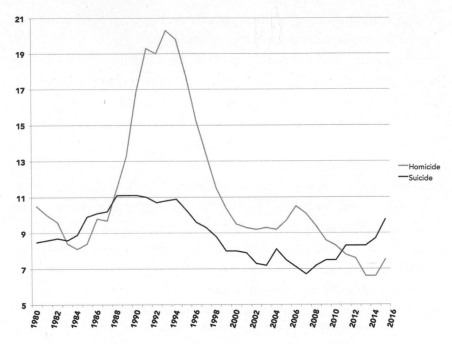

Figure 3.12. Homicide and suicide rates out of 100,000 population among 15- to 19-year-olds, 1980–2015. Centers for Disease Control and Prevention.

through their phones. Even if bullying is not involved, screen communication can be isolating, which might lead to depression and sometimes suicide. Of course, there are many causes of depression and suicide—too much technology is clearly not the only cause (after all, the suicide rate was even higher in the 1990s, long before smartphones existed). At the same time, it is distressing, and unacceptable, that so many more teens are killing themselves than did just a few years ago.

Caveman Brains, FOMO, and Soft Skills

All in all, in-person social interaction is much better for mental health than electronic communication. This makes sense: humans are inherently social beings, and our brains evolved to crave face-to-face interaction. In hunter-gatherer times, people who got kicked out of the tribe often died because they had no one to share food with (and no one to reproduce with—being a hermit was literally bred out of us). The legacy of this era lives in our brains, which are exquisitely attuned to social acceptance and rejection. I've studied this myself: I spent my postdoctoral fellowship researching the effects of social rejection in a series of projects led by the prominent social psychologist Roy Baumeister. We found that even a brief, randomly assigned experience of being socially rejected sent people into a tailspin, increasing aggression, creating feelings of hopelessness, and (my personal favorite) causing them to eat more cookies. Neuroscientists have found that when people are left out of a game by other players, the brain region involved in physical pain is activated. Apparently it's not a coincidence that many terms for social pain mimic those for physical pain, including "hurt feelings" and "heartbroken." (It's more as though your brain is broken, but the term comes from ancient times when people believed that the heart was the source of our thoughts and feelings.)

With our brains—perhaps especially teen brains—so attuned to social rejection, texting and social media are fertile grounds for negative emotions. Even when things go well, the cadence of electronic communication can be problematic. Unlike in face-to-face interaction, electronic communication often involves a delay between your side of the conversation and your friend's reply. Think about what happens when you send a text. If the other person doesn't write back right away, you might wonder why. Is she mad? Did he not like what I said? The same happens when you post something on social media—everyone wants to see the likes, and if they take too long to come or don't come at all, anxiety can follow.

One study had college students interact in one of two ways: online or in person. Those who interacted in person felt emotionally closer to each other, which makes sense given the conditions under which our human brains evolved. Think about it this way: humans experienced approximately 99.9% of our evolution when the only way to communicate with someone else was in person. Compared to a warm person right in front of you, electronic communication is a pale shadow.

Many iGen'ers say that their online lives make them feel they are walking a tightrope. "I find [social media] really stressful, actually," 19-year-old Sofia Stojic told the Australian newspaper *The Age*. "It's just the knowledge that it's there in the background. It's very hard these days to switch it off and be with your thoughts." The other iGen'ers interviewed in the article all said that they try to turn off notifications or their phone entirely so they can concentrate on other things, such as talking to a friend in person. But they find they can't, because they fear missing out. "It's not like you can ever get away from it. You can switch off your phone but it's still there," said Amy Bismire, 19.

Even when time on social media goes well and make us feel included, it is no substitute for actual, face-to face interaction. As 17-year-old Kevin says, "If you have contact person to person, you actually get true emotions if you hang out with them. If you do something together, accomplish something together, it just feels good, you know? You get to share emotions, like fighting and making up. You can't really get those kinds of feelings with social media."

iGen'ers still yearn for in-person interaction. Nearly all of the 18- and 19-year-olds in the SDSU freshman survey said they would rather see their friends in person than communicate electronically. "It is much more fun to have a conversation in person," wrote Bailey, 19. "When you are actually with someone it feels so much more personal and loving. Memories are created through experiences and that can't happen on the phone or computer," wrote Julian, 18.

For parents, teachers, student affairs professionals, and businesses, the big question is this: Will the decline in in-person social interaction lead to iGen having inferior social skills? Some preliminary evidence suggests it will. In one study, 6th graders spent five days at an overnight nature camp with no access to computers, cell phones, or TV. A control group continued their usual technology activities. All of the kids then took two social skills tests, naming the emotion (happy, sad, angry, fearful) expressed in a series of photos of people's faces or watching no-sound videotapes of social interactions. The kids who had spent five days away from screens improved their social skills significantly more than the control group did.

Athena, 13, thinks that today's kids are missing out on experienes that develop their social skills. "We grew up with iPhones," she says. "We don't know how to communicate like normal people and look people in the eye and talk to them." Her middle school drama teacher tells students, "Put your phone in the box, we're learning to look people in the eye." Athena thinks that phones have affected teen speech as well: "Sometimes it makes us, like, aliens. We don't know how to talk to people anymore."

Just as playing the piano takes practice, so do social skills. iGen'ers are not practicing their in-person social skills as much as other generations did, so when it comes time for the "recital" of their social skills, they are more likely to make mistakes onstage when it matters: in college interviews, when making friends in high school, and when competing for a job. Life's social decisions are still made primarily in person, and iGen gets less experience with such situations. In the next decade we may see more young people who know just the right emoji for a situation—but not the right facial expression.

Chapter 4

Insecure: The New Mental Health Crisis

UC Berkeley student Ilaf Esuf was home on a break from school when it hit. Returning from a shopping trip with her mother, she felt overwhelmed with sadness and began to cry. "I pulled into the driveway, my sleeves soaked from subtly wiping away my tears," she wrote in the *Daily Californian*. "My mom stood there, dumbfounded. She clutched my arm and asked me why I was crying, but I couldn't tell her. My unexplainable, occasional sadness lingered like my worried mother who stood by the door, heartbroken, waiting for things to make sense again." Ilaf isn't always sure why she feels depressed, and she struggles to explain her feelings to her parents. "I don't know what's wrong and I don't know why I feel this way, but I promise I'm fine and it will pass. That's what I tell myself when I'm walking down the street and I feel tears rolling down my face."

iGen'ers look so happy online, making goofy faces on Snapchat and smiling in their pictures on Instagram. But dig deeper, and reality is not so comforting. iGen is on the verge of the most severe mental health crisis for young people in decades. On the surface, though, everything is fine.

Everything Is (Not) Awesome

> You know what's awesome? EVERYTHING!
> —"Everything Is Awesome" from *The Lego Movie*

The Internet—and society in general—promotes a relentless positivity these days. Social media posts highlight the happy moments but rarely the sad ones: everyone is smiling in their selfies, unless they're doing a duck face.

This positivity has its roots in a trend begun by the Boomers, refined by Generation X, and brought to full force by the Millennials: the growing individualism of American culture. Individualistic cultures focus more on the self and less on social rules. Individualism is behind most fundamental cultural changes of the last few decades, from trends usually considered good (the growth of equality based on race, gender, and sexual orientation) as well as those seen as more negative (the sense of entitlement displayed by so many people). Individualism also encourages people to feel good about themselves—not just as good as they should but even better than might be justified. Positive self-views are one of the hallmarks of individualistic cultures, which encourage self-promotion and self-esteem. As the tide of individualism rose throughout the 1990s and 2000s, Millennials quickly gained a reputation for overconfidence and unrealistically high expectations—one justified by their more positive self-views, higher narcissism, and heightened aspirations compared to previous generations. Those trends tapered off with iGen'ers, who are not the overconfident optimists Millennials were at the same age. iGen'ers score lower in narcissism and have lower expectations, suggesting that the outsize entitlement displayed by some Millennials might be on its way out. Because overly positive self-views are mostly Millennials' story, not iGen'ers', those trends are discussed in the appendix instead (see Appendix E).

Millennial teens in the 2000s were also happier than the teens of the 1990s, the era when GenX'ers wore black T-shirts and talked about how depressed they were. With its emphasis on freedom and optimism, individualism is an advantageous system for teens, and greater happiness was the result.

Then iGen arrived, and teen happiness began to falter. For 8th and 10th graders especially, the gains of the 2000s have been wiped out in the years since 2011 (see Figure 4.1). Just as iGen entered the samples, teen happiness started to wane from its Millennial exuberance. Pop culture somehow saw this one coming, with teen movies veering from happy comedies about partying high schoolers (*American Pie*, *Superbad*) to tales of young people fighting their way through dystopian landscapes (*The Hunger Games*, *Divergent*).

Of course, the happiness question is just one item, and the decline is noticeable but not extreme. So it pays to look more deeply at trends in teens' psychological well-being.

The first serious rumbles of the oncoming crash in iGen'ers' outlook appear in their answers to questions asking whether they are satisfied with themselves and with their lives as a whole. From the 1980s to the 2000s, progressively more teens said they were satisfied. Then, when the first iGen'ers became high school seniors in 2012 and 2013, satisfaction suddenly

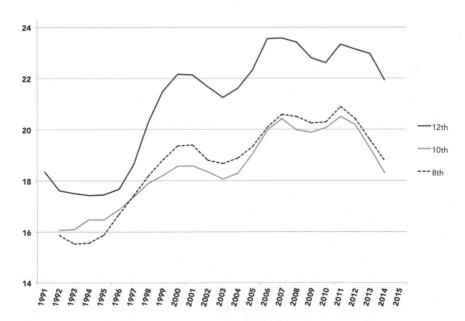

Figure 4.1. Percentage of 8th, 10th, and 12th graders who report being "very happy" (three-year moving average). Monitoring the Future, 1991–2015.

plummeted, reaching all-time lows in 2015 (see Figure 4.2). So as teens spent less time with their friends in person and more time on their phones, their life satisfaction dropped with astonishing speed.

With this sudden, cataclysmic shift downward in life satisfaction, the gains of more than two decades were wiped out in just a few years. And that, as it turns out, is only the tip of the iceberg.

Left Out and Lonely

Thirteen-year-old Grace Nazarian opened her Instagram page one day to find pictures of her closest friends at a birthday party—one she hadn't been invited to. "I felt like I was the only one not there," Grace told the *Today* show. ". . . I was thinking, they're having a good time without me. Then I just felt really, really bad about myself." Grace's experience is now common: whereas teens used to hear about social events through whispers and loose talk at

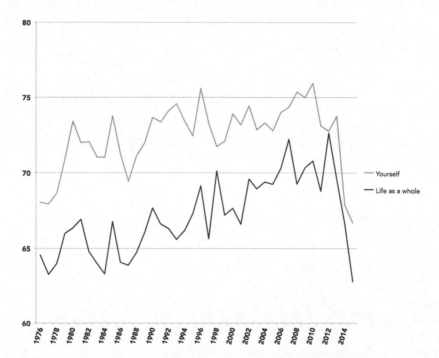

Figure 4.2. Percentage of 12th graders who are satisfied with their lives as a whole and with themselves. Monitoring the Future, 1976–2015.

school, they can now see up-to-the-minute pictures of exactly what they are missing. iGen has a specific term for this: FOMO (Fear of Missing Out). In many ways, it sounds like a recipe for loneliness.

Of course, electronic communication can also have the opposite effect, helping teens feel connected to one another even when they are apart. Teens stay in close touch with their friends via text and online, exchanging funny Snapchat pictures and constantly updating everyone on what they're doing. But that doesn't assuage their loneliness: in fact, they are lonelier than they were just five years ago. A stunning 31% more 8th and 10th graders felt lonely in 2015 than in 2011, along with 22% more 12th graders (see Figure 4.3). This is a monumental change in just four years. Teens are now lonelier than at any time since the survey began in 1991.

As might be expected in the age of FOMO, teens are also more likely to say that they often feel left out. Across all three age groups, feeling left out

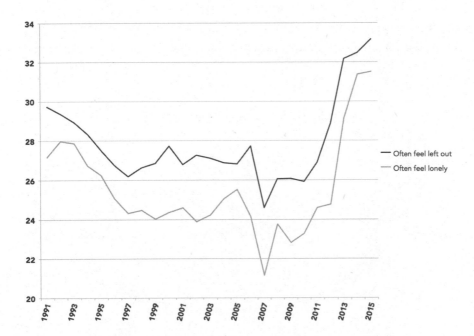

Figure 4.3. Percentage of 8th, 10th, and 12th graders who mostly agree or agree that "I often feel left out of things" or "A lot of times I feel lonely." Monitoring the Future, 1991–2015.

has reached all-time highs. Like the increase in loneliness, the upswing in feeling left out has been swift and large, with many more teens experiencing this feeling of exclusion (see Figure 4.3, previous page).

Such large changes over a short period of time are unusual, suggesting a specific cause with a big impact. Given the timing, smartphones are the most likely culprits, increasing loneliness both directly and indirectly by replacing in-person social interaction. With teens spending less time on activities that assuage loneliness, and more time on those that don't, it is not surprising that loneliness has increased. The likely mechanism looks something like Figure 4.4.

The decline in in-person social interaction is like a hit man hired by someone else: he commits the crime even though it wasn't his idea. Screen time both hires the hit man and, for good measure, fires a few shots herself.

One important note: this isn't a model of how screen time and in-person time work among individual people, because teens who spend more time on social media also spend more time with their friends in person—highly social teens are more social in both venues, and less social teens are less. It is instead a hypothesis for how these variables relate at the generational

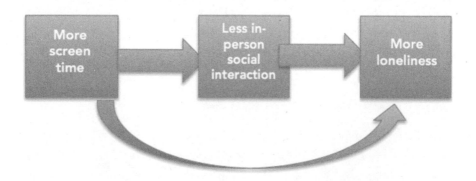

Figure 4.4. A possible model for the origin of iGen loneliness.

level: When teens as a group spend more time on screens and less time on in-person social interaction, loneliness will increase on average.

It's possible that loneliness causes smartphone use instead of smartphone use causing loneliness, but the abrupt increase in loneliness makes this alternative much less likely. If loneliness caused smartphone use, a sudden increase in loneliness with no known cause would lead to smartphones suddenly becoming more popular. It seems much more likely that smartphones became popular, screen time increased, and thus teens' loneliness increased. And, as we saw in the last chapter, several studies have shown that social media use leads to negative emotions rather than vice versa.

Although the trend toward feeling left out appears among both boys and girls, the increase was especially steep among girls (see Appendix F). Forty-eight percent more girls felt left out in 2015 than in 2010, compared to a 27% increase for boys. Girls use social media more often, giving them more opportunities to feel left out and lonely when they see their friends or classmates getting together without them. Social media are also the perfect medium for the verbal aggression favored by girls. Even before the Internet, boys tended to bully one another physically and girls verbally. Social media give middle and high school girls a 24/7 platform to carry out the verbal aggression they favor, ostracizing and excluding other girls. Girls are twice as likely as boys to experience this type of electronic bullying (known as cyberbullying); in the YRBSS survey of high school students, 22% of girls said they had been cyberbullied in the last year, compared to 10% of boys. iGen teen girls are living their social lives online and, as a result, are more and more likely to feel left out.

Afraid You're Gonna Live: Depression

In Laura's profile picture on Tumblr, she's a girl with wavy brown hair who looks no more than 16. Her site is titled "a depressed person life." Her pain is starkly evident in her posts, which include "That's how depression hits. You wake up one morning, afraid that you're gonna live," "I don't know why I am so stupid. I don't know why I am so sad," and "They all looked so damn happy to me. Why couldn't I look like that?" The web page's title appeared as one apt word: "Broken."

Depression like Laura's may be more common than it used to be. Many parents and educators worry that teens' constant smartphone use, especially the constant thrum of social media and texting, has created an emotionally fragile generation prone to depression. There's been a considerable amount of debate around this question, since much of what's been discussed in the media comes from the reports of those who staff college counseling centers. These administrators say that more and more students are seeking their help and that the students' problems are more severe than they were a few years ago. However, their perceptions could be influenced by a number of outside factors, including students' being more willing to seek help.

To really find out whether mental health issues are more common than they once were, it would be best to have data from anonymous surveys of a representative sample of teens (all teens, not just those who seek help), preferably before they enter college (to rule out any link between college attendance and mental health) and over several decades so we can compare their responses with those of previous generations at the same age. Fortunately, that is exactly what the MtF surveys of 8th, 10th, and 12th graders do, using the six-item measure of depressive symptoms introduced in the last chapter. The items measure feelings and symptoms rather than asking teens outright if they feel depressed. This helps minimize the possibility that they are more (or less) comfortable admitting to mental health issues. And of course, the MtF surveys are anonymous, explicitly telling students that their responses will not be identified. This measure of depressive symptoms is not equivalent to a clinical diagnosis of major depression, but it does capture the feelings and beliefs that are major risk factors for diagnosed depression.

The data from these surveys are stark: teens' depressive symptoms have skyrocketed in a very short period of time. The number of teens who agreed "I feel like I can't do anything right" reached all-time highs in recent years, zooming upward after 2011 (see Figure 4.5, next page). In all three age groups, feeling you can't do anything right also reached all-time highs in recent years. This isn't just a wave—it's a tsunami.

Social media might play a role in these feelings of inadequacy: many people post only their successes online, so many teens don't realize that their friends fail at things, too. The social media profiles they see make them feel like failures. If they spent more time with their friends in person, they might realize that they are not the only ones making mistakes. One study found that college students who used Facebook more often were more depressed—but only if they felt more envy toward others. The researchers measured envy using items many social media users would agree with, such as "I generally feel inferior to others," "Many of my friends have a better life than me," and "Many of my friends are happier than me." Megan Armstrong, a University of Missouri student who struggled with depression, put it this way: "You're constantly hearing about what this person did that was really awesome. It always makes me wonder, what am I doing? What should I be doing? Is it enough?"

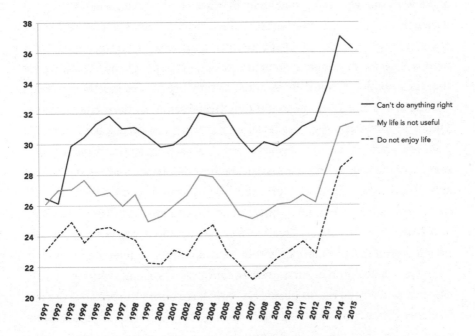

Figure 4.5. Percentage of 8th, 10th, and 12th graders who are neutral, mostly agree, or agree that "I feel like I can't do anything right," or "My life is not useful," or "I do not enjoy life." Monitoring the Future, 1989–2015.

Azar, the high school senior we met in earlier chapters, is an astute observer of the patina of positivity on social media covering the ugly underbelly of reality. "People post pretty Instagram posts, like 'My life is so great.' Their lives are crap! They're teenagers," she says. "[They post] 'I'm so grateful for my bestie.' That is b.s. You are not so grateful for your bestie, because in two weeks she's going to, like, cheat with your boyfriend, and then y'all gonna have a bitch fight and y'all gonna, like, claw each other's ears off. That is what a teenager's life is." Azar's assessment, funny and sad at the same time, captures the paradox of iGen: an optimism and self-confidence online that covers a deep vulnerability, even depression, in real life. That's the story of iGen'ers' life on social media, and it is increasingly the story of their generation. Like the ducks they imitate in their selfies, iGen'ers are calm and composed on the surface but paddling madly underneath.

It goes beyond just feeling inadequate, however. More teens in recent years agree with the depressing statement "My life is not useful," with feelings of uselessness reaching all-time highs (see Figure 4.5, previous page). In addition, fewer teens agree that "I enjoy life as much as anyone." Disagreeing with this item is a clear symptom of depression, as depressed people nearly always say that they no longer enjoy life as much as they used to. In just the few years between 2012 and 2015, more and more teens said they don't enjoy life (see Figure 4.5, previous page). Across all six items, depression has skyrocketed in just a few years, a trend that appears among blacks, whites, and Hispanics, in all regions of the United States, across socioeconomic classes, and in small towns, suburbs, and big cities (see Appendix F). On Tumblr, a microblogging site popular with teens, mentions of mental health increased 248% between 2013 and 2016. "If you wanted to create an environment to churn out really angsty people, we've done it," said Janis Whitlock, a Cornell University researcher. "They're in a cauldron of stimulus they can't get away from."

Just as with the rise in loneliness, girls have borne the brunt of the rise in depressive symptoms. Although teen girls and boys were once about equally likely to experience the symptoms of depression, girls now report markedly higher levels (see Figure 4.6, next page, and Appendix F). Boys' depression increased by 21% between 2012 and 2015, and girls' increased by

50%—more than twice as much. And girls spend more time on social media than boys do. "We're the first generation that cannot escape our problems at all," 20-year-old Faith Ann Bishop told *Time*.

College students' mental health is also deteriorating. In a major over-time survey administered by the American Collegiate Health Association, college students are now more likely to say they feel overwhelming anxiety and that they felt so depressed they could not function. Just as with high school students, anxiety and depression ticked up recently—just since 2013 (see Figure 4.7, next page).

The American Freshman Survey of entering college students shows sim-ilar trends. Every indicator of mental health issues on the survey reached all-time highs in 2016—rating emotional health below average (increasing 18% since 2009), feeling overwhelmed (increasing 51%), expecting to seek counseling (increasing 64%), and (perhaps most troubling) feeling depressed

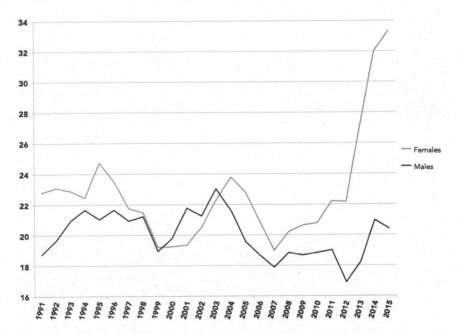

Figure 4.6. Depressive symptoms by sex, 8th, 10th, and 12th graders. Monitoring the Future, 1991–2015.

(increasing 95%, or nearly doubling), with noticeable jumps just between 2015 and 2016. In 2016, for the first time, the majority of entering college students described their mental health as below average (see Figure 4.8, next page). Overall, more and more college students are struggling with mental health issues—not just those who seek help at counseling centers but among representative samples completing anonymous surveys.

The sudden, sharp rise in depressive symptoms occurred at almost exactly the same time that smartphones became ubiquitous and in-person interaction plummeted. That seems like too much of a coincidence for the trends not to be connected, especially because spending more time on social media and less time on in-person social interaction is correlated with depression. With correlational data like this, social media could cause depression, depressed people could use social media more, or a third factor could explain the rise in both. Even if the second two explanations are true for individual people, they don't work very well for explaining why depression would

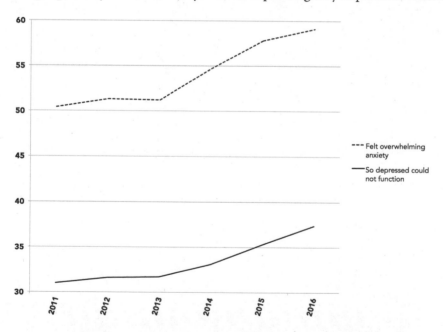

Figure 4.7. Percentage of undergraduate college students who felt overwhelming anxiety or who felt so depressed they could not function in the last 12 months, 2011–2016. American College Health Association (ACHA) survey of approximately 400,000 students on over 100 campuses.

increase so suddenly. That leaves the possibility of some unknown, outside factor that suddenly caused more depression among teens. Could the Great Recession of 2007–2009 be the outside factor? It did come on suddenly, but the timing is wrong. Unemployment, one of the best indicators of how the economy is affecting real people, peaked in 2010 and then declined, exactly the opposite pattern from depression, which was stable until 2012 and then increased. Smartphones, however, gained in popularity over that same time (see Figure 4.9, next page).

Why might smartphones cause depression? For one thing, not getting a reply to your text or social media message has a high potential for causing anxiety—a common precursor to depression. An exchange among three 16-year-old girls in Los Angeles captured this in *American Girls*. "I mean we all, like, overanalyze it," said Greta, referring to boys who don't respond to texts or Snapchats. "It goes both ways. I love it that, like, if I'm mad at a boy he can see that I've seen his message and he *knows* that I'm ignoring him."

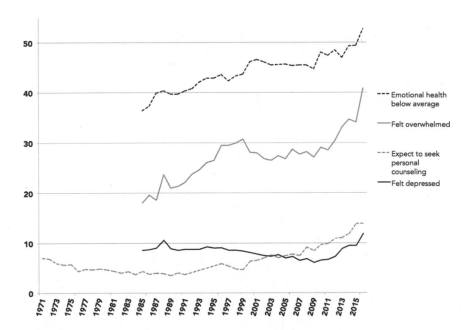

Figure 4.8. Entering college students reporting mental health issues. American Freshman Survey, 1971–2016.

"It causes stress, though, when it's you," said Melissa. "And depression," said Padma. "When they ignore your texts, and then you're like, Well, why am I even *alive*?"

Girls may also be uniquely vulnerable to the effects of social media on mental health. The emphasis on perfect selfies has amplified body image issues for girls, who often chase likes by taking hundreds of pictures to get just the right one but still end up feeling as though they've fallen short. "They make you think you have to change yourself, like lose weight or gain weight, instead of just being yourself," said a 16-year-old in *American Girls*. "Every day it's like you have to wake up and put on a mask and try to be somebody else instead of being yourself," said another, "and you can't ever be happy." Nineteen-year-old Essena O'Neill, a model who made her living by posting her photos on Instagram, suddenly took down her social media accounts in November 2015. She posted a YouTube video in which she said, "I spent hours watching perfect girls online, wishing I was them. Then, when I was 'one of them,' I still wasn't happy, content, or at peace with myself. Social media is

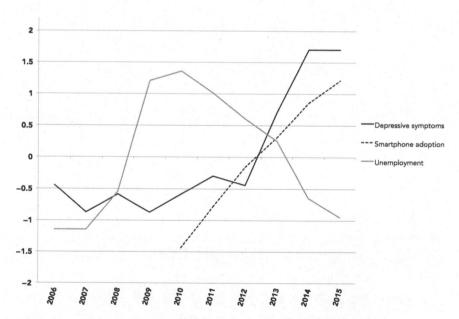

Figure 4.9. Smartphone ownership rates among Americans, yearly unemployment rate, and depressive symptoms among 10th graders. Monitoring the Future, 2006–2015. (Variables are standardized.)

not real life." Her photos, which looked like casual snaps, actually took several hours to set up and up to a hundred attempts to get right. Caring about her number of followers, she said, "suffocated me. . . . I was miserable."

Double standards of sexuality are also very evident online. Girls often feel that they can't win—a sexy photo will get lots of likes, but it also invites slut shaming. The usual girl drama of who said what to whom and who has a crush on whom is also heightened on social media, surrounding girls twenty-four hours a day with the back-and-forth of an often toxic interaction, all without the context of facial expressions and gestures. The perennial teen girl question "Is she mad at me?" is much harder to answer on a smartphone.

An Epidemic of Anguish: Major Depressive Disorder, Self-Harm, and Suicide

Madison Holleran was everything most young girls want to grow up to be: beautiful, academically successful, athletic. She was raised in New Jersey, one of five siblings in a close-knit family, and headed off to college at the University of Pennsylvania, where she ran track. Like many college students, she posted pictures on her Instagram page: track meets, friends, parties. "Madison, you look like you're so happy at this party," her mother told her. "Mom," Madison replied. "It's just a picture."

Madison's Instagram account didn't capture what was really going on: she was depressed. She was, she confided to her friend Emma, scared to grow up, terrified that she didn't know exactly what would happen next. She had yet to get a driver's license. After a tough first semester at Penn, she started seeing a therapist near her home in New Jersey. One day in January of her freshman year, her father called and asked if she had found a therapist in Philadelphia so she could continue her treatment when she was at school. "No, but don't worry, Daddy, I'll find one," she said. A few hours later, she jumped off the roof of a nine-story parking garage to her death. She was 19 years old.

So far, what we've discussed is variations in symptoms among the normal population: worrisome signs but not evidence of clinical-level depression. Those feelings are still very important, as they affect larger numbers of teens and are risk factors for more serious issues, yet most of the time they don't rise to the level of a debilitating mental illness. So it's fair to ask: Has the rise in feelings of loneliness, depression, and anxiety also been accompanied by changes in diagnosable depression and its most extreme outcome, suicide?

The National Survey on Drug Use and Health (NSDUH), conducted by the US Department of Health and Human Services, has screened US teens for clinical-level depression since 2004. The project sends trained interviewers to assess a nationally representative sample of more than 17,000 teens (ages 12 to 17) across the country every year. Participants hear questions through headphones and enter their answers directly into a laptop computer, ensuring privacy and confidentiality. The questions rely on the criteria for major depressive disorder documented in the *Diagnostic and Statistical Manual* (DSM) of the American Psychiatric Association, the gold standard for diagnosing mental health issues. The criteria include experiencing depressed mood, insomnia, fatigue, or markedly diminished pleasure in life every day for at least two weeks. The study is specifically designed to prove a benchmark for rates of mental illness among Americans, regardless of whether they've ever sought treatment. A study like this is about as reliable and valid as you can get.

The screening test shows a shocking rise in depression in a short period of time: 56% more teens experienced a major depressive episode in 2015 than in 2010 (see Figure 4.10, next page), and 60% more experienced severe impairment.

More young people are experiencing not just symptoms of depression, and not just feelings of anxiety, but clinically diagnosable major depression. With more than one in nine teens and one in eleven young adults suffering from major depression, this is not a small issue. Even more than the data on rising loneliness and depressive symptoms, these gold-standard data suggest that something is seriously wrong in the lives of American teens.

Just as with depressive symptoms and loneliness, the increase in major depressive episodes is far steeper among girls, the gender more likely to overuse social media. By 2015, one in five teen girls had experienced a major depressive episode in the last year (see Figure 4.10, next page).

Depressed teens are more likely to self-injure, such as through cutting. Fadi Haddad, a psychiatrist at Bellevue Hospital in New York City, told *Time*

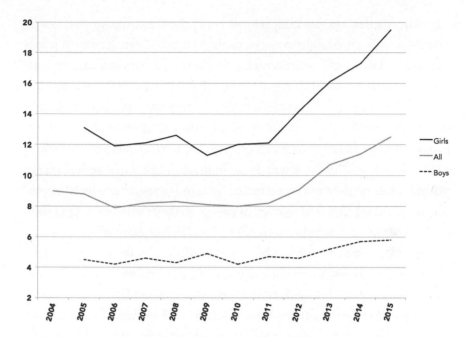

Figure 4.10. Percentage of 12- to 17-year-olds experiencing a major depressive episode or a major depressive episode with severe impairment in the last 12 months, overall and by sex. National Survey on Drug Use and Health, US Department of Health and Human Services, 2004–2015.

magazine, "Every single week we have a girl who comes to the ER after some social-media rumor or incident has upset her." Those ER visits are almost always caused by girls cutting themselves. Between 2011 and 2016, 6% more college students said they intentionally injured themselves (in the ACHA survey; see Appendix F). Some teens discuss their cutting on social media; one study found that the hashtag "#selfharmmm" zoomed from 1.7 million mentions on Instagram in 2014 to 2.4 million in 2015. The extra *m*'s are apparently to express pleasure, a cruel irony rooted in the feelings of release some cutters say they experience. Many parents have no idea what their children are doing on social media, and many feel helpless, Haddad says. One mother found that her self-harming daughter had seventeen Facebook accounts, which the mother promptly shut down. "But what good does that do?" asked Haddad. "There will be an eighteenth."

Major depression, especially if it's severe, is also the primary risk factor for suicide. A high school classmate once confided to Utah State student Whitney Howard that she didn't understand how anyone could commit suicide. How could things possibly be that bad? "Little did she know that I was suicidal myself," Whitney says. ". . . I tried overdosing on pain pills." Depression, she says, is "an emptiness, an absence of feeling. [It] numbs you and strips you of happiness, hope and enjoyment. Think of the Dementors from 'Harry Potter.'" Between 2009 and 2015, the number of high school girls who seriously considered suicide in the past year increased 34%, and the number who attempted suicide increased 43%. The number of college students who seriously considered suicide jumped 60% between 2011 and 2016 (see Appendix F).

Suicide, a carefully tracked behavior unaffected by the possible irregularities of self-report surveys, is the most extreme and sadly objective outcome of depression. If suicide rates have risen, it would be strong evidence that depression has reached problematic levels. Unfortunately, it has. After declining during the 1990s and stabilizing in the 2000s, the suicide rate for teens has risen again. Forty-six percent more 15- to 19-year-olds committed suicide in 2015 than in 2007, and two and a half times more 12- to 14-year-olds killed themselves (see Appendix F). These are heartbreaking numbers.

The rise in suicide is more pronounced for girls. Although the rate increased for both sexes, three times as many 12- to 14-year-old girls killed themselves in 2015 than in 2007, compared to twice as many boys (see Figure 4.11, next page). Although the suicide rate is still higher for boys (likely because they use more lethal methods), girls are beginning to catch up.

For an outcome such as suicide—the end of a young and precious life—this is an extremely worrisome rise. It's also surprising, because more Americans now take antidepressants (one out of ten in the last year, more than double the rate of the mid-1990s). Antidepressants are especially effective against severe depression, the type most strongly linked to suicide. Yet they haven't been enough to stem the growth of suicide among teens that started right around the same time smartphones became common. We can't say for sure that smartphones are to blame, but the timing is very suspicious. With twice as many young teens killing themselves, something clearly needs to be done.

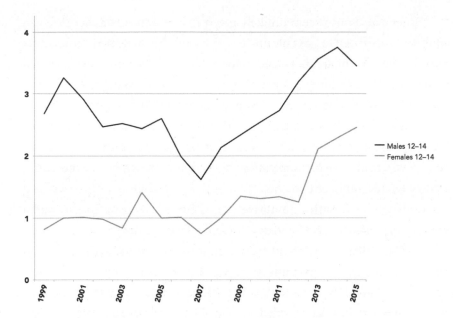

Figure 4.11. Suicide rate per 100,000 people, 12- to 14-year-olds, by sex. Fatal Injury Reports, Centers for Disease Control and Prevention, 1999–2015.

Why the Rise in Mental Health Issues?

Although the rise in anxiety, depression, and suicide has occurred at the same time as the rise of smartphones, it makes sense to consider other causes as well. An article in *The Atlantic* blamed teen mental health issues almost exclusively on academic pressure. "Students are challenged to take a demanding course of study, to get a high GPA. . . . School is more challenging," said one high school counselor. But one good indicator of academic pressure is the amount of time students spend on homework, and as we saw in chapter 1, time spent doing homework is less or about the same as in previous decades, with little change between 2012 and 2016, the years when depression skyrocketed. Plus, as we saw in chapter 3, students who spend more time on homework are actually *less* likely to be depressed. Thus, it seems highly unlikely that too much time spent studying is the cause of the rise in anxiety and depression.

Other causes also seem unlikely given the available evidence. We can apply a two-part test to possible causes: (1) it must be correlated with mental health issues or unhappiness (see chapter 3) and (2) it must have changed at the same time and in the correct direction. Time spent doing homework fails both tests; it's not linked to depression, and it didn't change much over that time period. TV watching is linked to depression, but teens watch less TV now than they used to, so it fails test number two. Time spent on exercise and sports is linked to less depression, but it didn't change much since 2012, so they fail test number two, too.

Only three activities definitively pass both tests. First, new-media screen time (such as electronic devices and social media) is linked to mental health issues and/or unhappiness, and it rose at the same time. Second and third, in-person social interaction and print media are linked to less unhappiness and less depression, and both have declined at the same time as mental health has deteriorated. A plausible theory includes three possible causes: (1) more screen time has led directly to more unhappiness and depression, (2) more screen time has led to less in-person social interaction, which then led to unhappiness and depression, and (3) more screen time has led to less print media use, leading to unhappiness and depression. In the end, all of the mechanisms come back to new-media screen time in one way or another. By all accounts, it is the worm at the core of the apple.

Of course, even with this evidence, these data can't definitively show that the shift toward screen time has caused more mental health issues. However, other studies can: experiments that randomly assign people to experience more or less screen time and those that track behavior over time have both found that more screen time causes more anxiety, depression, loneliness, and less emotional connection. It seems clear that at least some of the sudden and large increase in depression has been caused by teens spending more time with screens.

Another possibility is that iGen'ers are unprepared for adolescence and early adulthood due to their lack of independence. With iGen'ers less likely to work, manage their own money, and drive in high school, perhaps they are not developing the resilience that may come from doing things on your own. One study asked college students if their parents "supervised my every move," "stepped in to solve life problems for me," and didn't "let me figure things out independently." Students whose parents displayed those characteristics (often known as "helicopter parents") had lower psychological well-being and were more likely to have been prescribed medication for anxiety and depression. Thus, reduced independence passes both tests: it is correlated with mental health issues, and it changed at the same time.

The 2015 song "Stressed Out" by Twenty One Pilots captures this possible link between growing up slowly and mental health issues. In the music video, the band members ride oversized Big Wheels down a suburban Columbus, Ohio, street and drink Capri Suns with straws. Lead singer Tyler Joseph says he wishes they could "turn back time to the good ol' days when our momma sang us to sleep." Adulthood is also a sudden, unexpected reality: their parents, they say are "laughing in our face/Saying 'Wake up, you need to make money.'" He thought his fears would go away when he got older, he says, but now he's insecure and cares what other people think. The song was number two on the Billboard top 100 for 2015, and the video has more than 800 million views on YouTube. As Asbury University student Alyssa Driscoll wrote, the song "has exactly what we're thinking written in it. . . . [It] really GETS US."

In the video, Tyler wears black makeup on his neck and hands, which he says is a metaphor for stress. It represents "kind of a feeling of suffocation," he said in an interview. It makes sense: trying to find your way as an adolescent can be difficult when your childhood was a protected cocoon and you were always told not to care what anyone else thinks. Suddenly it matters what other people think, suddenly you have to be an adult, and that's stressful. Between student loans and tree houses, he sings, we'd all choose the tree house.

Stealing Sleep

Just before you go to bed, you check on your teen. It looks as though her light is off, but you're not sure. Then you see it: the faint blue light of her phone as she looks at it in bed.

Many iGen'ers are so addicted to social media that they find it difficult to put down their phones and go to sleep when they should. "I stay up all night looking at my phone," admits a 13-year-old from New Jersey in *American Girls*. She regularly hides under her covers at night, texting, so her mother doesn't know she's awake. She wakes up tired much of the time, but, she says, "I just drink a Red Bull." Thirteen-year-old Athena told me the same thing: "Some of my friends don't go to sleep until, like, two in the morning. "I assume just for summer?" I asked. "No, school, too," she said. "And we have to get up at six forty-five."

Smartphone use may have decreased teens' sleep time: more teens now sleep less than seven hours most nights (see Figure 4.12). Sleep experts say that teens should get about nine hours of sleep a night, so a teen who is getting less than seven hours a night is significantly sleep deprived. Fifty-seven percent more teens were sleep deprived in 2015 than in 1991. In just the three years between 2012 and 2015, 22% more teens failed to get seven hours of sleep.

As always, it's difficult to say for sure what the cause is in a trend over time. Still, the timing of the increase is suspicious, once again occurring just as most teens began to have smartphones, around 2011 or 2012. The

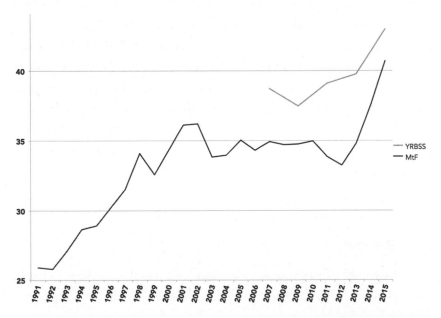

Figure 4.12. Percentage of teens who get less than seven hours of sleep on most nights, 8th, 10th, and 12th graders (Monitoring the Future) and 9th to 12th graders (Youth Risk Behavior Surveillance System), 1991–2015.

increase is also larger for girls than for boys (see Appendix F), and girls are more active on social media.

If teens who spent more time online also slept less, that would be further evidence that new media and smartphones might be behind the lack of sleep. That is indeed the case: teens who spent three or more hours a day on electronic devices were 28% more likely to get less than seven hours of sleep, and teens who visited social media sites every day were 19% more likely not to get adequate sleep (see Figure 4.13). The number of teens who don't sleep enough goes up after two or more hours a day of electronic device use and skyrockets from there (see Appendix F). An extensive meta-analysis of studies on electronic device use among children found similar results: children who used a media device before bed were more likely to sleep less than they should, more likely to sleep poorly, and more than twice as likely to be sleepy during the day.

Electronic devices and social media seem to be unique in their effect on sleep compared to older forms of media. Teens who read books and magazines more often are actually less likely to be sleep deprived—either reading puts them to sleep, or they can put the book down at bedtime. TV time is barely related to sleep time. Apparently, teens who watch a lot of TV can turn it off and go to sleep, while those on their phones do not. The allure of the smartphone, its blue light glowing in the dark, is often too much to resist.

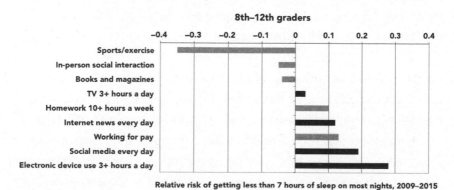

Figure 4.13. Relative risk of getting less than seven hours of sleep on most nights based on screen (black bars) and nonscreen (gray bars) activities. Monitoring the Future and Youth Risk Behavior Surveillance System, 2009–2015.

Other activities that take up a lot of time, such as homework and working for pay, also increase the risk of missing out on sleep. But since teens spent about the same amount of time working and on homework in 2015 as they did in 2012, those activities are unlikely to be the cause of the increase in sleep deprivation since 2012. Other activities that take time, such as exercising and spending time with friends in person, actually correlate with getting more sleep. New-media use is both the most strongly related to sleep deprivation and the only activity that increased significantly between 2012 and 2015. Thus, smartphones appear to be the primary cause of the recent increase in sleep deprivation, which means this new technology has adversely affected physical health as well as mental health.

Lack of sleep can have serious consequences. Sleep deprivation is linked to myriad issues, including compromised thinking and reasoning, susceptibility to illness, increased weight gain, and high blood pressure. Sleep deprivation also has a significant effect on mood: people who don't sleep enough are prone to depression and anxiety.

Sound familiar? Lack of sleep might be another reason why iGen'ers are more likely to be depressed. Teens who don't sleep enough are more than twice as likely to report higher levels of depressive symptoms (31% do, versus only 12% for those who sleep more). Teens who sleep less than seven hours a night are also 68% more likely to have at least one risk factor for suicide (see Figure 4.14, next page). Sleep deprivation is the ultimate buzzkill to mood, and over time it can snowball into serious mental health issues.

These risks look almost identical across gender, race, and socioeconomic status, so those factors are not the cause. Intriguing new research shows that the blue light emitted by electronic devices tells our brains it's still daytime, which makes the brain take longer to fall asleep. It probably doesn't help that social media exchanges, especially for teen girls, are filled with drama, not the best thing when you're trying to relax before bed. So smartphones could be causing lack of sleep, which leads to depression, or the phones could be causing depression, which leads to lack of sleep. It's all rooted in the allure of the phone: when the phone calls its siren song, teens crash into the rocks instead of crashing into their beds.

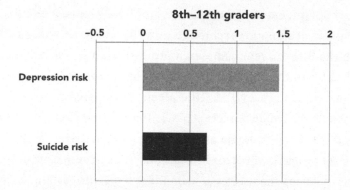

**Relative risk for depression and suicide of getting less than 7
hours of sleep on most nights, 2009–2015**

Figure 4.14. Relative risk of having a high level of depressive symptoms or
having at least one suicide risk factor based on sleeping less than seven
hours on most nights, 8th and 10th graders (Monitoring the Future) and 9th
to 12th graders (Youth Risk Surveillance System), 2009–2015.

What Can We Do?

According to his parents, Brian Go, a junior at Caltech, wrote an email to
a counselor at the university's counseling center asking for help. After a
breakup with a girlfriend, he wasn't sure he had the "will to go on," he wrote.
The counselor told him she couldn't get him an appointment for several more
days. Soon afterward, he killed himself.

Caltech disputed that account, maintaining that Brian had denied that
he continued to have suicidal feelings. Nevertheless, the case highlights a
nationwide problem: the often inadequate resources for mental health assis-
tance on college campuses. Waiting lists for appointments with therapists
can be long, and budget cuts have meant fewer staff to minister to more
students seeking help. Many campus counseling centers have limits on how
many times students can see on-campus therapists. After Shefali Arora ran
through the twelve sessions of on-campus therapy allowed for each student
at Tulane University, the office handed her a list of off-campus therapists.
"But I didn't have a car," she said. After taking a semester of medical leave,
she attempted suicide but, thankfully, did not succeed.

High school students and their parents are already seeking help for psychological issues at an unprecedented rate. In 1983, only 4% of high school seniors (in the MtF survey) had seen a professional for psychological or emotional issues in the past twelve months. That figure doubled to 8% by 2000 and then rose to 11% in 2015. Thus mental health providers are experiencing a larger caseload than in years past, a trend that is likely to continue. Practitioners need to prepare for an increasing wave of iGen clients.

The bigger problem will occur if young people don't seek help. In college newspapers, iGen'ers themselves are sounding the alarm, calling for more recognition of mental illness and less stigma around it. "I worry about the lack of understanding that always seems to accompany any talk of one's emotional well-being," wrote Logan Jones in the Utah State student newspaper. ". . . Seeing a therapist is still taboo. . . . Nobody likes the idea of putting a label on what can so easily be written off as some form of insecurity—nobody wants to be diagnosed." More often than not, depression goes untreated. Even in our age of greater awareness of mental illness, Cooper Lund argues in the *Daily Oklahoman*, depression is still stigmatized and undertreated. "If I thought I might have cancer, I'd go running to the doctor, but when I thought I had depression it took me four years to finally see a psychiatrist," he admitted.

Help for mental health issues is essential, but of course it would be even better to stop depression and anxiety before they start. To do that, it would help to know what causes these mental health issues in the first place. Though some people have genetic predispositions to anxiety and depression, the abrupt rise in mental health issues strongly suggests that genetics is not the whole story. Recent research confirms this, finding that genetics and environment interact. Among those predisposed to depression, only those who experience certain environments will actually become depressed. For example, sleep deprivation is linked to depression; as we saw, teens are not getting enough sleep, and that's probably one reason why more are depressed. The decline of in-person social interaction and the rise of smartphones are likely another reason. In other words, there is a simple, free way to improve mental health: put down the phone, and do something else.

Chapter 5

Irreligious:
Losing My Religion
(and Spirituality)

Boys hurl themselves onto plywood ramps, their skateboards rattling under them as they leap. It's cold outside, and they're enjoying having a place to board inside. But it's not just any skate park—the boys fly through the air under dramatically arched ceilings, silently watched by a stone sculpture of St. Joannes. Their skateboard park is the former Church of St. Joseph in Arnhem, the Netherlands.

Like many other churches across Europe, the Church of St. Joseph closed as more Europeans disassociated from religion. Another Dutch church is now used as a school for acrobats, and a third is a high-end women's clothing store. Many others sit empty. "The numbers are so huge that the whole society will be confronted with it," the Dutch religious heritage activist Lilian Grootswagers told the *Wall Street Journal*. "Everyone will be confronted with big empty buildings in their neighborhoods."

For decades, the United States has been a much more religious country than most of Europe. Even as churches in Europe have emptied, Americans have remained very religious in comparison. For a long time, scholars of

American religion maintained that religious practice and belief were relatively stable in the United States. The few changes that did appear, even among young people, were dismissed as "weak and slight." Nobody was going to skateboard in American churches.

Then came the Millennials. As studies by the Pew Research Center showed in the mid-2010s, one in three Millennials (then 20 to 34 years old) claimed no religious affiliation, much higher than the one in ten Americans over age 70 who did not affiliate. However, younger people have always been less religious and older people more so. Maybe Millennials are less religious just because they are young. Since the Pew data go back only to 2007, that survey can't tell us whether Millennials are less religious due to their age or to true generational and cultural change.

To really tell how the American religious landscape is changing, it's better to draw from data that reach back across the decades to compare young people now with young people of previous generations. With iGen'ers still emerging into adulthood, their religious orientation is a harbinger of what the United States will look like in the coming decades—whether that's shuttered churches or a new revival of American religion. Because most US teens who identify with a religion are Christian—68% of 10th graders in 2015— most of this discussion centers on Christianity and why teens are leaving it. Jewish, Buddhist, and Muslim teens remain small minorities in the United States (at 1.6%, 1.0%, and 1.5% of 2015 10th graders, respectively). The coming years may see more discussion of these faiths and how they impact iGen.

Part of the Flock: Public Religious Participation

Ben is a thoughtful 18-year-old from Illinois, one of the few iGen'ers I spoke with who loves paper books more than his phone. When I ask him whether he ever goes to church or religious services, he says, "Nope. Most of my friends don't, either." I ask if he was raised that way or if he gave up on religion at some point. "My parents just never took us to church. They both grew up quasi-religious, but they never had us doing anything," he says. "I know one or two people whose parents still go to church and want them to, but they stopped."

Affiliating with a religion was once a near-universal experience for young people: In the early 1980s, more than 90% of high school seniors identified as part of one religious group or another, meaning that only one out of ten chose "none" for his or her religious affiliation. As late as 2003, 87% of 10th graders affiliated with a religion.

Then that changed. Beginning in the 1990s and accelerating in the 2000s, fewer and fewer young people affiliated with a religion. The shift was largest for young adults, with the religiously affiliated dipping to 66% by 2016 (see Figure 5.1). Thus, a full third of young adults do not affiliate with any organized religion.

It's not just young people: iGen'ers are more likely than any generation before them to be raised by religiously unaffiliated parents. In the 2016 college student survey, 17% of students' parents did not belong to a religion, up from only 5% in the late 1970s. The drop in students' own affiliation is even

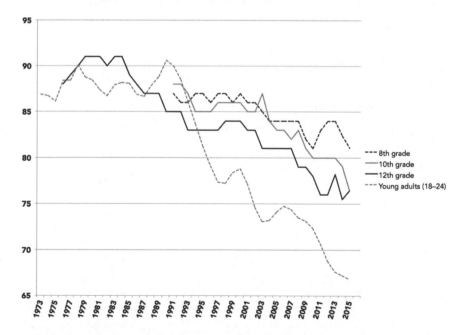

Figure 5.1. Percentage affiliating with any religion, 8th, 10th, and 12th graders (Monitoring the Future) and 18- to 24-year-olds (General Social Survey), 1972–2016.

steeper; by 2016, 31% did not affiliate with a religion. As Figure 5.2 illustrates, the gap between the religious affiliation of parents and their college student children has widened in recent years; though college students were always a little less likely to affiliate with a religion than their parents, the divide has now grown to a yawning gulf.

This suggests that two forces are working simultaneously to pull iGen'ers away from religion: more iGen'ers are being raised in nonreligious households, and more iGen teens have decided not to belong to a religion anymore. That seems to happen sometime between 8th grade and young adulthood, when adolescents begin to ask more questions and make decisions for themselves.

iGen'ers came of age in an era when disavowing religious beliefs became strikingly more socially acceptable. In 2009, Barack Obama became the first US president to include "nonbelievers" in an inaugural speech when listing religious groups. More and more Americans publicly challenge religion. "In the 21st century it has become clear that ancient religious texts are simply

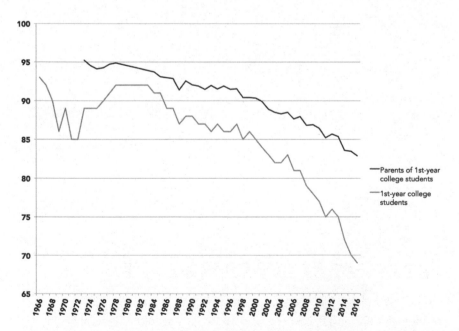

Figure 5.2. Percentage of college students and their parents who affiliated with a religion. American Freshman Survey, 1966–2016.

the creation of human beings. To believe otherwise is to define 'delusion,' "
wrote Brian Sheller of Columbus, Ohio, on the *New York Times* website in
2015. "Anything offered by religion can be found by another, less deluded
manner of belief or behavior."

Perhaps iGen'ers eschew affiliating with a religion but still go to religious services once in awhile. In the past, many religious scholars argued
that Americans were still as churchgoing as ever—or that any changes in
attendance at religious services were small.

But that's not true anymore. Attendance at services declined slowly until
around 1997 and then began to plummet. In 2015, 22% of 12th graders said
they "never" attended religious services (see Figure 5.3). That is a very low
bar; going to a service even once a year would still count as going. The picture
is the same for more frequent attendance: only 28% of 12th graders in 2015
attended services once a week, down from 40% in 1976.

Figure 5.3. Percentage ever attending religious services, 8th, 10th, and
12th graders (Monitoring the Future) and entering college students
(American Freshman Survey), 1968–2016.

In an interview on NPR, Father James Bretzke of Boston College acknowledged that only a small percentage of college students go to Mass but noted that his church in suburban Bedford is filled with young families. "They tend to come back to the Church because they want their children to have some sort of religious education," he said. That suggests that iGen'ers and Millennials are staying away from religious services because they are young—unsettled, childless, and far from situations such as death and sickness that religion comforts. Perhaps those generations will go back to religion later on when they have settled down.

However, age can't be causing the difference in these data over time: iGen'ers and the Millennials are less religious than Boomers and GenX'ers were at the same age. The recent data on Millennials, who are now in their family-building years, indicate that they are less likely to attend services than Boomers and GenX'ers were at that age. In fact, the decline in attending religious services for this group in their prime family-building years has been just as steep as that for young adults ages 18 to 24 (see Figure 5.4). Millen-

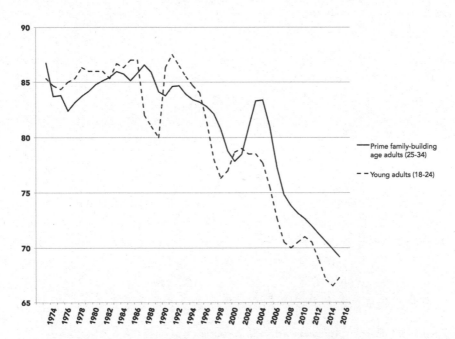

Figure 5.4. Percentage of young adults and prime-age adults who attend religious services at all. General Social Survey, 1972–2016.

nials have not been returning to religious institutions during their twenties and thirties, making it unlikely that iGen'ers will, either.

Faithful but Different

Even though it's 10 p.m., 20-year-old James is wide awake and ready to talk. He's just gotten out of a business class at his university outside Atlanta, and when I call and ask, "Is this James?" he answers with a cheerful "That's me!" After we chat for a few minutes about his major, his parents, and where he's from, I ask if he went to church growing up. He tells me about the mostly white Baptist church he and his family attended in suburban Atlanta, every Sunday at first but then less and less often. "They were very conservative. Very old-fashioned. Which is fine. We're an old-fashioned family. We have old-fashioned ideals," he says. Despite this, there were issues from the beginning: "Our family had a hard time . . . my father is black, my mother is white, and both of us are biracial, me and my brother. We would walk into the church and get stares from everyone."

Then his brother came out as transgender at the age of 14, which was an immediate issue at church. "Our church was not very LGBT-friendly at all," James says. Once, he says, the pastor mocked another church that was more accepting of LGBT people, saying they might as well accept cheaters and murderers, too. "Why would you celebrate sin?" the pastor asked. A few years later, James came out to his family as gay, after struggling with his feelings during middle school. He knew he was attracted to men, but he also knew that that wasn't accepted in his church. "It was just basically fear. Like you can't even think about that because you're going to go to Hell," he said. "In the church you had to put on major filters in order to be accepted. You couldn't be up-front with the things that you struggled with or couldn't be up-front with things that you believed in, or they were going to get shot down." Not surprisingly, James and his family stopped going to that church.

Yet, he says, "Right now all four of us are still very much Christian. All four of us still have very strong beliefs." His brother is "very involved with his friends who are religious. I feel like he has gotten a lot more of that spiritual learning, spiritual feeling from sources outside of the church." And even though James has moved away from church, he still longs for a religious connection. "It's very important to me that my relationship with God and my relationship with religion is sound in my own mind instead of trying to find fulfillment through the church," he says.

If James and his brother had been born fifty years ago, they might have stayed in the church and kept their identities hidden, at least for a time. But they are iGen'ers, and they are not going to hide who they are. Their challenge now is to find a church that supports both their identities and their deep Christian faith. That hasn't happened yet for James and his brother, but he's hoping it will once they are older. "Being in college now, being busy . . . He's eighteen. I'm twenty. Once I'm more secure and once my brother is more secure, finding a more permanent church would be a goal of ours," he says.

Losing My Religion: Private Religious Beliefs

When I ask 14-year-old Priya if she believes in God, she says, "I don't really know if there's, like, one person or a bunch of people or no one. So I'm keeping my views open—I'll figure it out." She only occasionally goes to religious services. "Sometimes my mom takes me along when she goes to the [Hindu] temple," she says, sounding uninterested. When I ask her if she ever prays, she says, "Not really. Sometimes I'm, like, 'Please please give me a B or higher on this essay.' So I guess I'm praying to the teacher. Or to some mysterious God of Essays that does not exist, I'm pretty sure."

For twenty years, headlines and academic articles declared that yes, fewer Americans affiliated with a religion, but just as many were praying and just as many believed in God. Americans weren't less religious, they said, just less likely to practice religion publicly. That was true for several decades: the percentage of young adults who believed in God changed little between 1989 and 2000.

Then it fell off a cliff. By 2016, one out of three 18- to 24-year-olds said they did not believe in God. Prayer followed a similar steep, downward trajectory. In 2004, 84% of young adults prayed at least sometimes, but by 2016 more than one out of four said they "never" prayed. Fewer young people believe that the Bible is the inspired word of God; by 2016, one out of four instead thought it was "an ancient book of fables, legends, history, and moral precepts recorded by men" (see Figure 5.5).

Thus it is no longer true that Americans are just as religious privately. More and more Americans, especially Millennials and iGen'ers, are less religious both publicly and privately. This is not due to shifts in ethnic or racial composition in the population: the trends are the same, and sometimes even stronger, among white Americans only (by 2016, only two in three white young adults ever prayed, and only 60% believed in God). The waning of private religious beliefs means that younger generations' disassociation from religion is not just about their distrust in institutions; more are disconnecting from religion entirely, even at home and even in their hearts.

I meet Max, 16, at his high school, sitting just outside his classroom as the lunch period is about to begin. With his buzz-cut dark blond hair and white-and-gray shirt, he would have blended in with teens in a 1950s school. His hobbies, though, are more modern: he spends all of his free time playing

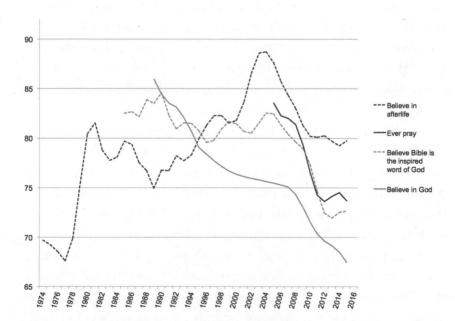

Figure 5.5. Private religious beliefs, 18- to 24-year-olds. General Social Survey, 1974–2016.

video games. When I ask Max if he goes to church, he says simply, "No." He gives the same simple answer when I ask if he believes in God or prays. When I ask him what he thinks religion is for, he says, "It's great for supporting people, like, if they're in a bad time. Like the saying, like, if you're in the trench and you're being bombed, everyone's praying." He says that some of his friends' parents "make them" go to church but his parents aren't religious.

Some iGen'ers who do pray aren't exactly engaging in traditional religious supplication. "I've stopped praying just to thank God; I only pray when I need something or when someone else needs something," wrote Tiara, 17. "To be honest, I kind of just forget to pray until a bad situation arises and I want it to change." Others do follow a more religious approach, though in their own way. "The way I pray is simply talking to God," wrote Marlee, 21. "I don't get on my knees or act 'churchy' about it. Prayer is personal."

For several decades, belief in the afterlife was a notable exception to the trend away from private religious beliefs: more young adults in the mid-2000s believed in the afterlife than had in the 1970s. Perhaps some young adults wanted to believe in eternal life even if they didn't want to go to religious services or believe in God. But even belief in an afterlife started to fade after 2006. Thus, late Millennials and iGen'ers are markedly less religious than their close generational neighbors the early Millennials, and that's true across all four private religious beliefs (praying, believing in God, believing the Bible is the word of God, and believing in an afterlife).

Another private feeling is the importance of religion in your life—and here as well, fewer teens are religious. By 2015, nearly one in four 10th and 12th graders said that religion was "not important" in their lives. The vast majority of teens said that religion was at least a little important to them until around 2000, when the number began to drop. Overall, iGen is, with near certainty, the least religious generation in US history.

Most iGen'ers do still participate in religion in some way. But there is now a relatively large segment of completely secular nonbelievers who don't participate in religion at all: they never attend religious services, don't pray, and don't believe in God. That growing segment is about one out of six 8th graders, one out of five 10th graders, one out of four 12th graders, and one out of three college students and young adults. Having such a large number of young people completely disconnected from religion is unprecedented. It's also a likely portent of what is to come in American religion: fewer and fewer believers and more and more churches closed down. We're not Europe yet, but that might be where we are headed.

Religion vs. the Twenty-First Century

It's a Monday around lunchtime when I reach Mark, 20, at his parents' home outside Fort Worth, Texas. "Is this still a good time to talk?" I ask. "Yes, ma'am," he replies, his choice of words momentarily transporting me back to my own Texas upbringing. Mark has been raised in a devoutly Christian home—"my parents are by-the-book Christians, by the Bible, all for the Bible," he says. He goes to church every Sunday, either to his parents' church or to a Dallas megachurch with his girlfriend. When I ask him if he prays, he says, "I do pray, every day. I pray for blessings over everyone that I know, hand of protection. I pray God will give me wisdom in life and that he'll make me the person he wants me to be." He says his life's goal is this: "I want to be able to get out of bed, and when my feet hit the floor, the Devil goes, 'Oh, crap, he's up.'" That, I thought as I laughed out loud, is real faith.

At the same time, Mark is iGen, and during the hour we talked I could almost visibly see the push and pull of his evangelical Christian faith wrestling with the twenty-first-century, iGen world he inhabits. When we talk politics, same-sex marriage never comes up in his list of important issues. When I finally ask about it specifically, he says, "Yes, I know same-sex marriage is wrong because it can never physically work out for the reproduction of life, but everybody has their own viewpoint and if they want to go out and have a same-sex lover, then there's really nothing you can do, it's not like you can force them to like the opposite sex."

Trying to decide whether to have sex before marriage also left him pulled in two different directions. He didn't get involved with the hookup scene at his public high school, but two years later he met his girlfriend—whom he describes as "the right person"—and they eventually decided to have sex. They plan to get married after college, he tells me. "It's tough, though, because who knows how long you're going to be in college, right?" I ask. "Exactly. Whether it's two years out of junior college, four years, six years, eight, ten years, I know people who have been in college for twelve years," he says. Still, he describes not waiting until marriage to have sex as a failure. "Ninety percent of people fail, and I was one of those who failed," he says. "You waited longer than most people, so I wouldn't call that a failure," I say. "Well, true, but I wouldn't mark it up as a victory, either. [My girlfriend] said it was the right thing to do, and it would have been nice to wait, but she said I'm glad we did what we did." (It turns out that he's in the majority: a recent study found that 80% of unmarried young adult evangelical Christians have had sex.) But Mark is still not sure. "If I could tell, like, a younger brother who was in my position, I'd say wait until marriage," he says.

Mark was both keeping his faith but also acknowledging the reality of his iGen world. His views may represent the future of Christianity: assuming that he and other iGen'ers like him keep their faith, they will usher in a new, more tolerant era of Christian belief that steps away from what people should *not* do to focus on what they *should* do.

"Spiritual but Not Religious" Has Become "Not Spiritual and Not Religious"

Another common narrative about trends in American religious belief says that spirituality has replaced religion. In 2001, the religious scholar Robert Fuller penned a book called *Spiritual but Not Religious* arguing that most Americans who eschew organized religion still have deep and dynamic spiritual lives. That theory is often mentioned in relation to young people; the assumption is that young people who are distrustful of traditional religion are still willing to explore spiritual questions.

That might have been true at one time, but no longer. iGen'ers are actually *less* spiritual as well as being less religious. iGen'ers and late Millennials ages 18 to 24 are the least likely of all age/generation groups to say they are a "spiritual person," showing a pronounced break even with older Millennials in their late twenties and early thirties (see Figure 5.6, next page). The age/generation differences look very similar to those in identifying as a "religious person"—older generations are the most likely to identify as both religious and spiritual and younger generations the least likely.

Of course, these differences could be due to age instead of generation; perhaps younger people have always been less spiritual. However, slightly fewer 18- to 24-year-olds in 2014–2016 (48%) described themselves as a moderately or very spiritual person than in 2006–2008 (56%).

Other data bear this out: in the American Freshman Survey, the percentage of college students who described themselves as above average in spirituality fell from 45% in 2000 to 36% in 2016. When sociologist Christian Smith interviewed young people about their religious beliefs in the late 2000s, most did not even know what he meant when he asked them if they were spiritual. "What do you mean, 'spiritual seeking'?" many asked. So the idea that young Americans in recent years are less religious but more spiritual doesn't hold up; they are *less* spiritual than their elders. Spirituality has not replaced religion among the young.

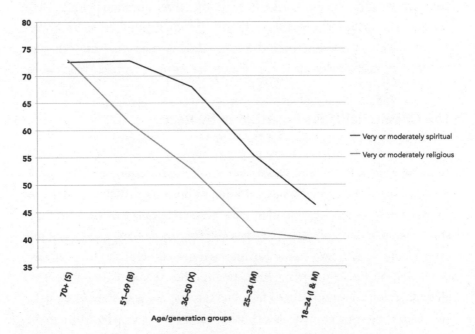

Figure 5.6. Percentage identifying as a "very" or "moderately" religious person or spiritual person, by age/generation group. General Social Survey, 2014–2016.

For years, religious scholars and observers have argued that the decline in American religious life is explained by other factors or isn't important: it's because this generation is still young; this generation just doesn't like institutions; Americans are just as likely to believe in God and pray; more young Americans are now spiritual instead; the changes are small. The most recent survey data, which you've seen here, knock down every one of those explanations: it's not age, because Boomers and GenX'ers were perfectly happy to be religious when they were young; iGen is less religious even in beliefs that don't require religious institutions; fewer Americans now believe in God or pray; fewer, not more, young adults are spiritual; the number who do not participate in religion has doubled.

iGen'ers are less religious and less spiritual, publicly and privately, and strikingly different from previous generations when they were young. The move away from religion is no longer piecemeal, small, or uncertain; it is large and definitive. More young Americans are thoroughly secular, disconnecting completely from religion, spirituality, and the larger questions of life. These complete nonbelievers are still a minority, but their numbers have swelled significantly in a very short period of time. More iGen'ers than any other living generation are unconnected to religion. Here's the question: Which ones?

The Chasm: Religious Polarization by Race, Socioeconomic Status, and Region

Not that long ago, religion was a nearly universal American experience. White or black, rich, middle class, or poor, in Boston or Atlanta, Americans went to religious services and identified with a religious tradition. The specific religion or denomination may have differed: more Baptists in the South, more Catholics and Jews in the Northeast, more Lutherans in the Midwest; more well-off Episcopalians; Christian churches segregated by race—but all demographic groups went to religious services at about the same rates.

iGen'ers have changed that, continuing trends begun by Millennials. Races, socioeconomic groups, and regions differ in their religious service attendance much more than they did a few decades ago. The religious landscape is now more polarized based on identity.

Most generational trends are remarkably similar across demographic groups. The correlation between race and religious participation is the largest exception to that rule, with strikingly different trends over time for white and black teens. In the early 1980s, black high school seniors were only slightly more likely than white ones to ever attend religious services, but by 2015, the gap was much larger (see Figure 5.7). Until very recently, black teens' religious service attendance barely budged while white teens' attendance plummeted.

Black iGen teens might be following the lead of white teens—the declines in religious service attendance since 2009 among black teens are the most consistent in decades. Black iGen teens might be the harbinger of a move away from religion in the black community that may take hold in the years to come. Still, the gap between white and black teens in religious service attendance, once small, is now a wide gulf.

Beliefs have also diverged. In the late 1980s, black and white American adults were nearly identical in their belief in God, but by 2016, blacks were

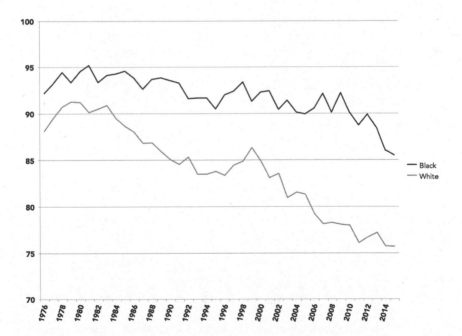

Figure 5.7. Percentage of black and white 12th graders who ever attend religious services. Monitoring the Future, 1976–2015.

much more likely to be believers than whites (see Figure 5.8; this is for adults of all ages to ensure that there are enough people in each group). So although black and white Americans could once assume they had belief in God in common, now the races are much further apart in this fundamental religious belief.

The 2016 election exposed the divide between working-class and college-educated Americans. Yet there is one class difference that is rarely discussed, perhaps because it is misunderstood: contrary to popular belief, teens from families with a college-educated father are actually *more* likely to attend religious services than those whose fathers did not attend college. That was not always true: in the 1970s and 1980s, teens from both types of families went to religious services at about the same, very high rate. That began to change during the 1990s, and in recent years teens from higher-SES families were more likely to go to religious services (see Figure 5.9, next page). The recent gap isn't as large as that for race, but it follows the

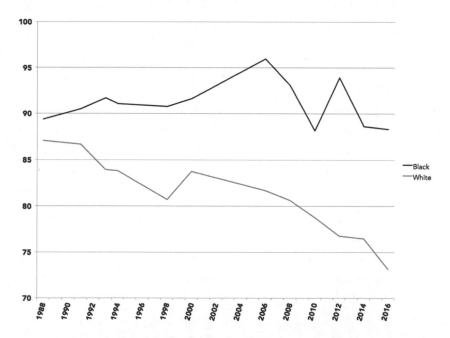

Figure 5.8. Percentage of all adults who believe in God, blacks and whites. General Social Survey, 1988–2016.

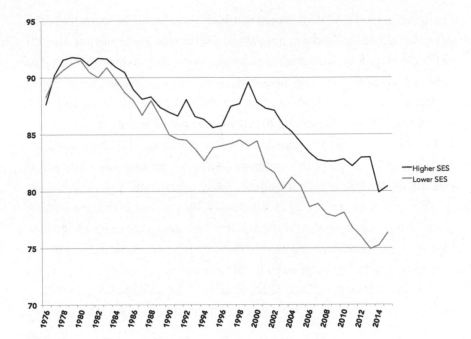

Figure 5.9. Percentage of 12th graders who ever attend religious services, lower and higher SES. Monitoring the Future, 1976–2015.

pattern of increasing polarization over time, with teens from different backgrounds having different religious experiences whereas they once had near-universal exposure to religious services. However, the same was not true for beliefs: the decline in belief in God was similar among all adults regardless of their education level.

Regions of the United States have also become more polarized. The South is often known as the Bible Belt, which I experienced firsthand growing up in Irving, Texas, which at one time claimed to have more churches per capita than any other city in the country. Religious service attendance didn't differ much by region in the 1970s and early 1980s (see Figure 5.10, next page). But by 2015, there was a larger gap in religious service attendance, with more southern teens attending services at least occasionally (the MtF survey stopped asking this question in California in 1997, so we can't compare residents of the West).

Belief in God has also diverged across regions. In the 1990s, the percentage who believed in God was once about the same in the South and the rest of the country, with southerners just a little more likely to believe. But views have sharply diverged since then, with a belief in one higher power barely budging in the South while it declined in the Northeast, Midwest, and West (see Figure 5.11, next page). By 2016, only one out of five white southerners did not believe in God, compared to nearly one in three white non–southern residents. The image of the godless North may be long-standing, but it became (partially) accurate only in the twenty-first century.

This religious division by region may be the product of the new choices Americans have enjoyed over the last few decades to move wherever they like. People cluster into neighborhoods of people like themselves, growing ever more isolated from those with different views.

As recently as the 1990s, religion was a near universal in America—whether black or white, northern or southern, rich or poor, a high school

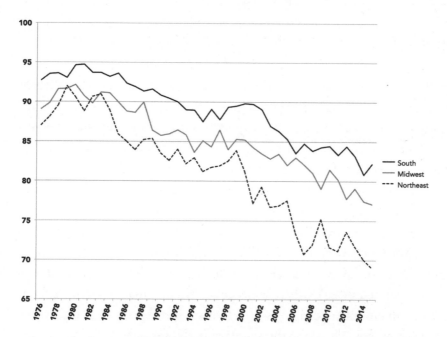

Figure 5.10. Percentage of 12th graders who ever attend religious services, by US region. Monitoring the Future, 1976–2015.

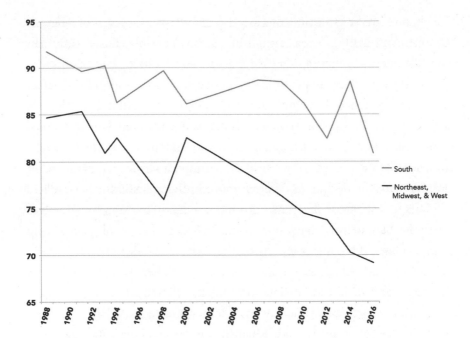

Figure 5.11. Percentage of white American adults who believe in God, South versus other regions. General Social Survey, 1988–2016.

student could look around her classroom and expect that those sitting around her were religious. Now, about one out of four are nonbelievers—but many more if you're in a classroom of mostly white students in the Northeast and many fewer if your classroom is mostly black students in the South. Over time, this polarization may lessen if black Americans and southern residents become less religious. For now, the chasm remains.

Too Many Rules: Why Religion Has Declined

"I don't pray, nor do I believe in an omniscient God," wrote Brittany, 19. "I like to think that your whole life isn't planned out already for you, and that your choices determine who you become."

Why has Brittany's view become more common? Why are young Americans now less religious? As with the other trends, we can identify things that changed at the same time that are also linked to lower levels of religious commitment. Brittany's reasoning hints at one possible cause: American culture's increasing focus on individualism—as she put it, "your choices."

To more precisely analyze the link between religion and individualism over time, I matched those indicators of individualism with teens' religious service attendance by year (so that each year was associated with an average level of, say, individualistic language in books and an average level of religious service attendance). The rise in these individualistic factors moved in lockstep with the decline in religion: more individualistic times were less religious times. That makes sense, given that religion by definition involves believing in something bigger than yourself. It also often involves following certain rules and joining groups, two other factors that don't fit particularly well with an individualistic mind-set. In a society where young people hear "If it feels good, do it" and "Believe in yourself," religion seems almost countercultural. As we saw in the stories of James and Mark, iGen faith often involves a careful balance of individualistic modern realities with traditional religious doctrines—particularly around issues of sexuality, gender identity, and sexual orientation.

Even religious teens often adhere to a more individualistic version of faith. When Christian Smith interviewed young people for his book *Soul Searching*, he found that many adhered to a belief system he labeled "moralistic therapeutic deism," which embraces a belief in God but also includes more uniquely modern ideas, such as the importance of happiness, feeling good about yourself, and the idea that "God does not need to be particularly involved in one's life except when God is needed to resolve a problem." Smith also found that most teens embraced "moral individualism," his label for teens' idea that "we are all different, and that's good." Twelve-year-old Harper, whom we met in chapter 2, sees an individualistic purpose for church: "Church is for people to express their beliefs. There's certain churches for certain people, like, what they believe in. It's a place that you can meet people who believe in the same thing as you."

In *You Lost Me: Why Young Christians Are Leaving Church . . . and Rethinking Faith,* his book about young former Christians, David Kinnaman reports that many young people feel a disconnect between their church and what they experience outside of it, including science, pop culture, and sexuality. For example, half of 13- to 17-year-olds want to pursue a science-related career. Yet only 1% of youth pastors say they have addressed any subject related to science in the last year. Kinnaman told the story of Mike, 20, who was invited to tell a room full of pastors why he no longer affiliates with Christianity. "I'm as nervous as an atheist at a pastor's conference," he began. But then he said, "It was tenth grade. I started learning about evolution. . . . I knew from church that I couldn't believe in both science and God, so that was it. I didn't believe in God anymore." If his church had not presented things as so black and white, he said, he might have stayed. Other iGen'ers echo that idea. "My father is an atheist and my mother is agnostic. We're science people," wrote Timothy, 23. "Religion, at least to people my age, seems like it's something of the past," says Matthew, whom we met in chapter 1. "It seems like something that isn't modern."

Then there's the elephant in the room: many Millennials and iGen'ers distrust religion because they believe it promotes antigay attitudes. More young people now associate religion with rigidity and intolerance—an automatic anathema to a highly individualistic and accepting generation. "I feel like some of the worst people, who are the most bigoted and closed-minded, are religious," wrote Sarah, 22. "My step-sister is constantly posting things on Facebook about how good she and her religion are, while posting hateful things about gays, people who eat pork, and anything else she doesn't agree with." That has hit some iGen'ers personally. "No, I do not pray," wrote Earnest, 21. "I'm questioning the existence of God. I stopped going to church because I am gay and was part of a gay-bashing religion."

A 2012 survey of 18- to 24-year-olds found that most believed that Christianity was antigay (64%), judgmental (62%), and hypocritical (58%). Seventy-nine percent of the nonreligious believed that Christianity was antigay. "I'm religious and I love God," wrote Michelle, 22. "But the rules are too strict. And some of them are prejudicial, like not liking homosexuality. How can you love everyone, except gays, transgenders, and people who don't believe in our God? I think people don't want to live with that kind of thinking anymore. It's a disgusting way to treat other people."

These views came up over and over again when I asked iGen'ers about religion. Kelsey, 23, told the story of a gay friend of hers who was "kicked out of Bible school in middle school because he was gay. He then hid being gay for years and felt horrible about it." She concluded, "That is why people do not want to associate with religion. Nobody wants to associate with something that tells people their sexual preference is a sin. God loves all. God just wants you to be nice." David Kinnaman's book *unChristian* reported that four out of ten young people outside Christianity have a "bad impression" of the religion. Why? As Kinnaman put it, "We have become famous for what we oppose, rather than who we are for."

Community college student Haley, 18, is not religious herself but works at a part-time job with many people who are. When we meet for lunch one day in San Diego, she tells me that many of her coworkers are intolerant toward gays, lesbians, and transgender individuals. She has no issue with their religious beliefs but does with their intolerance. "If you are religious, if that helps you become a better person, good, that's what religion should do—help you become a better person and treat others better," she says. "If that's not what it's doing, you're using it for hate, you're using it for your sole social and moral code, then you're going to be a messed-up person."

So what do iGen'ers want from religion? Many echo Kinnaman's assessment, saying they want religion to be more positive and less negative, to focus on what to do rather than what not to do, and to accept everyone. Tess, 21, grew up Catholic. "When my cousin was twenty-one, she learned she was pregnant and went to confession for guidance. Instead of the priest telling her of God's forgiveness and giving her hope for herself and her future child, he shamed her until she cried all the way home," she wrote. "How does something like that appeal to people? Even if it wasn't God directly shaming her, the leaders of the church are still the medium in which the message of the Lord comes through. God's word should foster happiness and faith. Not self-loathing and hopelessness." iGen'ers don't see the need for enforcing rules around sexuality, since most of them see these prescriptions as hopelessly outdated. Millie, 19, noted that the "ideals of religions conflict with what people believe to be normal in modern society. For example, the Bible says no sex before marriage, but in today's society, sex is considered a normal, healthy part of nonmarital relationships; people may even find it strange nowadays if you haven't had sex before marriage. Getting married just isn't considered a necessity to [us], but rather a choice in a variety of options."

iGen'ers want to interact with religion and not just be told what to do. Trevor, 20, wrote, "Young adults want answers about life and about who we are, why this even matters, what we can do. Instead we get told just to pray or a handout worksheet about Bible verses." Vanessa, 21, echoes this thought: "The church should make things more interactive to keep people actively thinking instead of just listening to someone speaking at them."

This suggests that religious organizations should focus on active discussions with iGen'ers that address the "big questions" they have about life, love, God, and meaning. Kinnaman found that 36% of young adults with a Christian background said that they didn't feel they could "ask my most pressing life questions in church." Just as education is moving away from the straight lecture format toward more interactive group discussions, religious organizations could consider gatherings that encourage parishioners to participate and to question. Mark, whom we met earlier, says he likes the megachurch he attends because "you're at church to learn more about God and know that you're not alone throughout whatever experience you're having. People give their testimonies all the time, and it's nice to know someone else went through the same thing you did and they turned out fine so you're going to be fine." There's progress on some counts, however: one church in Oregon invites parishioners to ask any question about faith—and questions can be asked via text and Twitter. iGen'ers don't want to be told exactly how to live their lives and what to believe—but that can be a strength, because if they come to beliefs themselves, they might be more likely to keep them.

Europe with Bigger Cars: The Future Religious Landscape

Many Americans see the trend away from organized religion as profoundly negative. "This is family," said Lorraine Castagnoli, who attended one of the eight Catholic churches shuttered in Westchester and Rockland, New York, in 2015. "With this church closing, a part of my soul and my heart is dying. We come together all the time and it's just sad." Religious leaders lament the loss of communities and note that religious people tend to be healthier and happier. "At the end of the day, most of us will figure out that we have a dimension that takes us beyond ourselves," said Father James Bretzke of Boston College. "There's a transcendental pull in our lives, and . . . [religion offers] deeper meaning [and] some deeper answers." According to a 2012 Pew Research Center poll, most Americans (56%) believe that the decline in religion is a bad thing, while only 12% believe it's a good thing.

Others see positives in religion's decline, such as Ronald Lindsay of the Center for Inquiry, which works to reduce the influence of religion on public policy. Americans, he theorized, are "no longer looking to the church as an authority on issues. These are issues they feel comfortable in deciding themselves. . . . People are still seeking community . . . but they're no longer seeking it in the context of organized religion." When the decline of religion is discussed online, many mention the negative history of religion in persecution and hatred, often specifically bringing up LGBT issues.

In Europe, half of the population disavows religion and many churches sit empty, and as more US churches close, charities run by religious organizations will begin to crumble. By the time iGen'ers have children of their own, the way the nation interacts with religion will look quite different.

Will any religions survive? Evangelical churches have not lost as many members over the last few decades as other Christian denominations have. That might be because they've recognized that iGen'ers and Millennials want religion to complete them—to strengthen their relationships and give them a sense of purpose. Some of those churches will begin to loosen their views on premarital sex, same-sex marriage, and transgender individuals as their acceptance becomes more mainstream, even among religious people.

Religion will survive, but it will be a flexible, open, equal religion that gives people a sense of belonging and meaning and that reaches less than half of Americans. It is unclear where iGen'ers will find community interaction to replace religion. Perhaps they won't find it at all, content to rely on their social media network, with deleterious impacts on their mental health. Or perhaps iGen'ers will affiliate with others who share their interests rather than building community through religion. Either way, the structure of American community will fundamentally change.

Chapter 6

Insulated but Not Intrinsic: More Safety and Less Community

The sun has just begun to burn off the morning's gray clouds when I arrive at my favorite San Diego sushi restaurant on a June day just before noon. Haley, 18, is already there, rising to meet me as I walk in. She's part white and part Asian, with a warm smile that lights up her eyes behind her glasses.

Over shrimp tempura and a dragon roll, we talk about everything from jobs to psychology to relationships. Haley has just finished her first year at a community college and is living at home with her parents. She has a part-time job but isn't taking any classes over the summer. "I need my summer," she says. "If I didn't have it, I'd go crazy." Like an increasing number of young people, Haley doesn't smoke, doesn't drink, and has had limited experience with romantic relationships.

The intriguing part is why. In short, it's because she doesn't think those things are safe. "Going out and partying when you're drunk, you're in such an altered state of mind, you behave in ways that you never would sober," she says. "There's drunk driving—and people take advantage of you when you're drunk. It's not safe. You're going to hurt yourself, or someone's going to hurt you. It's not my thing."

Haley's interest in safety extends beyond physical safety to a term I only recently learned from iGen: emotional safety. For example, Haley believes that high school is too young to have a romantic relationship, especially a sexual one. She points to scientific research to back up her conclusions. "With the release of oxytocin [during sex], you form emotional connections to someone whether you like it or not," she says. "I think it's dangerous to become emotionally reliant on someone, but especially at that age, when your brain is still developing."

Stay Safe

Like most generational trends, the interest in safety was not iGen's idea alone. The concern was already in the culture, in the air, when they were growing up. iGen's was the childhood of the car seat, of being picked up at school instead of walking home by yourself, of sanitized plastic playgrounds. Boomer and GenX kids free to roam around their neighborhoods have been replaced by iGen kids supervised at every moment. Even our language shows the growing attention to safety: in American books, the use of phrases such as "Keep safe" and "Stay safe" zoomed up in use in the early to mid-1990s, right when the oldest iGen'ers were born (see Appendix G).

This increasing interest in safety may be at least partially rooted in iGen's slower developmental trajectory: younger children are protected more than older ones, and children are protected more than teens. Notice how Haley immediately relates the danger of teen sex back to the notion of slow brain development—the study every parent cites when he or she doesn't want to give a teen the car keys. Now the kids quote it, too.

In many ways, this interest in safety has paid off. For starters, iGen teens are safer drivers: fewer high school seniors get into car accidents, and fewer get tickets. This is a recent trend, beginning only in the early 2000s for tickets and in the mid-2000s for accidents (see Figure 6.1, next page). As recently as 2002, more than one out of three 12th graders had already gotten a ticket, but by 2015 only one in five had.

iGen'ers also take it for granted that you should always wear your seat belt. More do so than among any previous generation—twice as many high school seniors said they "always" wore their seat belts in 2015 than in 1989. Some of this increase in seat belt use is likely due to the mandatory seat belt laws passed across the country during the 1990s—but of course laws have not always been successful in getting teens to do what's safe, and the increase has been gradual rather than all at once, as you'd expect if it were just an effect of the laws. A 2016 survey asked iGen teens what they wanted the most out of a car, comparing them to Millennial young adults who recalled their preferences as teens. The feature iGen wanted much more than Millennials? Safety. And remember: these were teens, not usually the group known for wanting Volvos. But that's iGen.

iGen teens are also less likely to get into a car driven by someone who's been drinking; the number who did so was cut in half from 40% in 1991 to 20% in 2015 (see Appendix G). One out of five is still too many teens getting

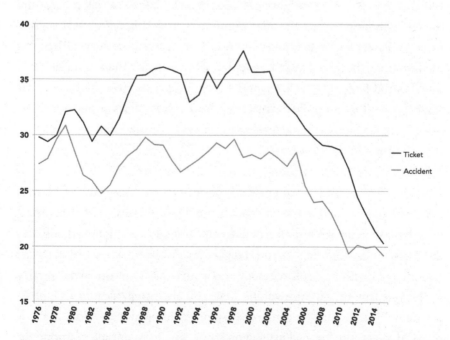

Figure 6.1. Percentage of 12th graders who got a traffic ticket or into a car accident among those who drove in the last year. Monitoring the Future, 1976–2015.

into a car with a potentially impaired driver. There's a possible twist to this, however: with iGen'ers less likely to have their driver's license and less likely to drink themselves, some of that 20% might be teens counting being in the car with Mom after she had a glass or two of wine (right before she got the text that asked, "Mom, can you pick me up at Tyler's?").

The Danger of the Drink and the Safety of the (Pot) Smoke

As we saw in chapter 1, fewer iGen'ers try alcohol at all. Merely trying alcohol isn't dangerous, but binge drinking—usually defined as having five or more drinks in a row at one time—is. That's the type of drinking adults warn teens about.

iGen'ers are less likely to binge drink—binge-drinking rates for 12th graders have been cut more than in half. Do they think it's safe? Here's where the trends get interesting. Until very recently, more teens binge drank than thought it was safe (see Figure 6.2, next page). Teens are risk takers, and they're willing to live on the edge a little to get plastered and have a good time. Well, teens *were* risk takers—until iGen entered the scene. Then, for the first time, the lines crossed: *fewer* teens binge drank than thought it was safe. Instead of going a little beyond safety and taking risks, iGen teens are staying *below* the threshold of what they think is safe. That's an attitude many of us associate more with older people than with teens, a vivid illustration of the generational shift toward safety.

Some attribute the decline in binge drinking to iGen's fear that your slobbered self will end up ridiculed all over Instagram. This is the first hint at a theme to come: for iGen, safety goes beyond just physical safety to encompass damage to one's reputation or even emotions as well. "I don't drink, and the reason is lack of safety," wrote Teagan, 20. Drinking, she said, "may lead to problems with law enforcement and embarrassment on social media. Employers [might] not hire you because you are unreliable and an embarrassment." Notice that Teagan's reasons for avoiding alcohol didn't include physical safety; she focused instead on emotions and economics, among the primary safety concerns of iGen.

Figure 6.2. Percentage of 12th graders who have had five or more drinks in a row on a single occasion (binge drinking) in the past two weeks and percentage who believe that binge drinking carries "no" or "slight" risk. Monitoring the Future, 1976–2016.

As we saw in chapter 1, iGen'ers are just as likely to use marijuana as Millennials were. If iGen'ers are so interested in safety, why is their marijuana use about the same? In short, because they believe it's safe. In fact, iGen'ers see regular marijuana use as safer than binge drinking, the first generation ever to do so (see Figure 6.3, next page). That might be why so many fewer are drinking alcohol as teens even as about the same number indulge in marijuana.

"I believe that marijuana is completely safe to use as long as you are not using machinery or a vehicle," wrote Brianna, 20. "It is far less harmful than alcohol, which is perfectly legal, but leads to far more problems that marijuana use ever could." Some iGen'ers embrace the idea that marijuana is not just safe but beneficial. "Weed has been proven to provide many health benefits," wrote Ethan, 19. "It helps with pain, cancer, and many other illnesses.

It can prevent people from getting addicted to other drugs that are way more harmful." Some iGen'ers use marijuana for medical purposes themselves. "I consider marijuana to be a very safe substance. I've personally been using it for three years for chronic spinal pain, depression, anxiety, and psoriatic arthritis," wrote Nellie, 21. "The withdrawal from my pain medication was among the hardest times in my life, but I was able to use marijuana to curb both the withdrawal and the heightened pain. I've never experienced any detrimental side effects in years of heavy use." Unfortunately, few iGen'ers seem to be aware of the long-term risks of marijuana use, which can include reduced intelligence and higher risks of schizophrenia, especially when use begins during adolescence. Marijuana is also now much more potent than the pot Boomers smoked in the 1970s.

Still, iGen'ers remain cautious. Even though they are more likely to see marijuana as safe, use hasn't gone up. Historically, pot smoking has come and gone with perceptions of its safety. But iGen'ers break that pattern, playing it even safer than they think they need to. Just as with alcohol, iGen is

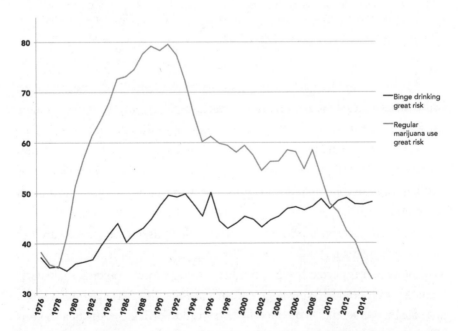

Figure 6.3. Percentage of 12th graders who agree that binge drinking and marijuana use are very risky. Monitoring the Future, 1976–2015.

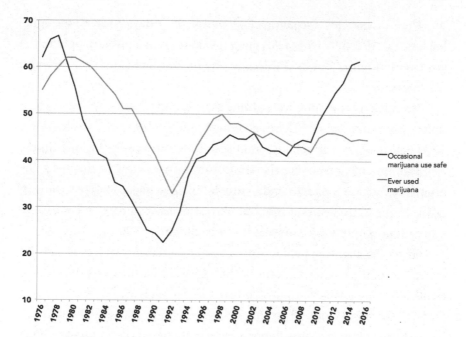

Figure 6.4. Percentage of 12th graders who have ever used marijuana and percentage who believe that occasional marijuana use carries "no" or "slight" risk. Monitoring the Future, 1976–2016.

the first generation in which fewer teens used marijuana than thought it was safe. Once again, the lines cross (see Figure 6.4).

For both alcohol and marijuana, iGen'ers ask first: Is it safe? Even if they think it is, many still hold back—an unusual choice at an age traditionally associated with risk taking. Teens just don't want to take chances anymore— so they stay at home, drive carefully, and use only substances in amounts they think are safe—or don't use them . . . because it's better to be safe.

The Decline of the Fight and the Waning of Sexual Assault

Most Boomers and GenX'ers can remember seeing a middle school or high school fight—a scuffle in the hallway, a brawl after school, fists thrown to settle a dispute. At my junior high in the early 1980s, the gauntlet would be thrown down the same way every time: "Meet me behind the KFC after school."

The KFC back lot is seeing a lot less action these days: iGen'ers are fighting less. In 1991, fully half of 9th graders had been in a physical fight in the last twelve months, but by 2015, only one in four had (see Figure 6.5 and Appendix G).

Many iGen'ers see physical fighting as risky and pointless, given the possibility of physical injury. "There's no point to physical fighting," wrote Aiden, 20. "I hate to see myself get hurt and I wish to see no one else be hurt either."

Extremes of violence are also less common: as we saw in chapter 3, the homicide rate among teens and young adults reached a forty-year low in 2014. In the YRBSS survey, the number of teens who carry a weapon to school is now only a third of what it was in the early 1990s.

Given the attention paid to sexual assault in recent years, especially on college campuses, you might think that it would be the exception to this trend of declining violence. But it's not: sexual assault is actually *less* common than it once was. From 1992 to 2015, the rate of rape was nearly cut in half in the FBI's Uniform Crime Reports, which are based on reports to police.

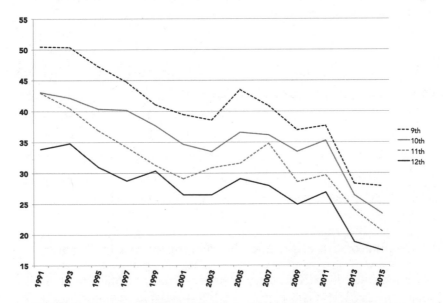

Figure 6.5. Percentage of high school students who have gotten into a physical fight in the last 12 months. Youth Risk Behavior Surveillance System, 1991–2015.

Of course, rape is a notoriously underreported crime—most studies suggest that the majority who experience it do not report it to the police. Thus, to understand the true occurrence of rape, it's better to rely on surveys of representative samples. One is the National Crime Victimization Survey (NCVS), administered by the US Department of Justice. In a 2014 report, the DOJ broke down the data by age and student status. Figure 6.6 shows the rate of rape for 18- to 24-year olds enrolled in a college or university, an important population given the recent attention paid to sexual assault on campus. Here, too, rape was less common in recent years, with the rate more than cut in half (from 9.2 to 4.4 per 1,000) between 1997 and 2013.

The number from the NCVS is the rate out of 1,000, while the FBI rate is out of 100,000; thus the survey actually shows a much higher rate than the FBI crime reports. Even this rate is lower (about half a percentage point) than the CDC's 2011 National Intimate Partner and Sexual Violence Survey, which

Figure 6.6. Rape (sexual assault) rates in the last year (1) from reports to police per 100,000 of the general population (FBI Uniform Crime Reports, 1960–2015) and (2) victim surveys of students and non-students ages 18 to 24, per 1,000 population (National Crime Victimization Survey, 1997–2013).

found that 1.6% of women had been raped in the last year using a broader definition of sexual assault. At the moment, the CDC sexual assault data are available for only 2010 and 2011, so we can't tell from that survey if rape is more or less common than it used to be. That survey also found that 19.3% of women—about one in five—have been raped during their lifetimes (this figure is much higher as it focuses on *lifetime* experience rather than just one year). Other summaries, such as one released by the Crimes Against Children Research Center at the University of New Hampshire, also show declines in sexual assault rates for child and teen victims.

Overall, much controversy surrounds the question of how sexual assault should be defined and measured; the data here are necessarily reliant on their particular definitions. The rate of sexual assault is unarguably still too high, but it is encouraging that it appears to be dropping—yet another piece of evidence that iGen is safer.

No Risk, Please

iGen'ers' risk aversion goes beyond their behaviors toward a general attitude of avoiding risk and danger. Eighth and 10th graders are now less likely to agree that "I like to test myself every now and then by doing something a little risky" (see Figure 6.7, next page). Nearly half of teens found that appealing in the early 1990s, but by 2015 less than 40% did.

iGen teens are also less likely to agree that "I get a real kick out of doing things that are a little dangerous." As recently as 2011, the majority of teens agreed that they got a jolt out of danger, but within a few years only a minority shared this view.

For the most part, this movement toward safety is a positive trend: it's good for everyone that fewer teens drag race, set stuff on fire, and play mailbox baseball. The nuance comes when we're talking about not just physical risk but intellectual, social, and emotional risks—the leaps of faith young people sometimes take that can lead them on their greatest adventures. Some wonder if iGen's interest in safety will stifle exploration and creativity. Former *Village Voice* rock critic Richard Goldstein, who now teaches at Hunter College, observes that his students are much more cautious than his Boomer

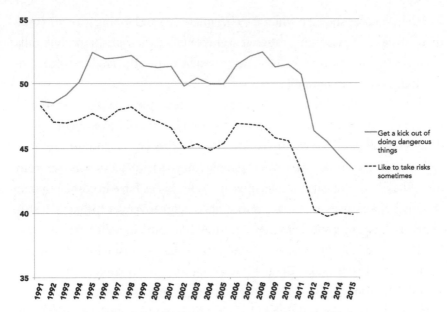

Figure 6.7. Percentage of 8th and 10th graders who like doing dangerous things or taking risks. Monitoring the Future, 1991–2015.

generation ever was. He praises his students' ambition, but writes, "I get that it's important to be safe, but I worry about the consequences of making that a priority. If you don't take chances, how can you invent yourself? If you aren't comfortable with instability, how can you create change?"

Wanting to feel safe all of the time can also lead to wanting to protect against emotional upset—the concern with "emotional safety" somewhat unique to iGen. That can include preventing bad experiences, sidestepping situations that might be uncomfortable, and avoiding people with ideas different from your own. That's where things get dicey—both for iGen and for the older generations struggling to understand them.

A Safe Space for All Students

When the writer Claire Fox arrived at a girls' high school in the United Kingdom for a debate, she expected the girls to challenge some of what she had to say. What she did not expect were tears. When the girls disagreed with her, she was shocked when they began crying and saying "You can't say that!" instead of presenting rational arguments for their positions. She calls iGen'ers "Generation Snowflake," apt to melt under the slightest pressure due to their extreme fragility.

This is the flip side of iGen's interest in safety: the idea that one should be safe not just from car accidents and sexual assault but from people who disagree with you. For example, take the most recent version of the "safe space," now known as a place where people can go to protect themselves from ideas they find offensive. In recent years, safe spaces have become popular on college campuses as responses to visits by controversial speakers: if students are upset by a speaker's message, they can come together in a separate location to console one another. Safe spaces echo not just iGen's interest in safety but their association of safety with childhood. Greg Lukianoff and Jonathan Haidt's much-discussed 2015 *Atlantic* piece on safe spaces and other campus controversies was titled "The Coddling of the American Mind" and was illustrated with a picture of a confused-looking toddler wearing a shirt that said "College." As Josh Zeitz put it in *Politico Magazine*, "Yesterday's student activists wanted to be treated like adults. Today's want to be treated like children."

Safe spaces began as places where (for example) LGBT or minority students knew they would be accepted—where they could congregate among themselves or with like-minded individuals without fear of judgment. In the last few years, however, the term *safe space* has broadened to include protecting anyone from any viewpoint that might offend them. This has spawned derision from many, including *South Park*, which featured the song "In My Safe Space." ("Everyone likes me and thinks I'm great in my safe space / We can face almost anything, but reality we can do without.")

James, the Georgia college student, believes it's beneficial to have safe spaces where LGBT people will not feel judged but does not agree that safe spaces should be created to protect students from controversial opinions. "Just because someone thinks differently from you or says something that you might find offensive or says something that might trigger you or whatever, that's a part of life," he says. "When you leave college, there's not going to be any rule that's going to protect your feelings." He thinks the current notion of safe spaces distorts the original idea behind them: "Safe spaces are supposed to be for people who need a place that they can express themselves without fear of being harmed verbally or physically. Safe space is not supposed to be for people who are just afraid of being offended. [That type of sensitivity] can hinder your ability to function in our world." It's an intriguing reversal: the original type of safe space promoted tolerance based on someone's identity or beliefs; the new version suggests that students should not tolerate another's identity or beliefs.

Eighteen-year-old Ben, the entering college student whom we met in chapter 3, sees safe spaces as an issue of emotional health. "The way [safe spaces] are meant to be used was if you were, like, in the midst of some kind of panic attack or something where you were feeling incredibly depressed or stressed or whatever, then a safe space would be available for you to, like, go in and just relax for a little bit," he says. Given that, he sees providing safe spaces as an individual right. "My view is, people know what's best for themselves, and if people are saying they need someplace to go because they're having a breakdown, then who are we to tell them they are not having a breakdown?"

My graduate student Hannah VanLandingham and I were curious how widespread these new beliefs about safe spaces were—is it just a few students at the extremes who thought safe spaces should be a place to retreat from contrary views? We surveyed more than two hundred SDSU students enrolled in introductory psychology, focusing on the iGen students aged 21 or under. As it turned out, support for safe spaces was widespread: three out of four students agreed that "If many students disagree with the views of someone who has been invited to speak on campus, the students should create a 'safe space' for students to come to during the speech." A whopping 86% agreed that "It is the responsibility of the university administration to create a safe space for all students to thrive." Thus, the vast majority agreed with the idea of safe spaces—both during controversial speeches and as a general goal for campuses. These are not fringe ideas but those embraced by the majority of iGen'ers.

The other common response to controversial speakers is "disinviting" a speaker from coming at all. Many disinvitations are framed in terms of preserving the "health" or "safety" of students—usually not physical health or safety but emotional health or safety. When Williams College "disinvited" a speaker, the campus newspaper editorialized that the speaker's presence on campus would have caused students—and here is a uniquely iGen phrase—"emotional injury." Protecting students from being distressed is considered more important than having a discussion of potentially uncomfortable ideas. If some people might be upset, the thinking goes, we'll ban the speaker. And why can't students who disagree simply choose not to go to the talk? I asked a few iGen'ers, but I never got a satisfying answer.

The embrace of safety and protection now extends to course readings, which must be sanitized to remove anything that might offend someone. In his piece "I'm a Liberal Professor, and My Liberal Students Terrify Me," Edward Schlosser noted that many faculty members have changed their syllabi for fear of being fired if students complain about offensive material in the course readings. One adjunct professor, he noted, was let go when "students complained that he exposed them to 'offensive' texts written by Edward Said and Mark Twain. His response, that the texts were meant to be a little upsetting, only fueled the students' ire and sealed his fate." The focus, he says, is now on students' emotional state rather than on their intellectual development, sacrificing challenging discussions for the possibility that a student might feel upset.

iGen college students' beliefs, and the campus incidents they create, have some common themes. One is equating speech with physical violence. When safety extends to emotional safety, speech can hurt. As Northwestern University professor Laura Kipnis wrote, "Emotional discomfort is [now] regarded as equivalent to material injury, and all injuries have to be remediated." Perhaps because they are so physically safe compared to previous generations, and perhaps because they spend so much time online, iGen sees speech as the venue where danger lies. In their always online lives, words can reach out and do damage even when you're alone. In 2016, the number one Billboard song of the year was "Stitches" by 18-year-old iGen'er Shawn Mendes. "Your words cut deeper than a knife," he sings. "I'll be needing stitches." The music video features Mendes being attacked by an invisible force that throws him to the ground, smashes his head into a car window, and pushes him through a wall, leaving visible bruises and cuts on his face. After he washes his face and stands up to look in the mirror again, the injuries are gone. Although on the surface the song is about a breakup, it can also be seen as an iGen metaphor for the cutting power of words—the pain that is mental rather than physical but (in iGen'ers' view) hurts just as much, even if it doesn't leave physical scars. With iGen'ers already mentally vulnerable due to higher levels of depression, words feel harmful. Unlike the rose-colored glasses worn by Millennials, the lenses iGen'ers use to see the world are much more blue.

To get a small window into this mind-set, I asked ten iGen'ers whether they thought safety also included "emotional safety." All thought emotional safety was important, and all could articulate why. "Safety has to do with avoiding danger. There is physical danger and emotional danger. Traumatic experiences can affect your mind and cause emotional suffering which can feel just as negative as physical suffering," wrote Owen, 20. Ivy, 20, sees emotional safety as even more important than physical safety. "Safe means caring for your physical and emotional needs," she wrote. "You could cause serious emotional harm to yourself, which can be even more detrimental [than] physical harm."

The difficulty, according to iGen'ers, is that it's harder to protect your mind than your body. "I believe nobody can guarantee emotional safety. You can always take precautions for someone hurting you physically, but you cannot really help but listen when someone is talking to you," said Aiden, 19. This is a fascinating, perhaps distinctively iGen idea: the world is an inherently dangerous place because every social interaction carries the risk of being hurt. You never know what someone is going to say, and there's no way to protect yourself from it.

Some students have taken this notion even further—beyond offensive or extreme speech to anything that makes them feel uncomfortable or challenges them to question their actions. Everett Piper, the president of Oklahoma Wesleyan University, said a student told him he felt "victimized" by a sermon on a passage in Corinthians about showing love. Why? Because it "made him feel bad for not showing love! In his mind, the speaker was wrong for making him, and his peers, feel uncomfortable." In this way of thinking, no one should ever say anything that makes a student feel bad, even if it might inspire him or her to do better. His university, Piper wrote, "is not a 'safe place,' but rather, a place to learn"—about caring for others, about channeling bad feelings into self-improvement. "This is a place where you will quickly learn that you need to grow up!" he concludes. "This is not a day care. This is a university!"

The idea that complaining students are like toddlers should not be applied too broadly; many campus protests and student complaints address legitimate issues, and protests are a long-standing tradition for voicing dissent. But when students want to ban anything that challenges them, they are questioning the core idea behind higher education and requesting to live in a protected, childlike world. A university is a place focused not on protection but on learning and questioning. Piper's example shows how far the movement toward safe spaces has gone, suggesting that ever feeling uncomfortable, for any reason, even your own failings, is something to be avoided at all costs. It's not; that's called learning.

The Safety of Home, Everywhere

In October 2015, the administration at Yale University suggested to students that they not wear Halloween costumes that might be considered offensive. Resident master Erika Christakis then wrote to the students in her dorm suggesting they decide for themselves what costumes to wear rather than having the administration tell them what to do: "American universities were once a safe space not only for maturation but also for a certain regressive, or even transgressive, experience; increasingly, it seems, they have become places of censure and prohibition. And the censure and prohibition come from above, not from yourselves! Are we all okay with this transfer of power? Have we lost faith in young people's capacity—in your capacity—to exercise self-censure through social norming, and also in your capacity to ignore or reject things that trouble you?"

Students called for her resignation, saying she was not creating a safe environment for minority students. A group of protestors then confronted Christakis's husband, Nicholas, on campus, surrounding him on a walkway. One student began saying Christakis should create "a safe space here for all students," and when he tried to respond, she barked, "Be quiet!" She went on, "It is your job to create a place of comfort and home for the students who live in Silliman. . . . By sending out that email, that goes against your position as master." "No, I don't agree with that," Christakis responded. The student then began yelling. "Then why the fuck did you accept the position? Who the fuck hired you?! . . . It is not about creating an intellectual space! It is not! It is about creating a home here!"

This focus on college as a "home," some have noted, might be part of iGen's slow developmental track. As Yale faculty Douglas Stone and May Schwab-Stone wrote in the *New York Times*, "Instead of promoting the idea of college as a transition from the shelter of the family to adult autonomy and responsibility, universities like Yale have given in to the implicit notion that they should provide the equivalent of the home environment." In other words, all of this focus on protection, safety, comfort, and home is the downside of teens growing up more slowly: they are unprepared to be independent and thus want college to be home. They love the idea of adult freedom that college offers (no curfew!) but still want to feel "safe" at all times.

It's Your Job to Protect Us and Keep Us Safe

A recurring theme in many campus incidents is the appeal to a higher authority to fix the situation rather than students' doing something about it themselves. That was the case at Yale, where the students were offended by the very idea that they work out the issues for themselves. The question is: Why are such issues now considered the purview of the administration instead of the students? The obvious answer is iGen'ers' long childhood: they want college administrators to be like their parents, seen by children as all powerful. But there may be other cultural shifts at work as well. In their article "Microaggressions and Changing Moral Cultures," the sociologists Bradley Campbell and Jason Manning argued that the United States has shifted from a culture of honor, in which people respond to a perceived slight themselves, to a culture of victimization, in which people avoid direct confrontation and instead appeal to third parties and/or public shaming to address conflict.

For example, when two students at Dartmouth College were insulted by a third student who said they were "speaking gibberish," the students did not confront the offender themselves. Instead, they reported the incident to Dartmouth's Office of Pluralism and Leadership. The Department of Safety and Security and Bias Incident Response Team then launched an investigation. "In other social settings, the same offense might have met with an aggressive response, whether a direct complaint to the offender, a retaliatory insult, or physical violence," note Campbell and Manning. "But in a setting where a powerful organization metes out justice, the aggrieved relied on complaint rather than action. In sum, the availability of social superiors—especially hierarchical superiors such as legal or private administrators—is conducive to reliance on third parties. . . . Even if no authoritative action is taken, gossip and public shaming can be powerful sanctions." This type of culture, the authors argue, is especially likely to arise among relatively high-status individuals who are not strongly connected to one another yet see one another as equals—virtually the definition of an iGen college campus.

iGen'ers' focus on safety also plays a role here. I asked Georgia college student Darnell what he would do if another student said something racially offensive to him. Would he confront the person or go to a staff member? He said he would go to a staff member. "Confronting somebody is never a good idea because you don't know what can happen or where that conversation's going to lead to," he said. "I think it's unsafe for other students and people in the general area. A fight could break out and next thing you know other people are popping in just for the ride, or maybe they have a knife on them—you just never know, and I don't like being in situations where I don't have control. So I'd take a step back and bring in the third party."

Darnell said he'd want to have a discussion with the other person and the staff member. "I'd want them to understand that I didn't like what they did, that it was offensive to me and I'd rather them not do it again, but because I can't tell them not to do it, they can do whatever they want, I'd rather they not do it in my presence. Or in the presence of people like me. If it was something racist and I feel like it was offensive, there are probably other people who look like me who would think it's offensive."

Darnell's point about the harm inherent in racist speech is a good one, and his concern about fights is shared by many iGen'ers. But there are also clear downsides to reporting to an authority. Appealing to the administration usually escalates rather than resolves the conflict, often leading the offender to react with defensive hostility. It also can make people afraid to say anything, silencing discussion about important issues. In *The Atlantic*, Conor Friedersdorf argued that reporting microaggressions (comments unintentionally harmful to women or minorities) to authority figures infantilizes students because they don't learn how to deal with such situations on their own "in an environment where the stakes are lower than a first job or group-house or marriage."

In March 2016, students at Emory University woke up one morning to find that someone had written "Trump 2016" in chalk on the sidewalks around campus. Some students said the messages made them feel unsafe, and protestors shouted at campus administrators, "You are not listening! Come speak to us, we are in pain!" The incident prompted widespread ridicule, including Larry Wilmore's show parodying one of the protesting students as saying "I had no idea I went to school with people who had different opinions from me. It's terrifying."

The iGen focus on appealing to a greater authority has resulted in several campus protests against the university administration when the offense was committed by others—even others not directly associated with the campus. That was the situation at the University of Missouri in fall 2015, where the university president eventually resigned even though he'd had no role in the incidents that had sparked the protests (which included racial epithets yelled at a student by men passing by in a truck). The students said that the president was not creating a safe environment for them.

Another incident occurred on my own campus of SDSU. In April 2016, students were upset when an off-campus pro-Israel organization posted flyers around campus naming specific students and staff members who "have allied themselves with Palestinian terrorists to perpetuate . . . Jew Hatred on this campus." The university president's first response to the flyers was an email statement supporting free speech but noting that the flyer should not have identified individuals.

Student protestors believed that the email was not critical enough of the group that posted the flyers, and put up a large banner reading "SDSU thinks we are terrorists." Later, students surrounded the police car in which the university president was riding and kept him from leaving for over two hours. They demanded that he apologize. "I wanted you to defend me," one student told the president. "They called us terrorists, and you didn't defend us." The incident left many wondering why the protests focused not on the group who had posted the flyers but instead on the administration.

Our survey of SDSU students—conducted just two weeks before that incident—presaged the protesters' focus on the university president. Two out of three students agreed that "If negative racial incidents occur on a college campus, the president of the university needs to apologize even if he/she did not take part in the incidents." Thus the clear majority of students agreed with the protesters that the apology should come from the administration, not the person or group responsible. SDSU students also strongly felt that creating a positive racial climate was up to the administration. Four out of five agreed that "If minority students feel unwelcome on campus, it is the responsibility of the university administration to do something about it."

In their *Atlantic* piece, Lukianoff and Haidt argued that the focus on safe spaces, trigger warnings, and microaggressions has things backward: the emphasis on protecting the emotions of students might actually be damaging their mental health. Cognitive behavioral therapy, the most common and empirically supported talk therapy for depression, teaches people to try to see things more objectively. Yet the language of safe spaces, trigger warnings, and microaggressions encourages the opposite—letting your feelings guide your interpretation of reality.

Others have argued that this climate ill prepares students for the workplace, where they will encounter people with beliefs different from their own—and will not be received kindly if they complain to their boss that someone hurt their feelings. In a *New York Times* op-ed critiquing safe spaces, Judith Shulevitz wrote, "While keeping college-level discussions 'safe' may feel good to the hypersensitive, it's bad for them and for everyone else. . . . Shield them from unfamiliar ideas, and . . . [t]hey'll be unprepared for the social and intellectual headwinds that will hit them as soon as they step off the campuses whose climates they have so carefully controlled." Some iGen'ers agree. College student James believes that people who are sensitive to certain issues need to make careful choices. "If you are constantly getting triggered by courses that are required for your major," he says, maybe that's not the right major for you. "My brother majors in criminal justice—those courses have trigger warnings since they're talking about murder cases. Well, sorry, police in the real world don't get to skate by on those kinds of things. You might have police officers who are not trained in all kinds of situations because they were triggered in college. That's where things go too far."

Ben, the 18-year-old entering college student we met earlier, sees the movement toward safe spaces and trigger warnings as a simple matter of mental health. "The perception seems to be that our generation is coddled and whiny and we don't have any kind of thick skin at all. But I think they are misrepresenting things," he says. "The trend is toward greater understanding for people's feelings and people's health. That looks like coddling because when my parents were kids lots of people were oppressed. It was really dangerous to be gay. People didn't recognize PTSD as a real disorder. Anxiety wasn't well understood. The fact that we are trying to be more understanding of that kind of stuff isn't bad." It's about safety and helping those who are vulnerable, he says: "We believe in PTSD as a medical condition that people need to be treated for, and we believe that people with anxiety need to be understood and not just called thin skinned." To Ben, and I suspect many other iGen'ers, they are being sensitive to the needs of others when they support trigger warnings and safe spaces, and it seems cruel not to.

How Did We Get Here?

iGen'ers' interest in safety may be at least partially rooted in their long childhoods. When parents treat children as younger, they protect them more; generally, the younger the child, the less we let him out of our sight, the bigger her car seat, and the more responsibility we feel for his safety. As 10-year-olds are treated like 6-year-olds, 14-year-olds like 10-year-olds, and 18-year-olds like 14-year-olds, children and teens spend more years fully aware that they are safe and protected in the cocoon of childhood. When they go to college, they suddenly feel unprotected and vulnerable and go about trying to recreate that feeling of home and safety that they were in just a few months before. Boomers and GenX'ers, more likely to have experienced freedom before they went to college, had a less jarring adjustment to make. Now they are the faculty and administrators who scratch their heads when iGen young adults want to be treated like children and flinch at the prospect of being emotionally upset.

Overall, children are much more carefully protected than they once were. As Hanna Rosin observed in *The Atlantic*, "Actions that would have been considered paranoid in the '70s—walking third-graders to school, forbidding your kid to play ball in the street, going down the slide with your child in your lap—are now routine. In fact, they are the markers of good, responsible parenting." These are not just perceptions. In 1969, 48% of elementary and middle school students walked or rode a bicycle to school. By 2009, only 13% did. Even among those who lived less than a mile from school, only 35% walked or bicycled in 2009, down from 89% in 1969. School policies often codify these choices. At my children's school, only 4th and 5th graders are allowed to ride bikes to school, and their parents must sign a form giving them permission and saying they will take responsibility for their child's safety. Rules like this, and the forms that accompany them, were unheard of during Boomers' and GenX'ers' childhoods.

An elementary school in Michigan banned the childhood favorite game of tag, saying it was dangerous. Another school banned cartwheels unless they were supervised by a coach. Many cities have banned street hockey (a game played with sticks and a rubber ball in the street; as demonstrated in *Wayne's World*, game play stops for traffic with the announcement "Car!"). One of the few city officials in Toronto who wants to bring back street hockey has set up a protected ring with a long set of rules—a very different game from the 1980s traditions of homemade goals and sticks, no helmets or pads, and rules worked out by the children themselves rather than adults.

In a recent poll, 70% of adults said they thought the world had become less safe for children since they were children—even though all evidence suggests that children are actually safer now. We protect children from danger, real and imaginary, and are then surprised when they go to college and create safe spaces designed to repel the real world.

The Upsides and Downsides of Protection

So: Is the interest in safety a good thing or a bad thing? Like many cultural and generational trends, it's likely some of both. The interest in safety began with the admirable goal of protecting children and teens from injury or death. The most prominent of those campaigns was car safety, including laws such as mandatory car seat use, mandatory seat belt use, "graduated" driver's license laws restricting teen drivers' privileges, and the raising of the nationwide drinking age to 21. Cars also became safer for those of all ages with the addition of air bags, antilock brakes, and softer materials in car interiors. Those measures were tremendously effective: death rates from car accidents have plummeted. The reductions have been the largest for the younger groups; less than a third as many children and teens were killed in car accidents in 2014 as in 1980 (see Appendix G).

This is unquestionably a good thing; fewer children and teens are dying in cars. Car seats, for all of the hassle they cause parents, save lives. So do seat belts and safer driving on the part of teens. This is the clear upside of the interest in safety—which doesn't really have a downside. It always bothers me when Boomers and GenX'ers observe about car seats and seat belts, "We didn't have any of that, and we survived." Sure, *you* did, but those who didn't are no longer with us to wax nostalgic about the days when they rolled around in the back of the station wagon.

Other safety measures have met with mixed reviews. For example, today's playgrounds are plastic, soft-surfaced, and—according to some— boring and not particularly interesting to children. Hanna Rosin argued in *The Atlantic* that the focus on safety has stifled children's natural need to explore and learn by making their own decisions. She profiled an alternative playground in the United Kingdom, modeled after the once common abandoned lot or junkyard where children roamed freely. The kids roll tires down hillsides, ride a rope swing that occasionally deposits them in a creek, and set fires in a tin drum. "If a 10-year-old lit a fire at an American playground, someone would call the police and the kid would be taken for counseling," she observed. A documentary about the playground features a shot of a child who looks about 8 sawing a wiggly board by himself. I am guessing I am not alone among modern parents in instantly thinking, "He's going to cut off his fingers." But he doesn't.

Rosin isn't the first to make the observation that we may have protected our kids into wimpdom. In her book *A Nation of Wimps*, *Psychology Today* editor Hara Estroff Marano argued that parental overprotection and hovering have made kids vulnerable because they don't learn to solve problems on their own. "Behold the wholly sanitized childhood, without skinned knees and the occasional C in history!" she wrote. "Kids need to learn that you need to feel bad sometimes. We learn through experience, and we learn especially through bad experiences." Lenore Skenazy made the case for the opposite approach to parenting, which she dubbed *Free-Range Kids* in her book of the same name. As she explains on her website, she's "fighting the belief that our children are in constant danger from creeps, kidnapping, germs, grades, flashers, frustration, failure, baby snatchers, bugs, bullies, men, sleepovers and/or the perils of a non-organic grape." In her view, the safety obsession has meant stifling kids' creativity and independence. "Society has forced us to always consider the worst case first and proceed as if it's likely to happen," she told the *Guardian* in 2016. ". . . Everything is framed that way and parents are scared to death. In response, they keep their kids in only supervised situations and . . . that's not fun." Because of iGen's fear, caution, and love for safe spaces, one friend of mine says I should instead call this generation "Gen P"—the *P*, he says, stands for *pussy*. (I told him I didn't think it was going to catch on.)

So why hasn't this increase in safety led to a generation of risk takers— kids who feel safe and thus can take risks? In short, because that's not how the human mind works. Generally, people overcome fears by confronting them, not by hiding from them. For example, the most effective treatment for phobias is having the phobic person work up to confronting her worst fear. When nothing bad happens, the fear lessens and then disappears. Without such experiences, the fear remains—and that might be iGen's story, too.

Like many generational trends, the interest in safety has trade-offs. iGen'ers are, by all accounts, the safest generation in US history, partially due to their own choices to drink less, fight less, wear their seat belts, and drive more safely. iGen'ers are markedly more careful, and as a result they are less likely to be killed in car accidents or through homicide. Yet they are more likely to die through suicide, perhaps an indication of their underlying fragility; as we saw in chapter 4, anxiety and depression have skyrocketed in recent years. iGen'ers seem terrified—not just of physical dangers but of the emotional dangers of adult social interaction. Their caution helps keep them safe, but it also makes them vulnerable, because everyone gets hurt eventually. Not all risks can be eliminated all the time, especially for a generation that believes someone disagreeing with you constitutes emotional injury.

Intrinsic No More

I glance at the clock in my personality psychology classroom, seeing we have enough time for a little discussion. I have just told the two hundred students, most in their early twenties, about two types of life goals—those labeled by psychologists as *intrinsic* (meaning, helping others, learning) and those known as *extrinsic* (money, fame, and image). "Which of these do you think is more important to your generation?" I ask. "And why?" A man near the back raises his hand. "Money," he says. "Because of income inequality." Several students nod, and a woman raises her hand. "It's harder now to afford what our parents had. We've got student loans, and everything is so expensive," she says. In other words, money is more important than meaning.

If you've read media portrayals of this generation, these views might surprise you; aren't today's young people increasingly interested in finding meaning? For example, a 2013 *New York Times* op-ed cited a survey finding that young adults named meaning as the most important thing they were looking for in a career. However, that survey queried only recent young people, with no comparison to previous generations when they were young—or even to older people at the moment. Data comparing the generations tell a different story.

In brief: money is in, and meaning is out. Entering college students are more likely to say it's important to become very well off financially (an extrinsic value), and less likely to say it's important to develop a meaningful philosophy of life (an intrinsic value; see Figure 6.8, next page; these numbers are corrected for recent generations' tendency to rate everything as more important—noted on the graphs as "corrected for relative centrality," which is explained in more detail in Appendix A). Even without the correction, the differences are large, with 82% of 2016 students saying that "becoming very well off financially" is important versus 47% saying "developing a meaningful philosophy of life" is important).

The vast majority of this shift occurred between Boomers (in college in the 1960s and 1970s) and GenX (in college in the 1980s and 1990s). Millennials' beliefs mostly stabilized at GenX levels in the 2000s, but then iGen continued the increase in the importance of being well off and the decrease in the importance of meaning. Even more than the Millennials just before them, iGen'ers think that making a lot of money—winning the economic race—is important. That's a far cry from the idea that the recession would reset the culture toward more meaning and less materialism—instead, the opposite occurred.

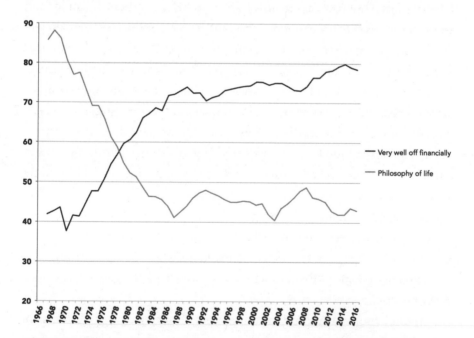

Figure 6.8. Percentage of entering college students who believe that life goals are "essential" or "very important," adjusted for relative centrality. American Freshman Survey, 1967–2016.

In the booming economy of the 1960s, Boomers figured they could count on getting a good job straight out of college, which freed them to contemplate philosophies of life. iGen'ers have no such faith in an easy economic road. They figure they need to focus on paying the bills, which include a staggering pile of student debt that may make it difficult for them to spend much time contemplating the meaning of life.

Another likely influence on the desire for wealth is screen time. Watching TV and surfing the web expose young people to more advertisements, more bling-bling-style wealth, and less intellectual stimulation. In general, modern TV and the Internet provide brief, vivid slices of opinion, often devoid of nuance, in contrast to the content of books. "We distract ourselves online with unimportant things and we are always being 'entertained,'" wrote Vivian, 22. "We have stopped looking at life and its deeper meaning and have instead immersed ourselves in a world where the big stuff people think about is how many likes they got on an Instagram post."

Focusing on money, fame, and image is a common pattern among people high in narcissism. Unlike Millennials, however, iGen'ers do not score particularly high in narcissism; scores peaked around 2008 and have been in decline ever since (see Appendix E). iGen'ers are not as overconfident, entitled, or grandiose as Millennials were at the same age, which in many ways is a positive development. However, some of that narcissism has been replaced with disengagement and cynicism—and that first appears in the classroom.

I'm Here Only Because I Have to Be: Attitudes Toward School and College

One student is slumped in his chair, half asleep or dozing—not just today but every day. Another sits upright, engaged and interested. Every teacher would rather have the second student in the classroom. So which one is iGen?

Unfortunately, more are now like the first student, disengaged and not so sure he wants to be there. Teens' interest in school took a sudden plunge beginning around 2012, with fewer students saying they found school interesting, enjoyable, or meaningful (see Figure 6.9). The strong push for technology in the classroom seems to have assuaged students' boredom during the 2000s, but by the 2010s little in the classroom could compete with the allure of the ever-tempting smartphone.

iGen'ers aren't even convinced that their education will help them get good jobs or give them information they will need later. Fewer 12th graders now believe that school will help them later in life, and fewer believe that doing well in school is important for getting a good job (see Figure 6.10, next page). Increasingly, high school students don't really see the point in going to school. High school teachers, whose jobs were already challenging, now face students who think that what they're learning is irrelevant to their lives and future careers. Within the space of a few years, both their intrinsic and extrinsic motivations for going to school have tanked.

Schools try to keep up with technology, but things change so quickly that they can never catch up, and students know it. Thirteen-year-old Athena says that at her middle school in Houston, Texas, "They want us to

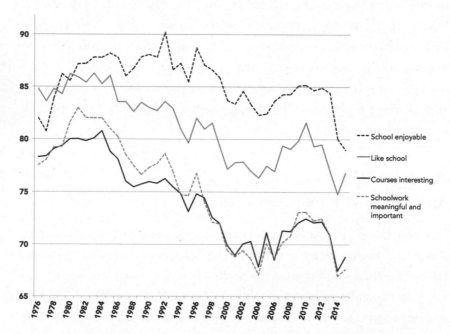

Figure 6.9. 12th graders' intrinsic motivation to go to school. Monitoring the Future, 1976–2015.

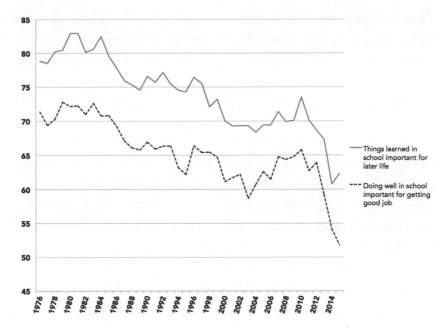

Figure 6.10. Extrinsic motivation for school, 12th graders. Monitoring the Future, 1976–2015.

learn everything out of a book, the same way they taught everybody fifty years ago, but that's not how we learn anymore. Books don't help us learn anything anymore, because it might not be true." She describes several cases in which the textbook and online sites disagreed over aspects of Texas history, a required 7th-grade class. "Which one, the book or what's online, do you think is right more often?" I ask. "Online," she answers. "Why do you think that is?" I ask. "Because the books are fifty years old, and stuff has been proven differently," she says. In her science class, she says, "everything's online. We get tablets—they give us websites we can look up, and then we look it up online and whatever pops up on those sites that we're allowed to go on, that's what we go off," she says. Their math books are updated every year, but, she says, "we don't use them—we just use our tablets. We have the book in case our tablet dies." Like Athena, many iGen students seem to see their schools as behind the times, irrelevant in a fast-paced world of constantly changing technology.

Even in college, where students have more of a choice about being there, a similar pattern emerges: compared to previous generations, iGen'ers are more focused on getting a better job and less focused on getting a general education (see Figure 6.11). iGen college students believe they are in class so that they can get a better job once they are out of class. Learning is less important.

Overall, iGen'ers are more practical than the generations before them. Career advancement has always been an important reason to go to college, but its importance has zoomed up in recent years. More iGen'ers find no joy in school, and more are cynical about its importance. School and college are now a means to an end—and high school students aren't even sure it is the right means anymore.

These attitudes have contributed to the college campus controversies of recent years. To Boomer, GenX'er, and even many Millennial faculty and administrators, college is a place for learning and exploration, and that includes being exposed to ideas different from your own. That, they believe, is

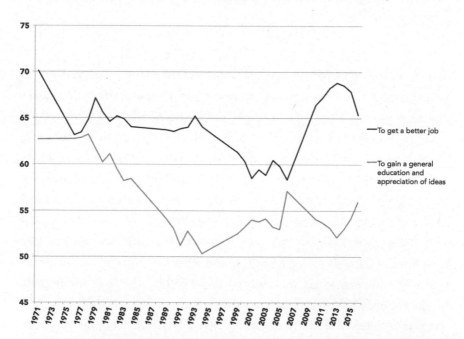

Figure 6.11. Reasons for going to college (corrected for relative centrality), entering college students. American Freshman Survey, 1971–2016.

the whole point of going to college in the first place. iGen'ers disagree: college, they feel, is a place to prepare for a career in a safe environment. Not only are different ideas potentially upsetting and thus unsafe, but there's no point in studying them because getting a good job is much more important. This "consumer mentality" of students arrived some time ago, during the GenX 1990s, but when iGen'ers combine it with their interest in safety, it ratchets up another notch. When exploring ideas was something your Boomer professor wanted, GenX'ers and Millennials could go along with that. iGen'ers' interest in safety leads them to balk at the idea that college should mean exploring new and different ideas—what if they aren't "emotionally safe"? And what does this have to do with getting a good job and earning money? This generational gulf in values, with Boomers favoring ideas and iGen'ers safety and practicality, helps explain why the two generations struggle to understand each other's viewpoints when controversial ideas arrive on campus.

Caring and Community

At the height of the Great Recession in 2009, *Time* magazine theorized that the economic collapse would mean "the end of excess," with the culture undergoing a "reset" that would banish the over-the-top indulgence of the mid-2000s and usher in a new era of caring and communalism.

iGen'ers were children and adolescents at the time, so many observers guessed that they would embody that silver lining to the recession, growing up more concerned for others and more involved in their communities. iGen is also the first completely post-Internet generation, and many people hope that the power of online communities will bring us together and effect change. After all, worthy causes are easier to publicize, and you can donate to a charity by merely sending a text. That has led some analysts to guess that iGen'ers will be more inclined to help others.

And they are—compared to the Millennials just before them, more iGen entering college students say it's important to "help others in difficulty" and more high school students say that "making a contribution to society" is important. More iGen high school seniors say they want jobs that help others and are worthwhile to society, bringing those values back to the levels of Boomers in the 1970s. From these data, we might conclude that iGen'ers want to make a difference in the world. They are dreaming big and including an altruistic vision in those dreams.

However, they have not quite mastered making those dreams a reality. Fewer iGen'ers express empathy for those unlike themselves. For example, more iGen'ers agree with or take a neutral stance on stark statements such as "It's not really my problem if others are in trouble and need help" and "Maybe some minority groups do get unfair treatment, but that's no business of mine." They say that helping others is important, but at least in some circumstances they don't think that help needs to come from them (see Figure 6.12).

The disconnect between statements and actions appears even more starkly in willingness to donate to charities (see Figure 6.12). Support for charities enjoyed a brief resurgence during the recession years but then con-

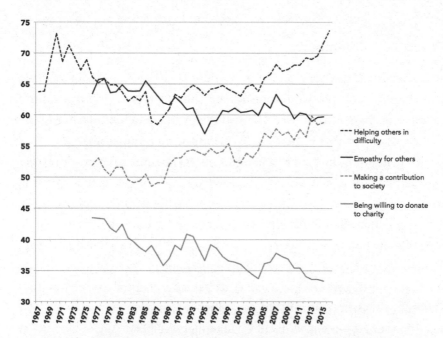

Figure 6.12. Percentage who agree that "helping others in difficulty" and "making a contribution to society" is important, average agreement with eight items on "empathy for others" and "being willing to donate" to nine different charities, 12th graders (Monitoring the Future) and entering college students (American Freshman Survey), 1968–2016.

tinued to slide, reaching an all-time low in 2015. (The survey asks about actual donations and willingness to donate to nine different types of charities, including international relief organizations, minority-group organizations, environmental groups, and charities fighting diseases.)

Overall, iGen'ers want to contribute but are not as inclined to take action. Apparently they agree that altruism is important but have trouble following through. Their always online lives, with lots of talk but not much action, may have something to do with that. "People will post on social media about 'helping more,' but a social media post isn't truly helping anything at all," pointed out Chris, 21. Online, this is sometimes called "slactivism." On the other hand, iGen'ers have mastered the art of joining the bandwagon of viral social media causes, which at least brings awareness to issues. iGen'ers may grow into adults who are skilled at forwarding links about worthy causes but not as skilled at actually getting involved. Or this may change or already be changing, with iGen'ers spurred to action to defend the cause of equality. If the 2017 women's march and protests against Trump's policies are the beginning of a new movement, iGen'ers might be taking steps toward action as well as talk.

What Are They Learning Online?

The Internet has tremendous potential for information gathering and activism. In 2011, young people in the Middle East used social media to organize protests and effect change in their countries during the Arab Spring. Many have hoped that the Internet would also increase civic engagement among US youths, allowing them to easily access news and information and gain empathy for others by interacting with people around the world.

So has it? To answer that question, we can look at the links between time spent online and important values and behaviors. We can contrast community involvement that focuses on helping others (thinking about social issues, being willing to solve environmental problems, and taking action to help others), with individualistic attitudes that focus on individual rights and individual pleasures (supporting gender equality, thinking it's desirable to have friends of other races, feeling entitled to wealth without putting in effort, and valuing materialism—these are a mix of what most consider "good" and "bad," but they are all features of individualistic societies).

The results are unequivocal: teens who spend more time on social media are more likely to value individualistic attitudes and less likely to value community involvement. Heavy users of social media are 45% more likely to believe it's important to own expensive material things such as new cars and vacation homes, and they are 14% less likely to say they think about the social issues affecting the nation and the world (see Figure 6.13). Overall, teens who use social media more are *less* engaged with larger social issues. The good news is that they are supportive of equality of race and gender, one of the primary outcomes of individualism. But they are also less civically engaged and feel more entitled to things even if they don't work for them.

Total time spent online is more weakly related to values. The community involvement of those who spend a lot of time online is about average: they are a little more likely than low-Internet users to think about social issues but a little less likely to want to help the environment, help starving people, or know what political party they belong to. Heavy Internet use is not as strongly linked to low civic engagement as heavy social media use is, but it also doesn't improve interest in community involvement. Like social media use, Internet use is linked to individualistic attitudes (see Figure 6.14, next page).

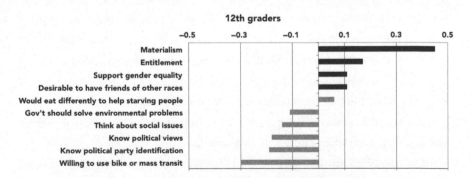

Figure 6.13. Relative risk of individualistic (black) and civic/caring (gray) attitudes and behaviors from spending 10+ hours a week on social media sites, 12th graders. Monitoring the Future, 2013–2015.

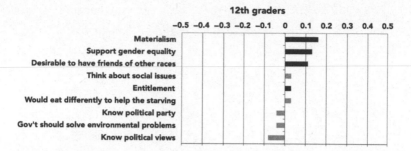

Figure 6.14. Relative risk of individualistic (black) and civic/caring (gray) attitudes and behaviors from spending 20+ hours a week on the Internet during leisure time, 12th graders. Monitoring the Future, 2013–2015.

Overall, Internet use does not mean high community involvement. That's true over time as well: as we'll see in chapter 10, the always online iGen is actually *less* interested in news and current events than previous generations were. iGen'ers can certainly use the Internet for community involvement, and many do. But those who spend the most hours online aren't doing that; they are playing video games with their friends, exchanging funny pictures on Snapchat, and watching YouTube videos of cats falling into toilets. The picture for social media sites is worse: they are not only no hotbed of community involvement but are most frequently used by teens who are less inclined toward interest in politics, social issues, and the environment.

The strongest legacy of iGen'ers' involvement in the online world may be their increased physical safety. They are spending more time on their phones and computers and less time driving and seeing their friends in person, and as a result their physical safety has reached unprecedented levels. They are less willing to take chances, and their definition of safety has expanded to include their emotions as well as their bodies. The more they use words to communicate, the less they put their bodies at risk and the more they put their emotions at risk. It's no wonder, then, that iGen'ers yearn for a safe space where they can be protected. Within that space, they are more likely to support the idea of helping others but less likely to venture out to actually provide that help.

Chapter 7

Income Insecurity: Working to Earn— but Not to Shop

Darnell, 20, chuckles a little when I ask him if he will need to find a job that will help him pay off his college student loans. "Absolutely," he says with a laugh that reminds me of Eddie Murphy's, friendly and ironic at the same time. Darnell is a junior majoring in business at a state university near Atlanta. He grew up in a midsize town near the Georgia-Florida line and attended a private high school that gave him the opportunity to get an internship at a bank. When I ask him how he decided to major in business, he says, "I felt like I'd be able to find a job. I didn't want to major in something and then not get a job in the field that I studied." I ask if he always wanted to go into business. "At one point I did want to be an actor, but that's a really competitive field and it's not a guarantee that you'll get a job. So I had to put that away," he said.

When I meet 18-year-old Haley for lunch in San Diego, one of the first things she tells me is that she is an artist and an actress, rattling off the titles of the plays and musicals she has performed in community theater and in high school. She and a friend have been working on writing a video game for two years. Creative endeavors are clearly her passion. "Are you going to pursue art or acting as a career?" I ask. "No," she says. "I wanted to go to art school to learn animation, but my parents were like, 'Mmm, you should probably pick something a little more practical.' And I get it, it's very, very competitive, and if you're not incredible and amazing and already know people, then you're not going to be successful. So I decided, second best thing, I want to be a forensic psychologist." She's still working on her video game and still draws, but these things will be hobbies instead of a career.

Nineteen-year-old college sophomore Ahmed, who's from Cincinnati, Ohio, decided to major in accounting and can tell you exactly why. "Job security is really good for accountants," he says. "You are almost never the one on the cutting block in downsizing or restructuring, [because] you are more privy to key operational data that cannot be easily replaced."

iGen'ers are practical, forward looking, and safe, a far cry from the "You can be anything" and "Follow your dreams" Millennials. With managers focusing on Millennial employees in the last decades, little time has been spent understanding what might motivate iGen'ers in their careers. That will soon change: iGen'ers already make up the majority of traditional-age college graduates and will soon dominate the pool of entry-level talent. Given the key differences between iGen'ers and Millennials, the strategies that leaders have been using to recruit and retain young employees may no longer work. The same is true for marketing to iGen'ers—with a decidedly different psychological profile, selling to iGen'ers varies considerably from selling to Millennials. Businesses and managers need to take note: a new generation is arriving on your doorstep, and its members might not be what you expect.

The Best Part of the Job

It's the day after New Year's when I arrive at my friend's house just outside Los Angeles. Her parents are visiting for the holidays, and they clatter pots and pans in the kitchen while my friend and I sit in the living room with her son Leo, 14, and daughter Julia, 16. Julia and Leo attend a private high school a fair distance from their house, and Julia uses her newly acquired driver's license to drive them back and forth to school. They're both quiet and introspective, but I finally get them talking when I ask what they want out of a job when they get older. "A job where I can make money—enough money, it doesn't have to be too much," Julia says. "I'd like to enjoy my job," Leo says. "I'd like to just not hate it," counters Julia. "I'd like to have a job that wouldn't take over my life and would pay enough money. I wouldn't want a job where I'd have to work so many hours—like a lawyer," she continues. They both say they would rank money first for what they wanted out of a job.

It's a different view than the common perceptions of young workers. The current trope is that Millennials want jobs that are interesting and inherently rewarding. Today's young employees, it's assumed, will leave unless they get a lot of enjoyment out of their jobs.

The data over time, however, paint a much more practical picture of iGen'ers—and even of Millennials. Compared to previous generations at the same age, slightly *fewer* iGen'ers and late Millennials are focused on intrinsic rewards, such as a job that is interesting, where you can learn new things, and where you can see the results of what you do (see Figure 7.1). Like Julia, many iGen'ers just want not to hate their jobs.

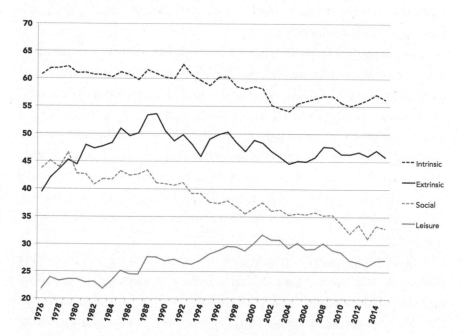

Figure 7.1. Job attributes judged as very important by 12th graders. Monitoring the Future, 1976–2015.

The other big story is the decline in the importance of the social attributes of a job, such as making friends at work and having a job where you can interact with lots of people. iGen'ers are less focused on this; just as they interact less with their friends in person during their leisure time, they are less interested in face-to-face social interaction at work. This is likely a surprise to many generational consultants who draw from one-time studies, who assume that Millennials and iGen'ers are more interested in the social aspects of work. However, young employees' interest in social activities might be more a function of their age than their generation: unmarried and without children, young people have more time and more need for social activities. But when compared to previous generations at the same age, iGen'ers are *less* interested in making friends at work.

Overall, the things that many Boomers and GenX'ers enjoy the most about their jobs—interesting work, friends—are just not as important to iGen'ers. They just want the job. "We should all be less interested in jobs that are interesting or encourage creativity because they don't pay anything. That's why you see so many people my age 100k in debt and working at a Starbucks," wrote Jordan, 23.

iGen's practical focus also appears in work-life balance—the idea that work should not crowd out the rest of life. When my colleagues and I analyzed these data back in 2006, the importance of leisure values was the largest generational difference: Millennials were significantly more likely than Boomers to say they wanted jobs that provided more vacation time, an easy pace, and little supervision and that left a lot of time for other things in their lives. iGen'ers have backed off those requests somewhat, returning the desire for work-life balance to where it was in the early 1990s. Perhaps because they grew up during the Great Recession, iGen'ers are more realistic about work and its demands.

iGen'ers might also be reversing one of the most striking trends in young people's work attitudes—their declining belief that work will be central to their lives. Millennials just didn't believe work was going to be as important to them as Boomers did; they wanted to focus more on other things in their lives. iGen'ers have turned that around, returning work centrality to the levels of GenX'ers in the 1990s—though that's still considerably lower than

Boomers' work centrality in the 1970s (see Figure 7.2). Disagreeing that "Work is nothing more than making a living" shows a similar trend, though here iGen'ers have arrested the downward trend but not improved it. Like Julia, many iGen'ers don't want to have jobs that "take over my life."

What about work ethic? Boomer managers often complain that their Millennial employees aren't as focused on work as they were. But maybe managers have always thought that about their young charges—after all, just about every manager wants his or her employees to focus more on work, and just about every older adult has exaggerated the virtues of their younger selves. In 2016, an article in *Forbes* made the bold statement that there was no evidence for generational differences in work ethic. However, it named only a few smaller studies, including one that could not separate age from generation, another with no generational comparison group at all, and one about the hours business students expect to work—not about the hours they would like to work. Those are not great data to determine whether there is a generational difference in work ethic.

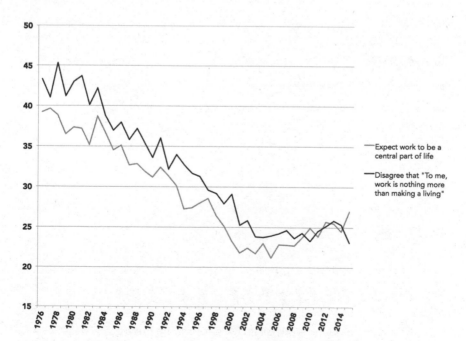

Figure 7.2. 12th graders' work centrality. Monitoring the Future, 1976–2015.

In fact, there *is* clear evidence for a generational shift in work ethic, and it validates managers' perceptions. The Millennials' work ethic was lower than Boomers' and GenX'ers' was at the same age—fewer were willing to work overtime, fewer wanted to work if they had enough money, and more said that "not wanting to work hard" might prevent them from getting the job they want (see Figure 7.3). Remember: this is based on what young people say about themselves, not others' judgments. As high school seniors in the 2000s, nearly 40% of Millennials said they didn't want to work that hard (an opinion embraced by only 25% of Boomers), and fewer than half definitely agreed that they would be willing to work overtime to do a good job.

But there might be relief around the corner for managers: the iGen'ers just arriving on their doorstep have a more substantial work ethic. Fifty-five percent of 2015 high school seniors agree that they are willing to work overtime, up from 44% in 2004. Fewer iGen'ers said they would want to stop working if they had enough money. However, iGen'ers have continued the

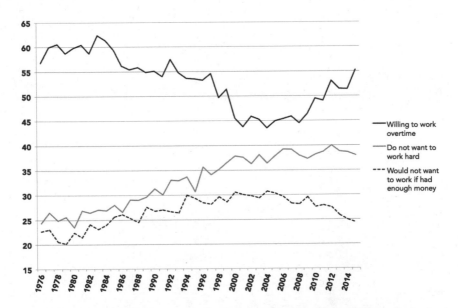

Figure 7.3. 12th graders' work ethic. Monitoring the Future, 1976–2015.

Millennials' trend toward saying they don't want to work hard. Apparently, iGen'ers know that they may have to work overtime, but they believe that many of the jobs they'd want would require too much effort. It's just too hard to succeed today, they seem to be saying.

This attitude may begin with the pressure iGen'ers feel to get a college degree. When I asked my students at SDSU how their lives differed from their parents', most mentioned the necessity of a college degree. Many of their parents were immigrants who had worked at low-level jobs but had still been able to buy houses and provide for their families. Today, my students say, they have to get a college education to get the same things that their parents got with a high school diploma or less. "My generation is stressed beyond belief because of college! When you graduate [from] high school, you are pushed to then go into college, get your masters then have this awesome job," wrote Jasmine, 21. "My father's generation was different. He was born in the 70's and despite never going to college he has a great paying job. That is not a reality for my generation. You are not even guaranteed a job after going to college! And once we graduate we are in debt up to our ears!"

It's true that Jasmine's statements have a tinge of entitlement ("What do you mean, I'm not guaranteed a job?"). But her comments also reveal an underlying exhaustion; she feels she needs to run twice as fast to get half as much. My students seemed envious of their uneducated parents, who could get good jobs without having to slog through four (or more) expensive years of college.

They have a point: the wages of Americans with just a high school education declined by 13% between 1990 and 2013, making a college education more crucial for staying middle class. At the same time, college has become more expensive: due to cutbacks in state funds for education and other factors, college tuition has skyrocketed, forcing many students to take out loans. The average student graduating in 2016 carried $37,173 in debt upon graduation, up from $22,575 in 2005 and $9,727 in 1993. iGen'ers are caught in a bind: they need to get a college education to get ahead, but they have to take out hefty student loans to pay for it. No wonder they are exhausted and just want a job—any job that can pay off their loans.

A Place to Work

Some observers have suggested that companies might have a hard time recruiting iGen and young Millennial employees because they all want to be their own bosses and start their own companies. A report by the advertising firm Sparks & Honey concluded that "entrepreneurship is in [iGen's] DNA" because it found that more high school students (as opposed to college students) wanted to start a business someday. But this could be a function of age; high school students may have always been more optimistic about owning their own businesses than college students are (not to mention that some of the true entrepreneurs might have left college). Nevertheless, many experts believe that the same entrepreneurial spirit is ascendant among Millennials. "Millennials are realizing that starting a company, even if it crashes and burns, teaches them more in two years than sitting in a cubicle for 20 years," the management professor Fred Tuffile told *Forbes*. "While they know their chances of creating another Facebook are low, they do think it's fairly easy to create a cool startup." Tuffile based his comments on a Bentley University survey finding that 67% of young people want to start their own business. But notice that that survey sampled only one generation at one time; there is no comparison group. Maybe Boomers and GenX'ers were just as likely, or even more likely, to want to be entrepreneurs when they were young.

As it turns out, iGen'ers are actually *less* likely to want to own their own business than Boomers and GenX'ers were at the same age, continuing a trend started by Millennials (see Figure 7.4, next page). Just as they are cautious about driving, drinking, and dating, iGen'ers are cautious about going into business for themselves.

Entering college students show the same trend: in 2016, only 37% said that "becoming successful in a business of my own" was important, down from 50% in 1984 (adjusted for relative centrality). So, compared to GenX college students, iGen'ers are *less* likely to be drawn to entrepreneurship.

These beliefs are affecting actual behavior. A *Wall Street Journal* analysis of Federal Reserve data found that only 3.6% of households headed by adults younger than 30 owned at least part of a private company in 2013, down from 10.6% in 1989. All the talk about the young generation being attracted to entrepreneurship turns out to be just that—talk.

Why the decline in entrepreneurship? Starting your own business is inherently risky, and, as we saw in chapter 6, risk is an iGen no-no. "A stable job means secure income, being able to buy the things we want, and feeling safe," says Kayla, 22, who is a week from graduating with her degree in nursing. To her, stability does not include starting your own business. "We saw lots of businesses failing in the last decade or so," she says. "I don't want to be living out on the streets. And neither does anyone else."

iGen'ers are also less drawn to having jobs in large corporations but more interested than Millennials were in industries they might perceive as more stable, particularly the military (the end of the wars in Iraq and Afghanistan may have something to do with that). They also express more interest in joining the police force. Even though those are potentially physically dangerous jobs, they provide a steady paycheck, with few layoffs. Overall, iGen'ers take a more neutral stance on various workplaces, rating

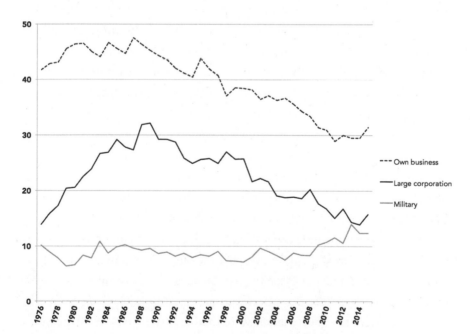

Figure 7.4. Percentage of 12th graders who believe that certain work settings are "desirable" places to work. Monitoring the Future, 1976–2015.

well-liked industries lower than Boomers did and rating less popular industries higher than Boomers did. Apparently, iGen'ers see these very different work settings as more similar than previous generations did; they are less likely to rate them high but also less likely to rate them low. They don't seem to care as much about where they will work; they just want . . . a job.

At least, some of them do.

Working Is for Old People

"Every time I see it, that number blows my mind," University of Chicago economist Erik Hurst said in 2016. The number he was referring to was the percentage of non-college-educated young men in their twenties who had not worked at all in the past year: about one out of four, according to his calculations of Bureau of Labor Statistics data. For nearly all of the twentieth century, men in their twenties were the most reliably employed of all demographic groups, with nearly 85% in the workforce. Not anymore.

I wondered if the trend extended to all men regardless of their education. It did: the employment rate of men in their early twenties reached all-time lows in the 2010s; by 2016, one out of four men in their early twenties was not working. The recent drop wasn't due to more men going to college; the number of men enrolling in college was fairly steady, yet fewer young men were working. (Hurst also concluded that school enrollment was not responsible for the decrease in employment.) It's also not solely due to the Great Recession; the decline in young men's employment began before the recession (around 2000) and has continued after it, with employment rates in 2016 (73%) still several percentage points below the rate in 2007 (79%). Those are years with similar low unemployment rates, but the unemployment rate does not include those who are not even looking for a job.

It's usually more difficult to compare the employment over time of men and women combined, because in past decades many young women were home with young children, and now that's less common. That's probably why the percentage of men and women (combined) who were employed increased steadily between the 1960s and 2000. But around 2000, that trend began to shift (see Figure 7.5, next page). In the decade and a half between 2000 and

2016, fewer and fewer young people held jobs. The slide follows a near-perfect progression by age, with young teens showing the biggest declines, followed by older teens, followed by those in their early twenties. Americans over 25, on the other hand, were working in 2016 at about the same rate as they did before the Great Recession, missing their prerecession employment rates by just a few percentage points. This graph bears a remarkable resemblance to the chapter 1 graph on alcohol use: the declines are the largest for the youngest groups and get progressively less steep, suggesting a postponement of the activity until older ages. Working, like drinking, is now for people over 21—and maybe over 25.

Like the trends for men only, this does not appear to be due to college enrollment, which increased substantially in the 1980s and 1990s but then leveled off after the mid-2000s. College enrollment also can't explain the drop in the employment of 16- to 17-year-olds, which was the largest.

So what are these young nonworkers doing instead of working or going to school? Hurst found a simple answer, at least for the men: they are playing video games. Young men had four more hours of leisure time a week

Figure 7.5. Percentage of Americans employed, by age group. Current Population Survey, Bureau of Labor Statistics, 1948–2016.

than they did in the early 2000s, and they used three of those hours (or three-quarters of it) to play video games. Twenty-five percent played video games three or more hours a day, and 10% played at least six hours a day. "The life of these nonworking, lower-skilled young men looks like what my son wishes his life was like now: not in school, not at work, and lots of video games," Hurst said. As we saw in chapter 2, video games take up an increasing amount of young men's time—about eleven hours a week on average by 2015.

Are young men playing video games because they are not working, or are they not working because they are playing video games? Hurst thinks that the latter might be the case—why work when you can live at home and play video games? "These technological innovations have made leisure time more enjoyable. . . . For lower-skilled workers, with low market wages, it is now more attractive to take leisure," he said.

Georgia college student Darnell, 20, tells me he spent a lot of time playing video games during his summer break last year, "which my dad was not pleased with. I was, like, it's the only break I get, I'm going to enjoy it." "Did your dad want you to get a job instead?" I ask. "Oh, my God, yeah, every time he got off work he was like, 'Did you get a job?' and I was like, 'Would you go away, please?'" Darnell's father finally insisted that he at least complete one job application a day. A retail chain eventually hired Darnell, but so late in the summer that he ended up not working at the store at all before he moved back to college. There, he says, he has to stay away from video games, because otherwise he'd never go to class.

Can I Make It?

Some iGen'ers might be staying away from work because they are convinced that what they do matters little in a rigged system. Take Amber, 20, writing about her generation in what sounds like one exasperated breath: "If we want to have a successful life, we have to go to college, but college is really expensive and we need to either take out loans or work full time in order to pay for it; if we take out loans, that is just going to make our future more complicated and stressful so we try to get a job but most well paying jobs you either need experience or an educational background, so we are often stuck in a minimum wage position, with part time hours because our employers don't want to give us benefits, which means we still have to take out loans." In other words, the cards are stacked against us.

Like Amber, many iGen'ers feel increasingly demoralized about whether they will be able to succeed. Psychologists call such beliefs *external locus of control.* Someone with an internal locus of control believes she is in control of her life, and someone with an external locus of control believes his life is controlled by outside forces. iGen'ers are markedly more external in their locus of control (see Figure 7.6). More say people should just accept their condition in life, and more say that they keep getting stopped from getting ahead.

Thus a growing number of teens think that success is just out of reach. This could be due to income inequality and the aftermath of the Great Recession: iGen'ers saw their parents and older siblings struggling to find good jobs during the economic downturn, and they anticipate having the same issues. The trend may also be connected to iGen'ers' more negative mental

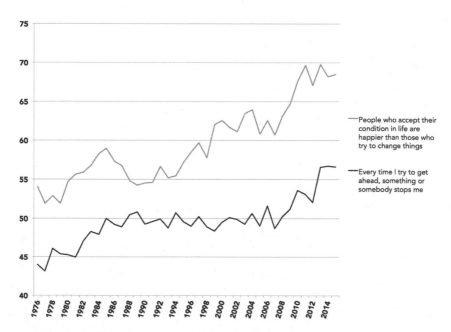

Figure 7.6. 12th graders' external locus of control beliefs. Monitoring the Future, 1977–2015.

state: as we saw in chapter 4, they report feeling more anxiety and depression, mental health issues that are linked to defeatist attitudes such as an external locus of control.

Compared to previous generations, iGen'ers also see more barriers in their way to success. More believe that their lack of ability will keep them from getting the job they want, that not knowing the right people will interfere, and that their family background will stand in the way. And, as we saw earlier, more also say that they think getting the job they want will involve too much work.

iGen sees another possible barrier to success: sexism. Much more than Millennials, they believe that women are discriminated against in jobs. The trend is even stronger for believing that women are discriminated against in getting a college education: compared to GenX'ers in the late 1980s, twice as many iGen'ers believe this (see Figure 7.7).

The previous peak in gender discrimination beliefs was in the mid-1990s, when gender issues were at the forefront in several high-profile

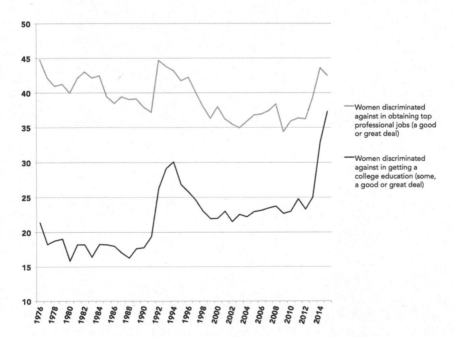

Figure 7.7. 12th graders' belief in gender discrimination. Monitoring the Future, 1976–2015.

cases, including the sexist vitriol directed at Marcia Clark during the O. J. Simpson trial. The recent rise in the prominence of gender discrimination suggests an awareness of continuing sexism, perhaps partially due to the recent attention paid to sexual assault on campus and the inequities pointed out in Sheryl Sandberg's 2013 book, *Lean In*. However, as women make up 57% of college graduates in the United States, it is somewhat surprising that teens perceive gender discrimination in getting a college education. Progress in the "top jobs in the professions," however, has been noticeably slower, with equality far from achieved in business, medicine, and politics. For example, a recent study found that female physicians make $20,000 a year less than their male counterparts, even taking specialty into account (some people call this the "Dr. Paid Less" effect). iGen is apparently more aware of these discrepancies and more willing to attribute them to gender discrimination.

Expectations: Has the Bubble Finally Popped?

Millennials were a generation of soaring expectations, raised on a mantra of "You can be anything you want to be." They arrived at their job interviews believing they already knew everything; when asked where they thought they'd be in five years, they answered, "The CEO of the company." (At least enough of them did for this story to circulate.) Hard data back up this perception: Millennials were strikingly more likely to believe that they would earn college and graduate degrees, while the percentage actually earning those degrees (especially graduate degrees) rose much more slowly. However, iGen'ers' expectations have moderated a bit and become more realistic: about the same number expect a four-year college degree or a graduate or professional degree as did Millennials ten years ago, while the number who actually earn those degrees has increased (see Appendix E). iGen'ers still have high expectations, but they are a little more in line with reality than Millennials' were.

The picture is even clearer for iGen'ers' expectations for the jobs they expect to work in when they are older. The trend for Millennials is worth discussing first: the percentage of high school seniors who expected to be a professional or a manager by age 30 skyrocketed between the 1970s-era Boomers and 2000s-era Millennials, even though the percentage of people who actually had those jobs stayed about the same. Students are also asked what they think their chances are for getting their chosen type of work. Since getting a job as a professional or a manager is more difficult than obtaining a lower-level job, Millennial 12th graders should have been less confident that they would be able to get the jobs they wanted. Instead, they were a little more confident than Boomers were. Confidence, after all, is the Millennial calling card.

Then came iGen. After iGen appeared in the 12th-grade samples around 2011, the percentage who expected to become professionals started to slide, and then in 2014 it suddenly fell sharply (see Figure 7.8). iGen took a long-standing trend toward high expectations and turned it around toward more realism.

Students also grew less certain that they could get their chosen type of work, with confidence reaching the 1970s level again by 2014 and sinking

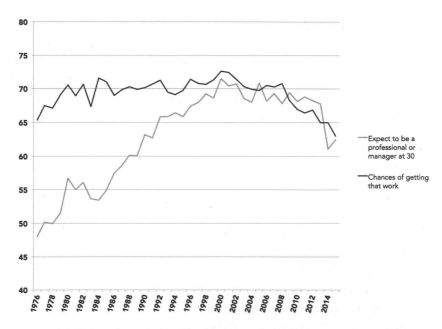

Figure 7.8. 12th graders' expectations for jobs. Monitoring the Future, 1976–2015.

below it by 2015. All in all, iGen'ers' expectations for jobs are more moderate than Millennials' were at the same age, and they are less convinced that they will get what they want.

This shift in attitudes could end up being an excellent opportunity for businesses looking to recruit young talent. Compared to the Millennials just before them, iGen'ers are hungry: they know they need to succeed to make it in an increasingly competitive world, but they lack the outsize bravado of the Millennials. They're not sure they are going to succeed and might be less disappointed with a midlevel job than Millennials were. Their work ethic is a little stronger, too. As they enter the workforce over the next few years, iGen'ers will likely need more encouragement than Millennials did, given their greater uncertainty about themselves and their prospects. iGen'ers are running scared—they want security in an insecure world. Managers who can give them some security, along with some nurturance, may well find themselves with the hardest-working group of young people to come along in a decade or even two.

What They Want: Marketing to iGen

What Millennials were to the 2000s, iGen'ers are to the late 2010s: the young people everyone is trying to reach and still trying to figure out. At 25% of the population, they will have $3.2 trillion in purchasing power by 2020. iGen'ers are out there, waiting for the products that will inspire them.

Even with their doubts about themselves and their prospects, iGen'ers are still fairly confident about their eventual standard of living (see Figure 7.9, next page).

Sixty percent of 2015 high school seniors expected to earn more than their parents, a little lower than the Millennial highs in the early 2000s (64%) but still 28% higher than the less optimistic Boomers. Somehow, iGen'ers thinks, they will make it. They have to: they are acutely aware that they need to succeed in an economy shaped by income inequality, and financial success is very important to them (recall that 82% of entering college students in 2016 said that "being very well off financially" was important—an all-time high in a survey going back to 1967). One out of four says they will be content only if they own more than their parents—about the same as Millennials and GenX'ers and 50% more than Boomers in 1976.

So this is good news for advertisers and marketers: contrary to some rumors, iGen does want to own stuff. The next question is how to sell to them. It's commonly assumed that Millennials and iGen'ers are immune to advertising and that young people today are postmaterialistic, focusing more on finding meaning. As we saw in the last chapter, that's not really true— iGen'ers are very interested in becoming well off and less focused on meaning than previous generations. iGen'ers are also accepting of advertising—more agreed that "There's nothing wrong with advertising that gets people to buy things they don't need." iGen'ers also embrace capitalism, with many more iGen'ers than Boomers agreeing that "People should be encouraged to buy since it helps the economy" (see Figure 7.10, next page).

So what do iGen'ers want to buy? For several years now, marketers have wrung their hands over Millennials' reluctance to buy big-ticket items such

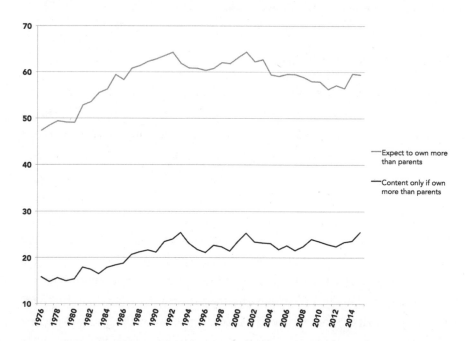

Figure 7.9. 12th graders' material expectations. Monitoring the Future, 1976–2015.

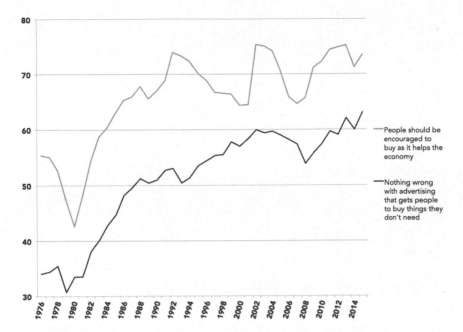

Figure 7.10. 12th graders' materialistic attitudes. Monitoring the Future, 1976–2015.

as cars. Millennials have also parked themselves in their parents' houses, slowing down the real estate market.

Apparently, that's not due to choice: as high school seniors, Millennials were very interested in owning their own homes. iGen'ers have continued this trend: of all the generations, iGen'ers are actually the most likely to think it's important to own a single-family house (see Figure 7.11, next page). This suggests that real estate should continue to be a good investment as young people grow up and buy houses. Assuming they do, sales of home appliances, furniture, and household goods would soon follow. If young Americans can find their economic footing, they will be more than willing to buy homes and everything that comes with them.

It's also often assumed that Millennials and iGen'ers don't want to buy cars. The survey question here asks about the importance of having a new car every two or three years—not an ideal measure since cars have become more reliable. Yet iGen'ers are still more interested in new cars than Boomers were

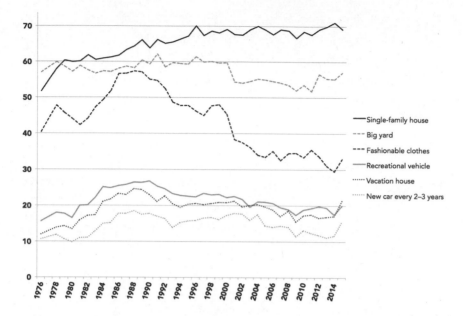

Figure 7.11. Percentage of 12th graders agreeing it is quite or extremely important to own six specific material goods. Monitoring the Future, 1977–2015.

in the late 1970s. A 2016 survey supports the idea that iGen'ers are not giving up on cars: 92% of 12- to 17-year-olds said they planned to own a vehicle. This is a one-time survey without a generational comparison, but it does at least show that forgoing car ownership is not the plan of the average iGen'er. iGen'ers' top reasons for wanting to own rather than ride-share reflect their psychological profile: driving your own car is "safer" and "more tailored to me," they say. Car manufacturers should take heart: despite the rumors, iGen'ers are not going to rely solely on Uber if they can possibly help it. They are too interested in safety, and too individualistic, to give up on having their own vehicle.

The largest change appears in clothes: iGen'ers are much less interested in having "clothes in the latest style." This may be individualism at work: fashion is now much more up to the individual and less of a pack mentality than it used to be. When I was a teen in the 1980s, styles for jeans changed every season—one year they were high, another low, one year dark, another light (or acid washed, or ripped, or faded, or . . .). Get caught wearing the wrong kind, and you were a dork. Things are different now: there are still certain styles that are in and out with jeans, but there seems to be more flexibility. In 2016, *Harper's Bazaar* ran an article on "The 12 Coolest Trends in Denim Now." In the 1980s, it would have been one trend, not twelve. iGen reflects this—having the latest style just isn't as important anymore.

The British writer Rachael Dove, 24, calls iGen "Generation Yawn." She observed that even their fashion choices are safe. "Young hipsters are embracing 'normcore,' a unisex trend characterised by bland, functional clothing," she wrote. ". . . The look dominated the autumn/winter catwalks: tennis shoes at Chanel, comfy nondescript knits at Stella McCartney, Steve Jobs-esque black rollnecks at Lanvin." Nothing too out there, too strange, or too risky for the new iGen era.

Although they like material things just fine, iGen'ers don't really see the point of material goods as messages to others or as a means to compete. Fewer iGen'ers say they care about having what their friends and neighbors have (often known as "keeping up with the Joneses"). Fewer say they care about having the latest fashion in their possession (see Figure 7.12). Even

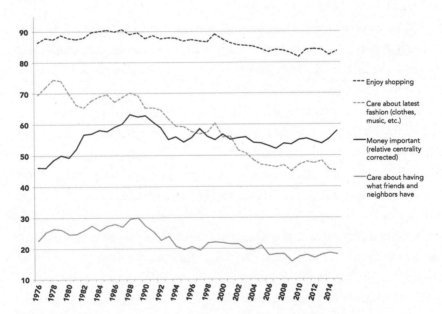

Figure 7.12. 12th graders' attitudes toward shopping, fashion, money, and "keeping up with the Joneses." Monitoring the Future, 1976–2015.

though money overall is still important, iGen'ers are just not as interested in following the crowd.

The 2016 survey about cars captured this attitude as well. Compared to Millennials recalling what they had liked as teens, fewer iGen teens said that the "style," "brand," or "popularity" of a car was important to them. They are just not as interested in fitting in; instead, they are more practical. Just as they just want a job, they just want a car.

iGen'ers are materialistic nonconformists, interested in using money to stand out instead of to fit in. As Rebecca, 23, wrote, "We like to maintain individuality, so we're more likely to buy products that other people don't already use." Ashley, 16, said she likes to shop, but "I don't buy things just because everyone else has them." Marketers have a great opportunity to sell to this generation, just not through telling them to fit in. iGen'ers want products that will be useful to them, make them feel unique, and provide them with the convenience or comfort they want. "I think we are just looking for a product to help us out in our daily lives," wrote Sophia, 21. "It's not about trying to keep up with others or fit in, we just need something that works and gets the job done."

Businesses have another challenge, however: iGen'ers do not like to shop as much as previous generations did when they were teens. Most teens still enjoy shopping. But they favor shopping in a certain way that caters to their impatience. iGen'ers have never known a world before Amazon.com; they are used to getting instant results online. They prefer to get the shopping over with quickly and get on to owning the stuff. Businesses that can make the shopping experience personal and fast will be most likely to attract iGen'ers' growing number of dollars. Some iGen'ers say they want experiences and necessities instead of lots of small things: "[We] need money to pay for important things, like housing, food, education, and medical care, and it's nice to buy experiences like travel, or nights out with your friends, or meals at interesting restaurants," wrote Daniel, 23. "The extra money isn't really just about buying more 'things' to fill up your place with, it's about quality of living."

A 2016 survey by Waggle Dance Marketing Research provides a further view into iGen'ers' consumer attitudes compared to those of Millennials. Of all the generations, Millennials (ages 25 to 34) were most likely to agree that

"I sometimes go shopping just for the fun of it"—more than iGen'ers (ages 18 to 24). As a one-time survey, any differences could be due to age instead of generation, but you'd expect teens to be more interested in shopping than young adults—which strongly suggests this is instead a generational difference. Millennials were also more likely than iGen'ers to agree that "I trust my heart over my head"—again an attitude more associated with teens and young adults than those over 25. Millennials were also more likely to agree that "If I think owning something will impress others, I am more likely to buy it" and "I am infatuated with someone who is currently famous." Both impressing others and having celebrity crushes are usually the realm of youth—yet the younger iGen'ers were less interested than the older Millennials. Overall, iGen'ers are more focused on practical things, less attracted to fame, and more likely to favor logic over emotions than the Millennials just before them. The same marketing messages are not going to work on them.

As advertisers start to reach iGen, we may see a return to the more fact-based ads of the past. Even if appeals stay more visual and emotional, they may be more likely to evoke iGen themes such as safety and security. Advertisers should also move away from appeals based on group conformity and instead emphasize what a product can do for the individual—its convenience, its safety features, the experience it provides. iGen'ers may also turn out to be less enamored with celebrity and fame than Millennials were.

iGen'ers' shift toward practicality should help them navigate a competitive job market and a sometimes confusing consumer marketplace. Their more realistic view of careers and their greater work ethic should serve them well with managers accustomed to the more demanding Millennials. Yet iGen'ers' material expectations are still considerable, focused not on the small things one associates with "shopping" but on big things such as houses, vacations, and the latest technology. More than Millennials, iGen'ers understand that they need to work hard and keep their expectations in check to make it in today's economy. They, more than anyone else, know that their future depends on it.

Chapter 8

Indefinite: Sex, Marriage, and Children

"Our 20s are meant to be the best years of our lives. The years in which we can be completely selfish, let loose, and ignore the consequences of bad decisions. . . . To be honest, sometimes a long-term relationship can just get in the way of all that fun," writes Leigh Taveroff on Today's Lifestyle. Taveroff's article was titled "8 Reasons Why Relationships in Your 20s Just Don't Work."

Not that long ago, the idea that romantic relationships should be avoided until age 30 would have been shocking, even nonsensical, to many people. As recently as the 1990s, most young women married in their early twenties, and many met their eventual husbands when they were still in their teens. Enter iGen'ers, who are taking a path that may permanently redefine adult relationships and families.

Eighteen-year-old Haley, whom we first met in chapter 5, had a boyfriend for six months but has otherwise avoided romantic relationships. "I am very glad I never got into a relationship [before] because I feel like I was able to develop into my own person and [be] independent," she tells me when we meet for lunch. "I tried to avoid building up emotional reliance on other people. I know a lot of people who started dating really, really young and became emotionally reliant on their boyfriend or girlfriend; now they have to seek that, and they can't stay single. They can't learn to be happy with themselves because they're always looking for that relationship. I think that's unhealthy. So I think not dating too young is safer, healthier."

iGen'ers' drumbeats of growing up slowly, individualism, and safety all manifest themselves in their exceedingly cautious attitude toward relationships. As we saw in chapter 1, iGen'ers are less likely than their predecessors to go out on dates and have sex as high school students, postponing romantic relationships until later. Even college is too early, according to some. "I think it's not good to be in a relationship at all during college because you need to focus, explore, make money, study [and] spend time with friends," wrote Harrison, 21. "Being in a relationship at that age makes you feel like you are smothered, brings drama and holds you back from your true potential. I saw a lot of talented people in my age group stop going towards their goals all because of a relationship. You can achieve more by not being in a serious committed relationship. No relationship, no problems."

With the rise of hookup culture—the twenty-first-century equivalent of a one-night stand—"no relationship" doesn't necessarily mean "no sex." So how pervasive is hookup culture, and what does iGen's sex life really look like?

Sex in the Tinder Generation

In 2015, a *Vanity Fair* article announced that Tinder and other hookup apps had created a "dating apocalypse." It was now the norm, it declared, for young people to easily locate multiple sexual partners and avoid committed relationships. "You can't be stuck in one lane. . . . There's always something better," noted one young man. "You can meet somebody and fuck them in 20 minutes," Brian, 25, told the reporter. "It's very hard to contain yourself."

Like most pieces documenting hookup culture, however, the *Vanity Fair* article was a collection of a few stories—mostly stories of people who hang out in bars. It vividly captured what a certain segment of the generation—the more promiscuous segment—is doing. However, it's tough to tell from talking to people in bars what the *average* young person is doing, because those who aren't as promiscuous aren't there. The reporter also didn't think to compare this scene to the bar and nightclub scenes of the 1970s and 1980s, where there was plenty of casual sex going on. To understand average behavior and how it's changed, it is of course better to rely on nationally representative surveys that compare generations. Fortunately, the General Social Survey has done just that.

It's true that iGen'ers' and Millennials' attitudes toward sex differ from those of young people just a decade before. As late as 2006, about 50% of 18- to 29-year-olds believed that sex between two unmarried adults was "not wrong at all"—about the same as in the 1970s. Then approval of premarital sex shot upward, with 65% of young people in 2016 declaring it "not wrong at all" (see Figure 8.1).

Even sex between young teens (those 16 or younger) became more accepted, with five times as many declaring it "not wrong at all" in 2016 than in 1986. iGen'ers are just less willing to label anything as "wrong"—it's all up to the individual. And with the average age of marriage rising to people's

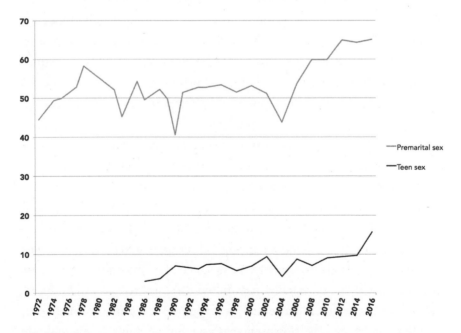

Figure 8.1. Percentage of 18- to 29-year-olds who agree that sex between two unmarried adults and sex between teens 16 or younger is "not wrong at all." General Social Survey, 1972–2016.

late twenties, iGen'ers may find the idea of waiting until they get married to be ridiculous.

With iGen'ers more willing to say it's just fine that unmarried people, even young teens, can have sex, you'd think they would then exercise this freedom and have sex with more partners. That's certainly the concern of parents and the assumption of the media—that with rampant Internet porn and a highly sexualized culture, teens are getting busy earlier, and young adults are hooking up with more partners than in the past, thanks to Tinder and online dating.

Yet iGen'ers are not more likely to have sex as teens and young adults; they are *less* likely. Let's start with teens. As we saw in chapter 1, iGen high school students are actually less likely to have had sex than their Millennial and GenX counterparts. The trend isn't due to shifts in ethnic composition—black, white, and Hispanic iGen teens were all less likely to have had sex, with an especially large decline among black teens (see Appendix H). As recently as 2007, the average high school boy had lost his virginity, but after 2009 only a minority of boys (43%) had had sex, along with 39% of girls. This is a reversal of a previous trend toward sex at younger ages: Boomer women born in the 1940s lost their virginity around age 19 on average, but GenX'ers born in the 1970s started having sex around age 17. Then the average age started to tick up again, settling around age 18 for those born in the 1990s.

There's some speculation that the decline in teen sexual intercourse is due to more oral sex. When Peggy Orenstein interviewed teens for her recent book *Girls & Sex*, several described oral sex as "nothing . . . it's not sex" and "a step past making out with someone." The theme of safety came up again as well. One 18-year-old from suburban Chicago told Orenstein that oral sex "doesn't have the repercussions that vaginal sex does. You're not losing your virginity, you can't get pregnant, you can't get STDs. So it's safer." Of course, that's not exactly true; sexually transmitted diseases (STDs) can be spread through oral sex, just not as easily as through intercourse. Nevertheless, infection rates for STDs fell among teens beginning in 2012—the only age group that saw declines (see Appendix H). Fewer teens having sex equals fewer with STDs.

If sex follows the pattern of alcohol use, young adults will make up for their abstinence during high school and indulge just as much as past generations did. Dating apps, which presumably make sex available at the tap of a smartphone, might make that even easier than it used to be.

That might be the popular narrative, but it doesn't seem to be true. In fact, more young adults are not having sex at all. More than twice as many iGen'ers and late Millennials (those born in the 1990s) in their early twenties (16%) had not had sex at all since age 18 compared to GenX'ers at the same age (6%; see Figure 8.2). A more sophisticated statistical analysis that included all adults and controlled for age and time period confirmed twice as many "adult virgins" among those born in the 1990s than among those born in the 1960s.

"I am not sexually active, and I am not looking to be either," wrote a 19-year-old woman who posted a comment after a *Los Angeles Times* news story covering these findings. "Relationships with that level of intimacy are

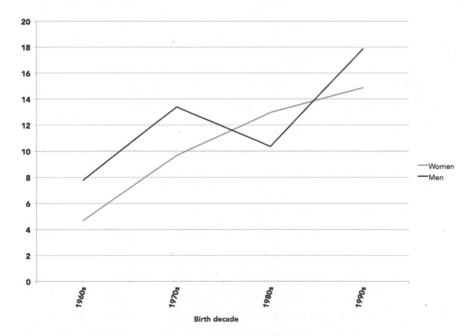

Figure 8.2. Percentage of 20- to 24-year-olds who have had no sexual partners since age 18, by birth decades and sex. General Social Survey, 1989–2016.

distractions." Another, presumably older, poster responded to her comment with "Distractions from what? Relationships are a part of life." To iGen'ers, self-focus and the race for economic success are more important, so sex and relationships are "distractions."

Some iGen'ers mention safety as the reason they have never had sex. "Sex . . . [is] not something I've ever sought out and I think that I would be pretty uncomfortable with it unless my partner made me feel safe and reassured," said Sam, 20, in an article in the Huffington Post. With more iGen'ers feeling lonely, depressed, and uncertain, more may be afraid of the physical and emotional vulnerability of sex.

Of course, if 16% of young adults have not had sex, 84% *have* had sex. So maybe a growing but small segment is opting out but the average Millennial or iGen'er is having sex with just as many people—or even more, given their reputation for hooking up. If that's true, they should report having more sexual partners than previous generations.

Except they don't. Even with age controlled, GenX'ers born in the 1970s report having an average of 10.05 sexual partners in their lifetimes, whereas Millennials and iGen'ers born in the 1990s report having sex with 5.29 partners. So Millennials and iGen'ers, the generations known for quick, casual sex, are actually having sex with *fewer* people—five fewer, on average. As Figure 8.3 (next page) shows, men born in the 1990s had nine fewer partners than those born in the 1970s, and women had about two fewer.

Is this due just to the larger number who don't have sex at all? No— among those who have had at least one sexual partner since age 18, GenX'ers born in the 1970s had 10.67 partners, and Millennials and iGen'ers born in the 1990s had 6.48 partners (after age was controlled). So even among the sexually active, iGen'ers and young Millennials had four fewer sexual partners than GenX'ers.

When I told a group of iGen'ers that their generation was actually less sexually active than previous generations, most didn't believe me—which isn't surprising, as young people often overestimate how many of their peers are having sex and the number of partners they're having it with. But they still came up with some plausible reasons that echo some of iGen'ers' cardinal traits, especially their concern with safety and their practical outlook.

"Teens are being scared into not having sex. When I was in high school the 'no sex' propaganda was strong. We watched videos of what diseased genitals looked like, and we heard all the stories about teen moms," wrote Kristen, 22. "Then that show 'Teen Mom' came out, and nobody wanted to be those girls. Their lives were sad and pathetic." Kristen is right that TV portrayals might have had an impact: one study found that teen births in the United States dropped significantly in the eighteen months following the premiere of MTV's *16 and Pregnant.*

Other iGen'ers mention their fears about sex, specifically sexually transmitted diseases. Tyrone, 20, believes that the decline in sex occurred "because of fear of pregnancy and disease. There's a bunch of commercials and television shows and stuff trying to teach you a lesson." Veronica, 20, wrote, "Sex is not something that is taken lightly. We talk more about sexually transmitted diseases and are more aware of what can happen to you when you have a lot of sexual partners."

The fear of sexual assault—and worse—might also play a role, especially for women. Amelia, 23, has never had sex. "There are just so many

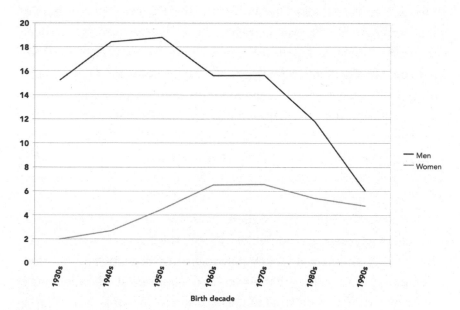

Figure 8.3. Number of sexual partners after age 18 by decade of birth, all adults, controlled for age. General Social Survey, 1989–2016.

risks . . . women in particular are very aware of the dangers in going with a stranger back to their house, and have legitimate concerns as to whether they will even make it out of there alive," she told the Huffington Post. Previous generations may have had those fears as well, but between today's constant media barrage and iGen'ers' interest in safety, the fears have become heightened.

iGen'ers may also have fewer opportunities for sex because they spend so much less time with their peers in person. As we saw in chapter 3, teens are hanging out with their friends and going out less, probably because they are Snapchatting or texting instead. Maybe they are naked Snapchatting or sexting, but they are less likely to take the extra step to be physically together and actually have sex. Sexting can't get you pregnant, and to many iGen'ers it feels safer. "I would do really graphic sexting in middle and high school or do stripteases on Skype," one East Coast college student told Peggy Orenstein in *Girls & Sex*. "I wasn't ready to lose my virginity, but I loved being the bad girl."

Internet access might be one of the primary reasons teen pregnancy declined in recent decades. One study found that the teen birthrate dropped significantly after the introduction of broadband Internet in an area, accounting for 13% of the decline in the teen birthrate between 1999 and 2007. That could be due to teens finding more information about birth control online, or it could be due to their communicating electronically instead. The data suggest the latter: birth control use among high school students has changed little (according to the YRBSS), suggesting that the birthrate decline is instead due to fewer teens going all the way. As a *Washington Post* article on the decline in teen sex put it, "Maybe they're too busy messing with their iPhones."

iGen and Millennial young adults may also have fewer opportunities to meet sexual partners. If you're not a looker, you'll get swiped left on Tinder even if you can reliably charm potential partners on the next bar stool. With fewer people on those bar stools—and those who are there looking at Tinder on their phones instead of the person next to them—a large group of people gets left out of the sexual scene. At one time, people who weren't into hooking up or who weren't conventionally attractive would find each other and get married young. With later marriage now the norm, some are not having sex at all.

Some might be opting out because they don't want to participate in hookup culture, which is often devoid of romance or even a hint of emotional intimacy. Tulane University student Claudia, 19, told the *Washington Post* that she wants an "old-fashioned" relationship but most Tulane students are into "very casual one-night stands, going to bars and going home with someone," which is not what she wants. Some young men these days are very direct about their desires—and that's often sex without strings attached or even foreplay. "I'll get a text that says, 'Wanna fuck?'" Indiana University Southeast student Jennifer, 22, told *Vanity Fair*. "They'll tell you, 'Come over and sit on my face,'" noted her friend, Ashley, 19. With serious relationships less common among young adults, and hookups the most reliable way to have sex, more young women might be choosing to not have sex at all. "Maybe Netflix has replaced sex?" asked Lucy, 26, in the Huffington Post. "All I know is catching a rare Pokemon is far more satisfying to me than chatting to uninteresting men on a dating app."

Some men feel the same way. Mark, 20, observed the hookup scene at his high school near Fort Worth, Texas, and decided it was not for him. "I was a virgin all the way through high school," he told me. "I saw all of the drugs and sex and I decided I'd never try to get into somebody's pants." Instead he waited to have sex until he met a young woman he was interested in as a long-term partner. After their first date went well, for their second date he decided "to upgrade to Olive Garden, a more fancy restaurant, a sit-down place, so we could really get to know one another." Soon afterward, he met her father, and a week later his parents met hers ("And all the parents like each other, which is a first for me"). Mark and his girlfriend first had sex when they had been dating for six months and plan on getting married when they are older. Mark is not alone: when the sociologist Lisa Wade interviewed more than a hundred college students for her book *American Hookup*, she found that most wanted a committed relationship. But many found that the only way to have sex on their campuses was through hookups, so they opted out.

Generation Porn

There's another possible reason for the decline in sexual activity that at first seems paradoxical: the easy accessibility of pornography online. As the musical *Avenue Q* charmingly put it, "The Internet Is for Porn."

More people are viewing pornography; one study found that for young adult men, watching a porn video in the last year went from a minority experience in the 1970s to a majority one by the 2010s. Even teens and children were watching porn—often after stumbling across it online. As early as 2005, 42% of 10- to 17-year-olds said they had seen some online pornography in the last year, two-thirds of them unwittingly.

You'd think the widespread availability of porn would make teens more interested in actual sex, but young people themselves often say the opposite. Hiro, 17, lives in Texas with his parents and older siblings. He says he first saw pornography when he was 9 years old, when he figured out how to turn off the child filter on his parents' computer. Porn led him to try to imagine what girls he knew looked like naked, so, he says, "I had two choices: hang out with girls and constantly think sexually about them, or avoid them entirely." He chose to avoid them. "I have never been in a relationship in my 17 years on this earth, and the big reason is porn and my association with it. At this point that makes me sad," he wrote. He concluded, "Pornography, especially on the internet, has desensitized teens into not enjoying or wanting sex and intimacy."

Some young men find that porn is enough to satisfy their sexual urges. Noah Patterson, 18, told the *Washington Post* he'd rather watch YouTube, play video games, or work than have sex. He's a virgin, though he has watched a lot of porn. When asked if he was curious about actual sex, he said, "Not really. I've seen so much of it. . . . There isn't really anything magical about it, right?"

A 2016 *Time* magazine cover story documented the growing number of young men who say their extensive use of pornography has left them unable to be aroused by actual sex. Noah Church, now 26, says he first saw pictures of nudity online when he was 9. By the time he was 15, he was masturbating to pornographic streaming videos several times a day. When he was a senior in high school, he and his date ended up naked in her bedroom, but he couldn't get an erection. "There was a disconnect between what I wanted in my mind and how my body reacted," he said.

In a widely viewed TED talk, 40-something Cindy Gallop described her experiences having sex with men in their twenties. "When I have sex with younger men, I encounter, very directly and personally, the real ramifications of the creeping ubiquity of hard-core pornography in our culture," she said. "Kids are able to access [porn] at a younger and younger age than ever before. There's an entire generation growing up that believes that what you see in hard-core pornography is the way that you have sex." In response, she originated the website Make Love Not Porn, a collection of helpful tips for men, including "A lot of women aren't into the idea of anal" and "Some women shave [down there], some women don't."

It's difficult to prove that increased pornography consumption has led to less sex. By definition, men and women who watch porn are more interested in sex in the first place, so they usually have more sex. For most people, porn likely doesn't decrease sexual activity. But there appears to be a measureable segment of people for whom porn is enough and real sex seems unnecessary. Why risk rejection, sexually transmitted diseases, relationship arguments, or having to meet up with someone when you can watch porn in the privacy of your own bedroom and do things your way?

Porn may be leading to sexual inactivity in another way, by influencing the kind of sex young people are having. College students told Lisa Wade that hookup sex was the norm and the only real route for entering a relationship. Hookups, they said, are ideally "emotionless or meaningless sex," an idea they might have gotten from pornography. As Wade told Minnesota Public Radio, "Pornography is hot sex and cold emotions. That is the same ideal that students will articulate if you ask them what hookup culture is all about. It's about having hot sex but being cold emotionally." She found that a third of students were sexually inactive in their freshman year. "Almost all of them were opting out specifically because they didn't want to have that kind of sexual encounter," she said. "They were okay with casual sex, they weren't opposed to that. But they didn't like the idea of having cold, emotionless, and possibly cruel sex with one another. They would have been happy to have hot sex and warm emotions. They wanted to at least be in like if not in love. And that is really off script in hookup culture." Other researchers who study sex have encountered similar attitudes among today's students. "I have students who say people should be able to have no emotions in sex, and if you can't, there's something wrong with you," says Debby Herbenick of Indiana University.

Catching Feelings

As her number one reason "why relationships in your 20s just don't work," Leigh Taveroff writes, "These years are extremely important: you're meant to be finding out who you are and building a foundation for the rest of your life. You don't want to get too caught up in someone else's problems, triumphs and failures, and forget to be experiencing your own. At the end of the day, your 20s are the years where YOU DO YOU. Be selfish, have fun and explore the world."

Taveroff clearly takes it for granted that self-exploration is the purpose of one's twenties—a notion that many 25-year-olds as recently as the 1990s might have found odd. By that age, most Boomers and GenX'ers were married, and many had children. That's not to say that one way is right and the other isn't, but they are very different viewpoints on the best way to spend the high-energy years of your life. "It's way too early," says Ivan, 20, when I ask him if most people in their early twenties are ready for a committed relationship such as living together or getting married. "We are still young and learning about our lives, having fun and enjoying our freedom. Being committed shuts that down very fast. We will often just leave our partner because we are too young to commit."

In general, relationships conflict with the individualistic notion that "you don't need someone else to make you happy—you should make yourself happy." That is the message iGen'ers grew up hearing, the received wisdom whispered in their ears by the cultural milieu. In just the eighteen years between 1990 and 2008, the use of the phrase "Make yourself happy" more than tripled in American books in the Google Books database. The phrase "Don't need anyone" barely existed in American books before the 1970s and then quadrupled between 1970 and 2008. The relationship-unfriendly phrase "Never compromise" doubled between 1990 and 2008. And what other phrase has increased? "I love me."

"I question the assumption that love is always worth the risk. There are other ways to live a meaningful life, and in college especially, a romantic relationship can bring us farther from rather than closer to that goal," wrote Columbia University sophomore Flannery James in the campus newspaper. In iGen'ers' view, they have lots of things to do on their own first, and relationships could keep them from doing them. Many young iGen'ers also fear losing their identity through relationships or being too influenced by someone else at a critical time. "There's this idea now that identity is built independent of relationships, not within them," says the psychologist Leslie Bell. "So only once you're 'complete' as an adult can you be in a relationship." Twenty-year-old James feels that way. "Another person could easily have a large effect on me right now, and I don't know if that's necessarily something that I want," he says. "I just feel like that period in college from twenty to twenty-five is such a learning experience in and of itself. It's difficult to try to learn about yourself when you're with someone else."

Even if they go well, relationships are stressful, iGen'ers say. "When you're in a relationship, their problem is your problem, too," says Mark. "So not only do you have your set of problems, but if they're having a bad day, they're kind of taking it out on you. The stress alone is ridiculous." Dealing with people, iGen'ers seem to say, is exhausting. College hookups, says James, are a way "to find instant gratification" without the trouble of taking on someone else's baggage. "That way you don't have to deal with a person as a whole. You just get to enjoy someone in the moment," he says.

Social media may play a role in the superficial, emotionless ideal of iGen sex. Early on, teens (especially girls) learn that sexy pictures get likes. You're noticed for how your butt looks in a "sink selfie" (in which a girl sits on a bathroom sink and takes a selfie over her shoulder Kim Kardashian style), not for your sparkling personality or your kindness. Social media and dating apps also make cheating extremely easy. "Like your boyfriend could have been talking to somebody for months behind your back and you'll never find out," 15-year-old Madeline from the Bronx said in *American Girls*. "Love is just a word, it has no meaning," she said. "It's very rare you will ever find someone who really likes you for who you are—for yourself, your originality. . . . Rarely, if ever, do you find someone who really cares."

There's another reason iGen'ers are uncertain about relationships: you might get hurt, and you might find yourself dependent on someone else—reasons that intertwine with iGen's individualism and focus on safety. "I think it's good for people to be on their own for a while, too. People who are so heavily reliant on relationships for their whole source of emotional security don't know how to cope when that's taken away from them," says Haley, 18, whom we met earlier. "A relationship is impermanent, everything in life is impermanent, so if that's taken away and then you can't find another girlfriend or another boyfriend, then what are you going to do? You haven't learned the skills to cope on your own, be happy on your own, so what are you going to do, are you just going to *suffer* through it until you can find someone else who will take you?" Haley's view is the famous couplet "Better to have loved and lost/Than never to have loved at all" turned on its head: to her, it's better *not* to have loved, because what if you lose it?

This fear of intimacy, of really showing yourself, is one reason why hookups nearly always occur when both parties are drunk. Two recent books on college hookup culture both concluded that alcohol is considered nearly mandatory before having sex with someone for the first time. The college women Peggy Orenstein interviewed for *Girls & Sex* said that hooking up sober would be "awkward." "Being sober makes it seem like you want to be in a relationship," one college freshman told her. "It's really uncomfortable." One study found that the average college hookup involves the woman having had four drinks and the men six. In *American Hookup*, one college woman told Lisa Wade that the first step in hooking up is to get "shitfaced." "When [you're] drunk, you can kind of just do it because it's fun and then be able to laugh about it and have it not be awkward or not mean anything," another college woman explained. Wade concluded that alcohol allows students to pretend that sex doesn't mean anything—after all, you were both drunk.

The fear of relationships has spawned several intriguing slang terms used by iGen'ers and young Millennials, such as "catching feelings." That's what they call developing an emotional attachment to someone else—an evocative term with its implication that love is a disease one would rather not have.

One website offered "32 Signs You're Catching Feelings for Your F*ck Buddy" such as "You guys have started cuddling after sex" and "You realize that you actually give a shit about their life and want to know more." Another website for college students offered advice on "How to Avoid Catching Feelings for Someone" because "college is a time of experimentation, of being young and wild and free and all that crap, the last thing you need is to end up tied down after the first semester." Tips include "Go into it with the attitude that you're not going to develop feelings towards this person" and "Don't tell them your life story." It ends with "Don't cuddle. For the love of God, this is a must. Whether it's while watching a film, or after a steamy session in the bedroom, do not go in for the hugs and snuggles. Getting close to them literally is going to mean getting close to them emotionally, and that's exactly what you don't want. Don't indulge in those cuddle cravings, and if needed make a barrier of pillows between you. Hey, desperate times call for desperate measures."

Maybe I'm just a GenX'er, but this sounds like someone frantically fighting against any kind of actual human connection because he has some idealized idea about being "wild and free." Humans are hardwired to want emotional connections to other people, yet the very concept of "catching feelings" promotes the idea that this is a shameful thing, akin to being sick. As Lisa Wade found when she interviewed iGen college students, "The worst thing you can get called on a college campus these days isn't what it used to be, 'slut,' and it isn't even the more hookup-culture-consistent 'prude.' It's 'desperate.' Being clingy—acting as if you need someone—is considered pathetic."

Then there's "ghosting." That's when someone you've been talking with, flirting with, or hooking up with suddenly stops texting you back. It's the most passive way to break up ever invented, worse than the dreaded GenX Post-it note. Ghosting, wrote Columbia University first-year student Madison Ailts, "isn't your run-of-the-mill rejection. This is rejection that leaves you in a state of utter confusion." Ailts believes that ghosting is a product of the constant array of choices offered by digital media: "We are hardwired to constantly search for the best thing possible, even if it's at the expense of someone else. This has resulted in a new social norm: to suddenly pretend like that person doesn't exist." It also sounds like a generation without the social skills to know how to break up with someone.

Many Millennials and iGen'ers have ended up someplace in the middle, not merely hooking up but also not settling into a committed relationship. As Kate Hakala wrote on Mic.com, there's a new status called "dating partner" that's somewhere between a hookup and a boyfriend. Dating partners have emotionally deep conversations but don't move in together or meet each other's parents. Hakala calls it "the signature relationship status of a generation" and explains, "It might all come down to soup. If you have a cold, a fuck buddy isn't going to bring you soup. And a boyfriend is going to make you homemade soup. A dating partner? They're totally going to drop off a can of soup. But only if they don't already have any plans."

Here's the irony: most iGen'ers still say they want a relationship, not just a hookup. Two recent surveys found that three out of four college students said they'd like to be in a committed, loving relationship in the next year—but about the same number believed that their classmates only wanted hookups. So the average iGen college student thinks he is the only one who wants a relationship, when most of his fellow students actually do, too. As Wade says, "There's this disconnect between brave narratives about what they think they should want and should be doing and what, in a way, they do want." As a 19-year-old put it in *American Girls*, "Everyone wants love. And no one wants to admit it."

I'll Get Married . . . Someday

Will iGen eventually catch up in the relationship department? Maybe. iGen'ers are just as likely to say they want to get married—77% of 12th graders said so in 2015, exactly the same as Boomers in 1976. There's also been little change in the percentage who say they would prefer to have a mate for life or who definitely want to have children.

iGen'ers' attitudes toward marriage are a little less positive than previous generations' views, but not for the reasons you might expect. iGen'ers are more likely than their Millennial predecessors to question marriage because there are so few good ones and are less likely to say their lives will be happier if they marry. However, that's not because they think having just one partner is too restrictive; fewer iGen'ers believe this than Boomers or even Millennials did. By far the largest shift: iGen is more likely to believe that it's a good idea to live together first before you get married (see Figure 8.4). So iGen sees marriage as less mandatory and questions the institution more, but it's not due to some longing for a perpetually promiscuous life.

The bigger question is: What are iGen'ers' priorities—do they think marriage and family life are important? Given iGen'ers' move away from in-person social interaction, it's worth considering what they think of marriage and family, the primary social interactions of adult life. In 1976, Boomer high school seniors rated "having a good marriage and family life" higher than any other life goal. By 2011, however, marriage and family had slipped to fourth (behind finding steady work, being successful at work, and "giving my children better opportunities than I had"—the last likely focused on economic issues). Marriage and family remained at fourth in 2015. Overall, significantly fewer iGen 12th graders felt that "marriage and family life" were important compared to Millenials, and fewer college students believed that "raising a family" was important (see Figure 8.5, next page).

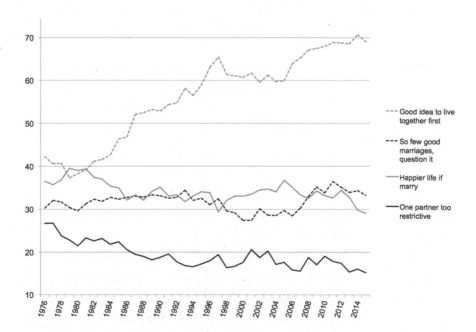

Figure 8.4. 12th graders' attitudes toward marriage. Monitoring the Future, 1976–2015.

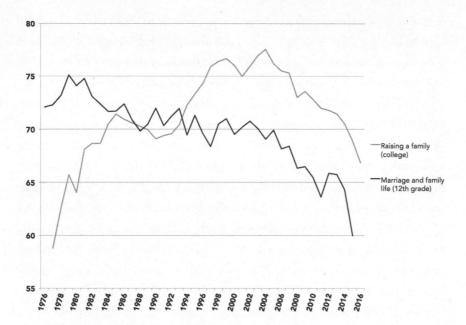

Figure 8.5. Importance of marriage and family among 12th graders and entering college students (corrected for relative centrality). Monitoring the Future and American Freshman Survey, 1976–2016.

When the Boomers, GenX'ers, and Millennials were in college, students rated raising a family either highest or second highest; during the Millennial years of 2002 to 2007, raising a family was rated highest each year. By 2008, though, "being very well off financially" had muscled its way to first place. By 2015, raising a family had slipped to third on the priority list (behind "being very well off financially" and "helping others in difficulty"), the first time that had occurred since it was included on the list of life goals in 1969. It stayed in third place in 2016. Marriage and children are just not as high on iGen's priority list.

iGen'ers' uncertainty about their economic prospects may play a role in their rejiggering of priorities. "I think the biggest problem in having children is [wondering whether] I'll be able to provide a secure and comfortable lifestyle for them," wrote Miles, 22. "I don't want to have a child when I'm not sure if I'm going to have a job tomorrow."

iGen'ers may also see marriage as less important due to their own child-hood experiences. Thirty-six percent of iGen babies were born to unmarried mothers, up from 25% during the Millennial birth years. Perhaps as a result, more did not live with their father or even a stepfather (see Appendix H). These statistics contradict the common view that iGen was more carefully nurtured by fathers ("Having a dad at home or even around was more common," claims *GenZ @ Work*). Actually, it's the opposite: fewer fathers even lived in the same household as their kids.

Then there's the question of timing: when do high school seniors expect to get married? In the 1970s, most expected to get married in the next five years, but by 2015 only 39% did. That's a 22% decline just since 2007, suggesting that iGen'ers will continue the trend toward later marriage begun by GenX'ers and Millennials. "A lot of people are putting off [marriage] so they can fulfill their dreams and desires without having to answer to someone else," wrote Andrew, 22.

The shift in the average age at first marriage since the 1960s has been enormous, increasing by seven years over five and a half decades. In 1960, the median age at first marriage for women was 20—thus half of the women getting married for the first time back then were teenagers. That rose to only 21 in 1970, when the first wave of Boomers was coming of age. Then the age started to climb, and it hasn't stopped since. In 2015, the median age at first marriage for women was 27.1. The average age for men also shot up, from 23 in 1960 to 29 in 2015 (see Appendix H). Marriage is beginning to be seen as something only old people do. As Caitlyn, 22, puts it, "Marriage is boring because you're stuck with the same person for the rest of your life. It's like having chicken every night for dinner. So people are waiting until they don't have any other option but to get married."

Think about it: When was the last time you received an invitation to the wedding of two 23-year-olds? The percentage of 18- to 29 year-olds who are married was cut in half in just eight years, from 32% in 2006 to 16% in 2014. Getting married young is now so uncommon that when Barnard College student Melyssa Luxenberg got engaged in 2015, the campus newspaper ran a story on it, headlined "Engaged at 20."

Whereas previous generations married young and figured out their economic prospects together, many iGen'ers have a long list of things they think need to be in place before getting married. "You'd better have a job that is stable and is high paying or be close to your ideal life before getting married," wrote Harrison, 21. "Settling so young without an education and no business skills is gonna be a disaster down the road. You need to get all this right before being in a committed relationship." The requirement of having a steady job in place is especially problematic for this generation, in which one out of four men in their early twenties is not working at all (see Appendix H).

Americans aren't just waiting longer to get married; fewer are getting married at all, with the US marriage rate reaching all-time lows in the 2010s. This is likely to continue for iGen: more iGen'ers than any other generation were raised by unmarried parents or single mothers. Marriage does not feel mandatory to them. "Marriage is not a necessity anymore," wrote David, 22. "We live in a society no longer blinded by social dogma, and people are allowed to do what they want."

Okay, so maybe more people are living together—after all, high school students are now much more likely to say that's a good idea. Sure enough, more young couples now live together while unmarried than in previous generations. But in the last decade, something interesting has happened: the percentage of unmarried young adults living with a partner has stayed about the same, while the percentage who are married has plummeted. That means that more young people are truly single—not married and not living with anyone (see Figure 8.6, next page).

Millennials and iGen'ers are putting off not just marriage but live-in relationships entirely, with fewer young people living with a partner at all. By 2014, more 18- to 34-year-olds were living with their parents than with a spouse or romantic partner. So not only are high school students less likely to date and young adults less likely to have sex, fewer are living in committed relationships and fewer anticipate marriage and family being a priority. iGen'ers are also less likely to hang out with their friends, at least in person. All in all, iGen'ers are increasingly disconnected from human relationships—except perhaps with their parents.

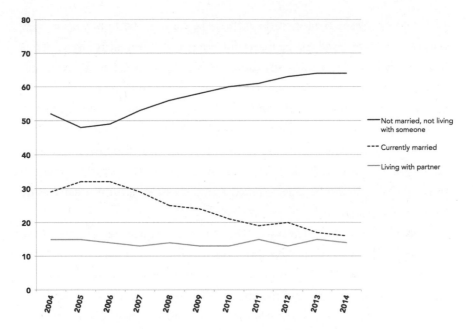

Figure 8.6. Percentage of 18- to 29-year-olds who are married, living with a partner, or neither. Gallup, 2004–2014.

Not Sure if I Want Kids

The economic squeeze facing Millennials and iGen'ers makes having children challenging. College debt loads are at record levels, housing costs have soared, and child care often costs more than rent. Children are expensive, and it's tough to be able to afford to have more than one. "While I would like to have children at some point in my life, I think one of the major challenges in doing so would be financial," wrote Tyler, 23. "It just seems so costly to raise kids and being able to afford them would probably require more than one income." Ava, 22, says, "I already have a child, and the most challenging thing has definitely been the money management of it all. It takes a lot of money to raise a child." With iGen'ers prioritizing financial success over family and many facing economic challenges, more of them will not have children, plunging the birthrate to all-time lows.

Economic woes may be part of the reason Millennials, right before iGen, are waiting longer than any previous American generation to have kids.

In the 1950s, women aged 20 to 24 had the highest birthrates of any age group. Just since 1990, the birthrate for women in their early twenties has plunged by 36%. Over the same time, the birthrate for 35- to 39-year-olds has increased by 63% (see Appendix H).

iGen'ers will undoubtedly continue the trend toward later motherhood, with more women having their children in their 30s, often their late 30s or early 40s (which is about the age limit of both natural fertility and current fertility techniques, including IVF). It remains to be seen whether new fertility technology will be able to extend fertility even later; if it can, many Millennials and iGen'ers will be interested.

The profound shifts in attitudes toward sex, marriage, and children have fundamentally altered the reproductive lifecourse. On average, Boomer women had their first child only about two and a half years after they first had sex. With earlier sex and later births, GenX lengthened that interval to seven and a half years. Millennials and iGen'ers wait to have sex *and* to have children, with 8.3 years from first sex to first birth. For the first time, the entire reproductive timeline has shifted later (see Figure 8.7, next page).

This can be a difficult waiting game for iGen'ers; evolution has shaped humans to want to reproduce earlier in life, and the time between sexual maturity and reproduction keeps growing. "I have seven siblings and all I have wanted since I was eight is a family of my own. I really scared my mom all through high school when I kept telling her that I just want to have a baby," wrote Janelle, 18, a nursing major at SDSU. Yet her typical-for-iGen fears and lack of experience with relationships don't make contemplating marriage easy. "Marriage scares me," she admits. "I have never been in a long-term committed relationship so the thought of spending the rest of my life with one person is frightening." All in all, iGen'ers want kids but fear they might not be able to afford them and are frightened of the long-term adult relationships that often go along with having them.

What will the future hold? There are several possible scenarios. First, iGen'ers will have children but will choose to do so in more unconventional arrangements. With their caution around relationships, more may choose to have babies on their own, and fewer will feel the need to live with their partner if they do get pregnant accidentally. Take Louis Tomlinson of the boy

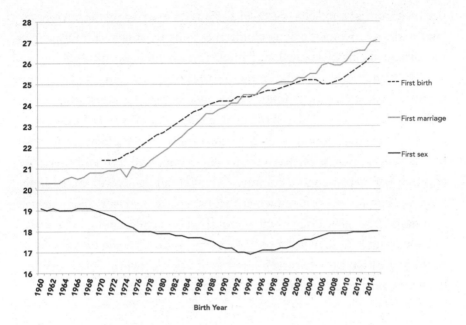

Figure 8.7. Women's ages at reproductive milestones, 1960–2014. Finer & Philbin (2014), U.S. Current Population Survey, and Centers for Disease Control and Prevention.

band One Direction, whose former flame Briana Jungwirth announced in 2015 that she was pregnant when they were both 23. "[The pregnancy] was a surprise at first, but he and Briana are very, very close friends and this has brought them even closer," a friend of the two told *People*. "Although they aren't in a relationship, their friendship is extremely strong and they are both really excited about the baby." Perhaps this will become the new iGen model of parenthood: we won't get married or even live together or be in a relationship, but we will be good friends and raise our baby together. (Or not—by 2016, Tomlinson and Jungwirth were embroiled in a custody dispute that had begun when Tomlinson started dating someone else.)

Such situations make it difficult to have more than one child, and many people want to raise children with a partner. If committed relationships become less common, the birthrate might decrease, too. Several signs point in this direction. Fewer Americans are having children outside marriage: after rising for decades, the percentage of babies born to unmarried mothers declined from 52% in 2008 to 40% in 2015. With marriage being put off ever later and fewer women having children outside marriage, childbearing is increasingly being postponed until one's thirties, if it happens at all.

The trends all seem to be going the same way: fewer young adults are having sex, fewer are in committed relationships, and fewer prioritize marriage and family. The high cost of housing and child care make having children, particularly more than one, economically challenging. All of these trends suggest that fewer iGen'ers will ever have children and that only children will become more common. The United States will increasingly resemble Europe, where birthrates are below replacement level and marriage is optional. The move away from relationships and children might be a permanent trend instead of just a postponement. If so, iGen will be on track to be the generation with the largest number of single people in US history and the lowest birthrate on record.

Chapter 9

Inclusive: LGBT, Gender, and Race Issues in the New Age

When the Supreme Court ruled in June 2015 that same-sex marriage was legal nationwide, Snickers tweeted a picture of a rainbow-wrapped candy bar inscribed "Stay who you are." AT&T turned its globe logo to rainbow hues, and American Airlines tweeted, "We're on board. Diversity strengthens us all & today we celebrate #MarriageEquality."

It's rare for companies to chime in on social issues, as they'd rather not alienate their customers. For a company like American, headquartered in Texas, that could be a lot of customers. But American and other companies are looking toward an iGen future, seeking to appeal to the young consumers who will fuel their bottom line in years to come. Companies know that embracing equality is not just an expectation for iGen; it's a requirement.

From LGBT identities to gender to race, iGen'ers expect equality and are often surprised, even shocked, to still encounter prejudice. At the same time, equality issues are far from resolved, creating divisions within iGen as well as generation gaps that can seem like unbridgeable gulfs. The equality revolution has been breathtaking but incomplete, leaving iGen to come of age after 2017, when issues around LGBT rights, gender, and race were suddenly back in contention.

LGBT: Love Wins

Cameron has always known about gays and lesbians; his uncle is gay, so he can't remember a time when he thought same-sex relationships were out of the ordinary. Perhaps as a result, he takes it for granted that same-sex marriage should be legal. "There's no plausible reason to be against same-sex marriage," he says. "Saying you can't marry who you want to doesn't let gays and lesbians exist as equals."

The oldest iGen'ers were starting preschool when *Will & Grace* (the first sitcom with a gay man as a central character) premiered in 1998 and in elementary school when shows such as *Queer Eye for the Straight Guy* made being gay not just mainstream but fashionable. iGen teens grew up watching *Glee*, which featured several gay, lesbian, and transgender teen characters, and they saw numerous celebrities come out. Compare that to Boomers, who were young when gay men were still getting arrested at Stonewall; GenX'ers, who were teens during the extreme homophobia of the AIDS crisis; or Millennials, who were adolescents when President Bill Clinton signed the bill outlawing same-sex marriage and Ellen DeGeneres found her sitcom abruptly canceled after she came out. In contrast, many iGen'ers will barely recall a time before same-sex marriage was legal, and they'll remember Ellen as a popular talk show host married to the actress from *Arrested Development*, which they watch on Netflix.

As the country singer Kacey Musgraves, 28, sings, "Make lots of noise and kiss lots of boys/Or kiss lots of girls if that's something you're into"—not exactly your father's country song. But it is iGen's country song. "I believe people should do what they want with their own bodies," Musgraves says. "The majority of the younger people that listen to my music don't think twice about the things I'm singing about."

The 2000s and 2010s ushered in a sea change in attitudes toward lesbian, gay, bisexual, and transgender (LGBT) people. These are some of the largest and most rapid generational and time-period differences in existence (see

Figure 9.1). Even many conservative Republican iGen'ers now support same-sex marriage. Anthony Liveris, the vice president of the University of Pennsylvania College Republicans, said in 2013, "A true conservative should endorse empowering Americans to marry whom they love, not limit them." The vast majority of iGen'ers see no reason why two people of the same sex can't get married.

In this graph, the differences aren't due to age, since everyone is 18 to 29 years old, but we don't know how much of the shift is due to a generational trend (affecting only young people and not older people) and how much to a time-period trend (with people of all ages shifting in their views). Because the General Social Survey (GSS) includes adults of all ages, we can compare the views of all ages and generations in recent years to see the current generation gaps.

By 2014–2016, Boomers, GenX'ers, Millennials, and iGen'ers were all nearly universally supportive of a gay man teaching at a local college—only

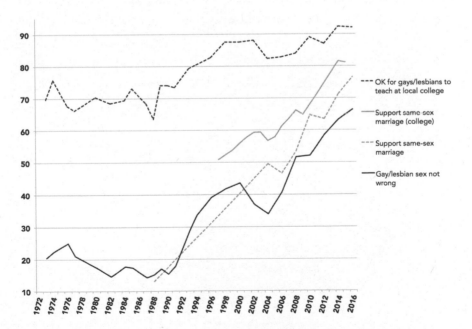

Figure 9.1. Attitudes toward gays and lesbians, 18- to 29-year-olds (General Social Survey) and entering college students (American Freshman Survey), 1973–2016.

Silent generation members over 70 weren't as sure. Views of gays' and lesbians' personal lives, however, differ more by generation. In 2014–2016, a slim majority of GenX'ers still found something questionable about sex between two same-sex adults. In contrast, two-thirds of iGen'ers and younger Millennials saw nothing wrong with gay/lesbian sexuality. Support for same-sex marriage follows a similar pattern. Even in recent years, LGBT issues have produced a significant generation gap (see Figure 9.2).

For many iGen'ers, LGBT issues are tightly linked to their innate individualism. They take acceptance of others so much for granted that you can almost hear them yawn. "My view of LGBTQ is the same as on other people having sex before marriage: I don't particularly care," wrote Riley, 17. "I wouldn't do it, but it has nothing to do with me, it doesn't affect me in the slightest, and I have no right to tell other people what to do or believe. . . . I wouldn't go to a protest for it or anything, but they can do what they want." Twelve-year-old Harper captures the view of a generation who likely won't remember a time before same-sex marriage. "I've never really thought anything about it," she said when I ask her what she thinks about

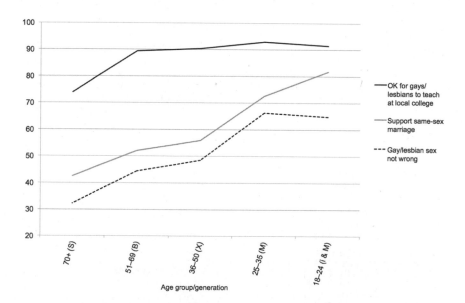

Figure 9.2. Attitudes toward gays and lesbians, all adults, by age/generation group. General Social Survey, 2014–2016.

same-sex marriage. "When you see two people [of the same sex] together it's just like you think it's normal, you never really thought they were different or weird. You kind of just thought they're the same people as you, just, like, a different gender."

Even many religious teens embrace same-sex marriage. Emily, 14, whom we met in chapter 2, attends church regularly with her family in suburban Minneapolis. When I talk to her older brother, he tells me that their church views marriage as between a man and a woman. But when I ask Emily about same-sex marriage, she says, "I'm proud for those people—they fought through everything. It's letting everyone be themselves, and everyone can be happy." When I ask her how she thinks her generation is different, she says, "People aren't afraid to be who they are." Even in the South, the issue is not at the forefront as it once was. At his historically black church in Georgia, 20-year-old Darnell says the pastors "never, like, bring it up—I think because the LGBT community is so big now, maybe we don't touch that."

Even with the large changes in attitudes, a third of iGen'ers still have some issues with same-sex sexuality, and one in four questions same-sex marriage. These young people often struggle to reconcile their iGen upbringing with their religion's viewpoint that homosexuality is wrong. Sofia, 18, and I meet for lunch at the food court on her university's San Diego campus. She was born in South America and came to the United States as a small child, growing up in a small town in the high desert of California. A strikingly pretty young woman with beautiful brown eyes and a kind smile, she attends church every Sunday and believes that sex should be saved for marriage. She and her boyfriend, who was her first kiss in 8th grade, have already discussed getting married someday.

When I ask Sofia what she thinks of the Supreme Court's ruling on same-sex marriage, she says, "That's a tough one for me. I don't think some people are less deserving of happiness than others. God made everyone in his perfect image—there's not a mistake, 'Oh, she likes girls.' It makes me really sad when Christians condemn other people for who they are. That's not really the point of being a Christian at all, it's supposed to be the complete opposite, accepting people for who they are and still love them anyway, because that's what Jesus did, and that's something they forget quite a lot." Yet, she says, it's problematic when gays and lesbians "act upon" their desires. "God didn't say they are sinful for being gay—their choice is more acting upon it, and acting upon their sexual desires. That's where it becomes difficult, since marriage was meant for a man and a woman. But I don't believe they are less deserving of happiness—and when they don't act on it, they're missing out on some of that happiness." Sofia has reconciled her Christianity and her belief that "people should be who they are" but has not yet accepted the realities of homosexuality or same-sex marriage. Yet Sofia is the exception among iGen'ers, and with the legalization of same-sex marriage, acceptance will continue to grow.

If younger generations are more likely to believe that there's nothing wrong with gay and lesbian sex, does that mean they are more likely to have it themselves? They are: the number of young women who have had sex with at least one other woman has nearly tripled since the early 1990s. More men now report having had a male sexual partner as well (see Figure 9.3). It's possible that more people are simply willing to admit to such experiences, rather than more actually having had the experience. Either way, reporting of same-sex sexual experience is on the rise.

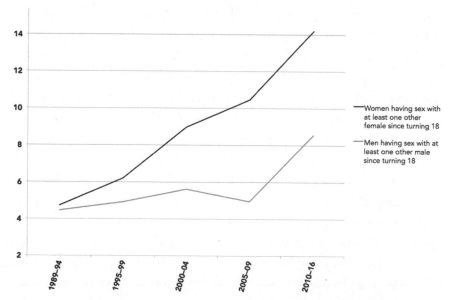

Figure 9.3. Percentage of 18- to 29-year-olds who have had at least one sexual partner of the same sex since turning 18. General Social Survey, 1989–2016.

There is a particularly large generation gap in lesbian sexual experience. Among women born in the 1940s and 1950s, only about six in one hundred had had a lesbian partner during her lifetime by 2014–2016. But among those born in the 1980s and 1990s, nearly one in seven already had even though she'd lived decades less. Millennial and iGen women are much more likely than their predecessors to have had sex with another woman.

Bisexuality—having sex with both male and female partners—is also on the rise. The percentage of adult Americans with bisexual experience during their lifetimes tripled between 1990 and 2016, from 3% to 11%. This might reflect recent trends on college campuses known as LUG ("lesbian until graduation") or BUG ("bisexual until graduation")—women who have lesbian relationships while young and then date and marry men (also called "hasbian"). Overall, the large increase in bisexual experience suggests that many people are having sex with both men and women without necessarily identifying as gay, lesbian, or bisexual—generally, only about 4% of the population identifies as LGBT, but many more have had some experience with same-sex sexuality.

This flexibility around the gender of sexual partners has led some iGen'ers to say that people should no longer be labeled based on their sexual orientation. Twenty-year-old Georgia college student James says, "I'm not much of a label person. I would date someone because they make me happy, not because of what their gender is." He told his parents he was gay instead of bisexual because, he told me, "I know they don't understand that ambiguity that our generation deals with." Several Millennial celebrities have also resisted labeling their sexual orientation. Raven-Symoné said, "I don't want to be labeled 'gay.' I want to be labeled 'a human who loves humans.'" Miley Cyrus says she's had relationships "that weren't 'straight'" and notes, "I'm not hiding my sexuality. For me, I don't want to label myself as anything. . . . I am ready to love anyone that loves me for who I am! I am open."

Young and Trans

iGen will likely be the first generation to understand what the term *transgender* means from an early age, partially due to Caitlyn Jenner's transition from male to female in 2015. Transgender individuals are coming out at younger and younger ages. In January 2017, *National Geographic* featured Avery, a 9-year-old transgender girl, on its cover. Jazz Jennings, 14, was born a boy but knew since she was 2 that she was really a girl. Diagnosed with gender dysphoria when she was 5, the iGen'er stars in her own reality show, *I Am Jazz*. She now questions the idea that she needed to be "diagnosed" at all. Looking up the definition on her phone during an interview for *Cosmopolitan*, she says, " 'Diagnose: Identify the nature of an illness or other problem by examination of the symptoms.' Do I look like I have an illness? Do I look like I have a problem? Being transgender is not a problem. It is not an illness. It's just who you are."

Full acceptance of transgender individuals may take some time. James has a transgender brother. At first his parents assumed his sibling was a lesbian. "Then, when he came out as trans, my dad was like, 'What's that?' " James says. The relationship between my brother and my dad was very, very rocky, and very awful for a long time." His father just didn't seem to understand what being transgender meant. "He said, 'I have a daughter. That's who she is.' He would reference it as a game, [saying] 'He goes around and he wants to be dressed as a boy, he wants to be dressed as male, and all his friends are playing along with it. He can say he's male all the time, but when you take the clothes off you still have a biological female there.' [My father] didn't understand. He couldn't comprehend that."

Most of the teens I interviewed weren't sure what to think about transgender issues, finding it difficult to reconcile their individualistic "be who you are" philosophy with the reality of someone who feels he or she is a different gender from his or her body. Emily, who supports same-sex marriage, is not as sure about her attitude toward transgender individuals. "I disagree about changing your gender, because I think you were born how you're supposed to be," she said. When I ask high school senior Kevin about transgender people, he replies, "Like Bruce Jenner? It's kind of weird for me, because they actually change their own sex. They weren't born that way. I feel like they're denying their previous existence. They're not true to themselves and I kind of don't like it." Athena, 13, says, "I don't agree with being transgender because I think the way God made you is the way you should stay.

God made everybody on this planet the way He wanted it. I don't know why you would want to change the way God made you. They're just confused."

Other teens, especially those who had learned about transgender people in psychology classes or who knew a transgender person, were more understanding. Ben, the 18-year-old from Illinois, knew a transgender boy at his high school. Ben and his friends accepted him, but the process was far from easy; among other things, it took an extraordinarily long time for the boy's name to be changed in all of the school records. And not everyone knew what to do. "Everyone wanted to be supportive, but no one really knew how to be supportive," Ben said.

Leo, the Los Angeles high school freshman, disagrees with those who say things such as "God doesn't make mistakes." "It's not their business to tell people what to do and what not to do," he says. Transitioning "is something transgender people are doing for themselves and not hurting other people. If they want to be transgender, then they can be transgender." Leo's viewpoint will become increasingly common. Once iGen'ers understand more about transgender people—that by changing their sex they *are* being true to themselves—their acceptance will follow, and quickly. But many are not there yet.

Gender Roles: Who Does What?

Gender is not what it used to be. One Stanford University psychology professor asked her class to divide up into gender categories—whatever categories they chose, and it could be more than two. Most divided into male and female, but a sizable minority decided that their group would be called "Fuck Gender." They didn't want to be categorized into one gender, they said—they preferred no gender label at all.

Partially inspired by transgender individuals, there's a nascent movement to declare that gender is "fluid"—not just changeable but also not easily contained by just two categories. Will Smith's son Jaden, 16, caused a sensation in 2015 when he wore a skirt to his prom. College senior Justice Gaines, interviewed for the student newspaper at Brown in 2016, asked to be identified with the pronouns xe, xem, and xyr; thus, the article contained the sentence "xe felt pressure to help xyr peers cope with what was going on, xe said." Others prefer to use "they" as a pronoun for a single person, such as Miley Cyrus's 2015 date Tyler Ford, whom she described on Instagram as "a queer, biracial, agender person, whose pronouns are they/them/theirs." "My whole life I was led to believe that there were only two genders," Tyler said. "I thought I had to shrink myself to fit into a box that was never going to contain me."

This movement toward gender fluidity may be picking up steam, but it's still far from the average response or average experience. In the public eye, you are either male or female, and there is no acceptable in-between state. When Caitlyn Jenner transitioned from male to female, she did an interview with Diane Sawyer as a man—in which she had slightly longer hair but wore men's clothes—and then went underground for four months to modify her appearance to become female. She conformed to the traditional idea of gender as a binary—one interview as a man, then a sexy, barely clothed *Vanity Fair* cover as a woman. She was not allowed (or didn't wish) to be in between, at least not publicly.

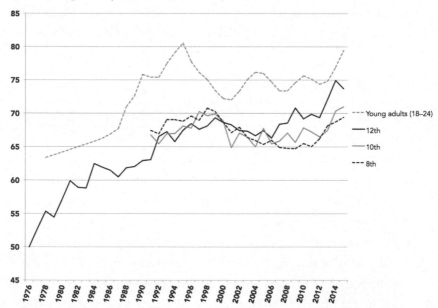

Figure 9.4. Percentage who agree that working mothers can have just as warm a relationship with their children, 8th, 10th, and 12th graders (Monitoring the Future) and young adults ages 18 to 24 (General Social Survey), 1976–2016.

Not only is gender not fluid, but American society continues to struggle with gender equality. Many debates center on family responsibilities: Who takes care of the baby? Who cleans the house? Who goes to work? In a video I show to my psychology classes, young children asked these questions don't hesitate: they point to the Barbie doll for who takes care of the baby and who cleans the house and to the Ken doll for who goes to work.

The movement toward accepting working mothers has been fruitful but incomplete. Between 1977 and the mid-1990s, more and more Americans agreed that working mothers could have just as warm a relationship with their children as mothers who did not work (see Figure 9.4, previous page). After 2010, support for working mothers steadily grew until three out of four high school seniors believed a working mother could have just as good a relationship with her children as one who stayed home.

In addition, a majority of iGen'ers disagree that "A preschool child is likely to suffer if the mother works" (see Figure 9.5). Priscilla, 18, sees benefits

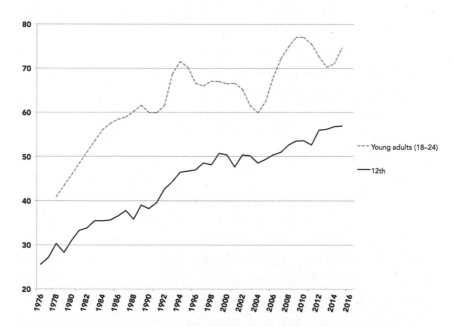

Figure 9.5. Percentage who disagree that "A preschool child will suffer if his or her mother works," 12th graders (Monitoring the Future) and young adults ages 18 to 24 (General Social Survey), 1976–2016. (Note: This question did not appear on the 8th and 10th grade surveys.)

for both mothers and children when mothers work. "Kids get a lot out of going to preschool and socializing with other kids their age," she wrote. "As much as I can't wait to have a child, I know that I will also want to continue to work. I think a child will see their mother's work ethic and develop strong ones of their own." iGen'ers are unprecedented in their beliefs in gender equality. That might be due to their own childhood experiences: two-thirds of 2015 high school seniors said their mother had worked all or most of the time when they were growing up—more than double the number of Class of '76 Boomers who had that experience.

However, supporters of gender equality shouldn't celebrate too soon. The surveys also ask whether it's best for the man to achieve outside the home and the woman to take care of the family. Disavowing such rigid family roles peaked during the early 1990s but then lost ground. Twelfth graders who disagreed that "the husband should make all the important decisions in the family" also peaked in the 1990s (at 70%), falling to 61% by 2015. Even set against the backdrop of the previous gains, it is shocking that two decades of progress for women in the workplace have resulted in *more* traditional attitudes toward family roles. However, there are early signs, just since 2014, that iGen teens and young adults are turning this trend around, bringing it into line with their other views of gender equality and banishing the backlash created by Millennials (see Figure 9.6, next page).

It's possible that this shift toward the traditional stems from the trends we explored in the last chapter: with fewer young people in relationships, teens may view male-female partnerships in increasingly traditional terms. If you want to avoid these gender roles, they might think, don't get married or even live together. Or perhaps iGen'ers believe that working mothers don't harm children but it's still "best" (as the question puts it) when she can stay home. Alternatively, sociologists David Cotter and Joanna Pepin point out that these two questions, unlike those about working mothers, explicitly mention men, suggesting the shift toward conservatism may be due to a longing for men to return to their traditional role as breadwinners. Women may have to work, they seem to say, but wouldn't it be great if men could be men again?

Figure 9.6. Percentage who disagree that "it's best for the man to achieve outside the home and the woman to take care of the home and family," 8th, 10th, and 12th graders (Monitoring the Future) and young adults ages 18 to 24 (General Social Survey), 1976–2016.

Some iGen'ers think it would be best to have a traditional division of labor, but they also recognize that's not always economically feasible. "Personally if I had a kid I would like to stay home at least until they were in school, but that's just me and I'm one person. Other people have different needs and desires," wrote Carly, 19. "I'm sure a lot more women would stay home if they COULD, but they can't, because nowadays both parents have to work and families are still just barely making ends meet." Vanessa, 19, isn't sure she could both work and have kids. "Even if you get, say, 6 hours of free time after work, you're going to be completely exhausted and won't be able to pay as much attention to your kid as they maybe need. I think maybe it is best if at least one parent doesn't work, but that might not be realistic," she wrote. Twelve-year-old Harper told me, "I feel like it would be pretty stressful trying to work and have little kids at the same time because, like, you never really get a break because you're at work and then you have to come home and work with them. I would rather just take time off of work and stay home than be tired all day and then having to deal with, like, three kids." Studies find that children do just fine, both academically and emotionally, when both parents work, but these iGen'ers seem more concerned with the effects on themselves and their partners. They sound tired before they've even begun.

Just as with LGBT attitudes, we can look at recent data to see the generation gaps as they are right now. They show a surprise for gender roles: only small generation gaps between iGen'ers, Millennials, and GenX'ers. Not until you reach the Silent generation in their seventies do attitudes shift decisively toward the more traditional. At least on these questions, iGen'ers and younger Millennials are only a little more progressive in their gender views than GenX'ers in their forties are, and indistinguishable from older Millennials in their late twenties and early thirties (see Figure 9.7).

In other words, the generational change in gender-role attitudes has stalled. This is in contrast to LGBT issues, where iGen'ers and Millennials show a notable generation gap from previous generations.

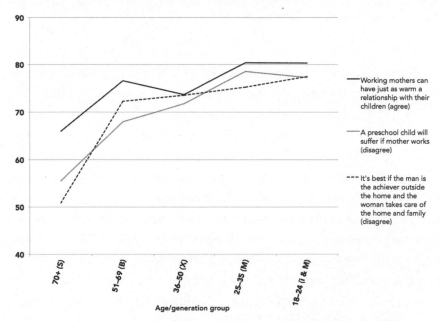

Figure 9.7. Gender-role attitudes, all adults, by age/generation groups. General Social Survey, 2014–2016.

Race: All Together Now, but Somewhat Reluctantly

"All that crap about people's race or sexuality or whatever—no one our age cares about any of that," said a young man in a college course recently, according to the *New York Times*. The professor of the class says that's the norm— she's continually impressed by "the total ease [with] which black, Hispanic, Asian, and white students of all ethnicities interact with one another. Over several years, I've never had a single incident of disrespect."

Yet that same school year, protests over racial issues rocked college campuses around the country. Men driving by in a truck yelled the N-word at the student body president of the University of Missouri. At Clairmont McKenna College in California, a Latina student posted on Facebook, "I feel uncomfortable as a person of color every day on this campus." University of Wisconsin students started a Twitter hashtag (#TheRealUW) to tell their stories of racism on campus: "Frat boys telling you you're cute for a black girl," "When you get told to 'go back to Mexico' by a person in your class," "I hear racist things toward Asians every day on campus but no one here cares. I've never felt fully respected here."

Depending on whom you believe, iGen is either the most racially equal generation in history or rapidly ushering in a return to old-fashioned racism. Which view is right?

Mostly the first, but there's still a long way to go. On the subject of iGen'ers supporting racial equality, they and the Millennials are much more likely to support Black Lives Matter than are older generations—in a 2016 Pew Research Center poll, 60% of white adults ages 18 to 30 said they supported Black Lives Matter, compared to 37% of 50- to 64-year-olds (GenX'ers and Boomers) and 26% of those 65 and older (Silents). "I am white and I support the Black Lives Matter movement. I think it is important that people express frustration with the way police are treating minorities in this country," wrote Jason, 20. "I think it is good that attention has been called to corruption and poor policing—it probably should have happened sooner."

On August 9, 2014, 18-year-old Michael Brown was shot dead by a police officer in Ferguson, Missouri. Several other high-profile cases of blacks shot by police followed, and teens' attitudes about the police and racial tensions shifted abruptly. In just one year—from the spring of 2014 to the spring of 2015—29% more 12th graders believed the police were doing a poor job, and two and a half times as many thought that black-white race relations had gotten worse, attitudes last seen during the racially charged 1990s (see Figure 9.8). This rise in racial discomfort in 2015 also presaged the racially polarizing presidential campaign of 2016 and the rise of the white nationalist "alt-right." For a decade or so, it looked as though Americans had worked things out—we'd elected a black president, anointed Beyoncé the queen of all media, and flocked to Shonda Rhimes dramas on ABC. But it was a fragile truce—and by all appearances it's over. In a March 2016 Gallup poll, 54% of college students said there had been protests on their campus about diversity and inclusion in the last school year.

Issues around race are particularly salient for iGen'ers, who have been surrounded by racial diversity their entire lives. In 2015, most 12th graders said their high school was at least half another race, double the number in 1980. Three times more said their close friends were of other races.

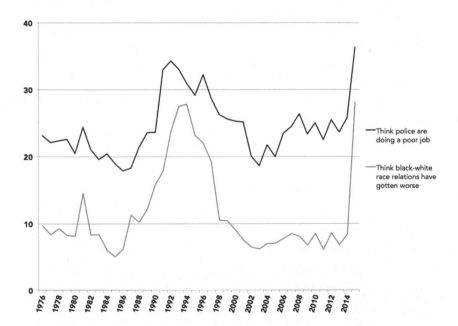

Figure 9.8. 12th graders' attitudes toward police and toward race relations. Monitoring the Future, 1976–2015.

iGen'ers don't just go to diverse schools; they also interact with people of different races in many different settings and say they have gotten to know people of other races this way (see Figure 9.9). College student Darnell, who is black, says, "I've been blessed to be surrounded with Latinos, white people, black people, Asians, all type of people, and I think that broadened my horizons." Carly, 19, also views living in a diverse neighborhood as a positive. "I live in Ypsilanti, Michigan, which is like 40% black, and in my surrounding neighborhood almost all my neighbors are black or Hispanic," she wrote. "I am white so that makes me a minority here. I grew up in a town that was 99% white and I was nervous moving here—like an idiot—but it turns out that it is exactly the same as anywhere else, except there are more black people."

iGen teens have experienced a record-setting amount of diversity in their schools, neighborhoods, and activities. But what would they *prefer* to experience? Here the picture is more complex. On the side of progress toward racial equality, the number of white teens who think an all-white

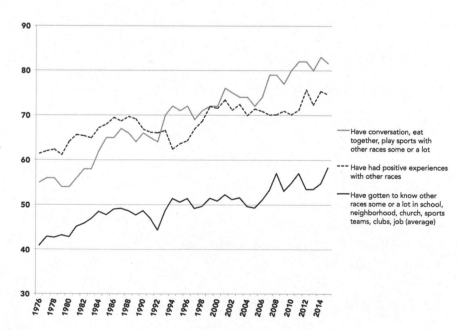

Figure 9.9. 12th graders' interaction with other races. Monitoring the Future, 1976–2015.

environment is best has been cut in half to a small minority. In addition, the number who think primarily other-race environments are desirable has doubled.

But that's not the whole story. Surprisingly, the number of white teens who say that diverse environments—those in which "some" people are of another race—are desirable is just one out of four and has not budged since the 1970s (see Figure 9.10). The number is only somewhat higher among black and Latino teens: one out of three. Despite iGen'ers' greater experience with those of other races, and even though most say those experiences have been positive, most of them describe diverse environments as merely "acceptable," not "desirable." If a racially diverse environment is merely acceptable, it goes a long way toward explaining why racial incidents continue to occur on college campuses and why the 2016 election season gave voice to a white nationalism some had thought no longer existed. Apparently the average iGen teen tolerates diversity but is not sure it's the ideal system.

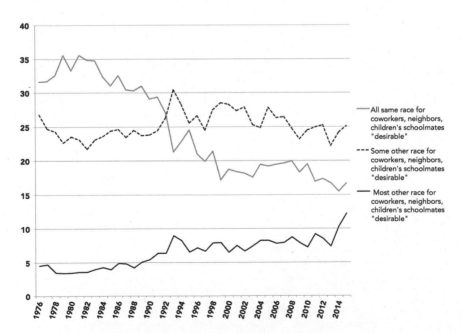

Figure 9.10. Percentage of white 12th graders who rate certain racial compositions as "desirable." Monitoring the Future, 1976–2015.

The same trend appears in personal relationships. White teens who say that having a close friend, boss, or next-door neighbor of another race is "desirable" are in the minority. That number is about the same as in the 1990s—though iGen has started a trend toward changing that just in the last few years (see Figure 9.11). Black and Latino teens are a little more likely to favor cross-race relationships, with half viewing having a close friend of another race "desirable" in 2015. Overall, these preferences help explain why the white kids still sit together in the high school cafeteria.

When I interviewed iGen'ers about this, most said diversity is "acceptable" instead of "desirable" for a quintessentially iGen reason: race doesn't matter. Living with other races "would be acceptable because I honestly do not understand what the fuss is about racism. The color of skin is just that—a color. It doesn't tell you what they feel inside, what their motivations are, or their goals in life," wrote Lori, 21. "I don't care if my neighbors and coworkers were different, I don't care if I'm the only white person. As long as everyone

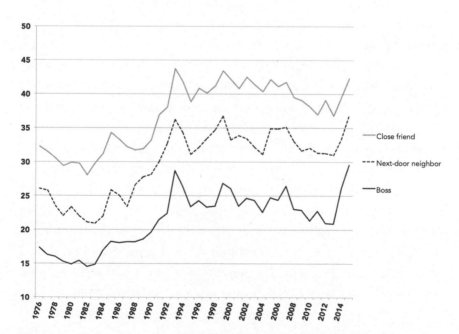

Figure 9.11. Percentage of white 12th graders who rate having a close friend, boss, or next-door neighbor of another race as "desirable." Monitoring the Future, 1976–2015.

can treat everyone with the same respect then I don't see a problem." William, 20, found that mutual interests are more important. "As a black guy, I'm really into metal and other kinds of rock music," he wrote. "I'm also a huge World War I buff. Not too many people in my area (mostly black) are into those things. I just happened to meet a cool guy that was into that stuff and he happened to be white. I don't go out of my way looking for white people to be my friend—it just comes naturally. People get so caught up on race, if they look a little deeper they might find that people are not so different after all."

I got the impression that these iGen'ers didn't want to choose between diversity being "acceptable" or "desirable" because they saw the whole question as ridiculous. As Heather, 20, wrote, "Race has nothing to do with qualifications of a person's ability to be a manager. What is this, the 50's?" Francie, 20, wrote, "In this day and age, it seems silly to still be seeing in color with regards to dealing with humans. I'm white, but I don't care about color when it comes to my friends because it's idiotic and close minded to be trapped in an archaic mindset." Saying that diverse environments were "desirable" might have indicated a little too much interest in race, and if you are iGen you aren't supposed to notice race.

This iGen theme of ignoring race crops up again when we consider how racial issues are discussed on college campuses. Not seeing race has advantages, but it also overlooks the different experiences of students of color and ignores the reality that people do of course "see" race. (When a conservative guest on *The Daily Show* said, "I don't see color," host Trevor Noah responded, "Then what do you do at a traffic light?") The idea of ignoring race might also be at the root of the surge of white nationalism, if some whites feel that their race is not being recognized. The history of 2014–2016 might well suggest that pretending race doesn't exist is not a viable strategy.

In other ways, however, racial attitudes in the United States have shifted substantially toward equality. The percentage of whites who wouldn't want a close relative to marry a black person plummeted from 54% in the early 1990s to 10% in the 2010s (see Figure 9.12, next page). Many iGen'ers can't even comprehend why anyone would oppose interracial marriage. "I'm honestly not too sure why interracial marriage was ever an issue in the first place, but I think it's more accepted now due to the public's shift toward racial acceptance," wrote Anthony, 19. "Most people in America have access to information that can refute claims about purity of race, which is a racist idea created by white people in the first place. That mixing races was ever seen as 'bad' or 'immoral' honestly confuses me."

The percentage of whites opposed to living in a mostly black neighborhood or who support housing discrimination has been cut in half. Yet about the same percentage of white adults believe that blacks are lazy. Jaden, 21, thinks this might be due to media coverage. "While there is coverage of other races also doing crime, there seems to an incredible focus on showing African Americans doing illicit activities," he wrote. "This nonstop negative portrayal of African Americans on news programs and documentaries has a significant effect on how people view them."

It's also interesting to explore the generational divisions in recent years (2014–2016). The biggest differences are between the Silents (those 70 and older) and everyone else (see Figure 9.13, next page). There are also some surprises: white iGen'ers and young Millennials are the generations most

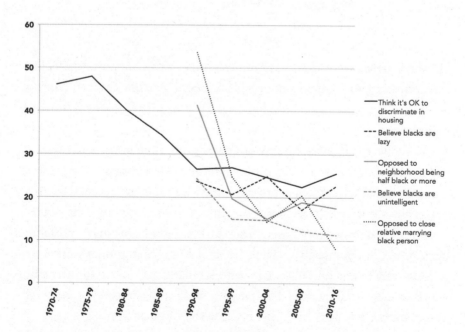

Figure 9.12. Negative attitudes toward blacks, white 18- to 24-year-olds. General Social Survey, 1972–2016.

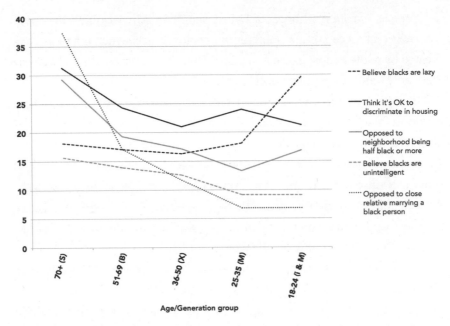

Figure 9.13. Whites' negative attitudes toward blacks, by age/generation group. General Social Survey, 2014–2016.

likely to believe that blacks are lazy, and are slightly more opposed than older Millennials are to living in a mostly black neighborhood. This could be the ignorance of youth, or it could be a sign of the return of a form of white nationalism.

On college campuses, discussions of race often center on issues such as affirmative action in university admissions and scholarships. With income inequality and high student loan debt, some white students resent what they perceive as the special treatment of students of color. One University of Wisconsin student posted to Yik Yak, "There's a black girl on my floor constantly bitching about oppression . . . bitch I scored 12 pts higher than you on my ACT, yet you have a full ride & I got zero scholarships." When Rutgers University student Yvanna Saint-Fort was admitted to seven colleges, her high school friends told her it was only because she was black.

Reverse racism resonates with iGen. In a survey of 14- to 24-year-olds conducted by MTV, 48% of whites agreed that "discrimination against white people has become as big a problem as discrimination against racial minority groups" (27% of people of color agreed as well). The vast majority, 88%, believe that favoring one race over another is unfair, and 70% believe it's never fair to give preferential treatment to one race over another, regardless of historical inequalities (that includes 74% of whites and 65% of people of color). iGen'ers believe in their version of equality so much that many find it difficult to support affirmative action. When racial preferences collide with economic burdens, racism on campus is sometimes the result.

iGen may usher in a new era of affirmative action, but based on class rather than race. In 2015, 52% of entering college students (in the American Freshman Survey) agreed that "Students from disadvantaged social backgrounds should be given preferential treatment in college admissions," up from 37% in 2009. iGen'ers are fiercely supportive of equality, but they see equality as going beyond race.

All in all, iGen'ers have had more experience with racially diverse environments than any generation before them, and the vast majority say they believe in equality. Whites are much more willing to have black neighbors or relatives by marriage, though these shifts have appeared among older generations as well. The number of white teens who think an all-white environment is desirable has been cut in half, but the number who think a diverse environment is desirable has barely budged. Social psychology studies have found that mere contact among the races is not enough; the contact must be positive and among equals. Although iGen'ers are clearly more racially progressive than previous generations at the same age, they are far from postracial. They are also not postgender, and for both race and gender issues they look similar to Millennials and GenX'ers in recent years. iGen'ers do stand apart on LGBT issues, however; that's where there is a sizable generation gap, with iGen'ers leading the way toward more equality and acceptance.

Safe Spaces, Disinvitations, and Trigger Warnings

In the past few years, college campuses have erupted in protests, many of them focused around equality issues. But there are other themes as well. Many protests focus on eliminating not just discrimination but offensive speech, which has drawn criticism that iGen'ers exhibit a hair-trigger sensitivity. This is where the movement for equality collides with the First Amendment. To the distress of free speech advocates, campuses have "bias reporting systems" that allow students to report incidents that offend them. Faculty members have been suspended for leading discussions about race. Controversial speakers are increasingly "disinvited" or their talks disrupted.

Is this really a cultural change, or have college students always been this way? The over-time data show that things really have changed: iGen'ers are more likely to support restricting speech (see Figure 9.14).

Young adults in general are also more likely to agree with speech restrictions. The Pew Research Center found that 40% of Millennials and iGen'ers agreed that the government should be able to prevent people from making offensive statements about minority groups, compared to only 12% of the Silent generation, 24% of Boomers, and 27% of GenX'ers.

When people answer these questions about speech restrictions, they are likely thinking about blatant racism or sexism—someone who uses a

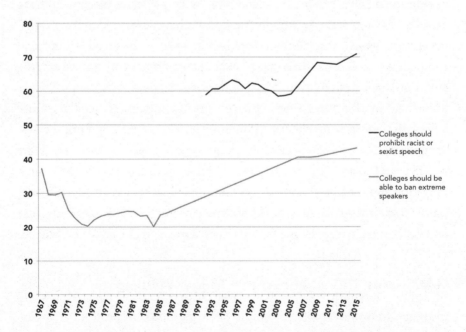

Figure 9.14. Entering college students' attitudes toward speech on campus. American Freshman Survey, 1967–2015.

racial epithet in anger or contempt or someone who says, "All [insert group here] are [insert negative trait here]." When two white fraternity brothers at the University of Oklahoma were caught on tape leading a chant taunting that "[N-word]s" would never be allowed in the fraternity, including the line "hang 'em from a tree," they were promptly expelled and the fraternity was shuttered. The case ignited a furious debate over the limits of the First Amendment, which legal scholars agree protects even such vile and hateful speech. As Supreme Court Justice John Roberts wrote in the majority opinion on a different First Amendment case, "Speech is powerful. It can stir people to action, move them to tears of both joy and sorrow, and . . . inflict great pain. On the facts before us, we cannot react to that pain by punishing the speaker. As a nation we have chosen a different course—to protect even hurtful speech on public issues to ensure that we do not stifle public debate."

Blatantly racist incidents such as the one in Oklahoma clearly push the limits of free speech. What's changed recently is that more and more statements are deemed racist or sexist and more and more speakers are deemed "extreme." A Latino student was offended that a white friend used the Spanish word *fútbol* to refer to playing soccer. Students at Oberlin College complained that the undercooked rice in the cafeteria sushi was offensive to minority students. A Colorado College student was suspended for two years (later reduced to six months) for responding to a Yik Yak social media discussion of #blackwomenmatter with the anonymous post "They matter, they're just not hot." A faculty member at the University of Kansas was suspended after a candid classroom discussion about race on campus. As sophomore Rachel Huebner wrote in the *Harvard Crimson* in 2016, "This undue focus on feelings has caused the college campus to often feel like a place where one has to monitor every syllable that is uttered to ensure that it could not under any circumstance offend anyone to the slightest degree."

This is the dark side of tolerance; it begins with the good intentions of including everyone and not offending anyone but ends (at best) with a reluctance to explore deep issues and (at worst) with careers destroyed by a comment someone found offensive and the silencing of all alternative viewpoints.

This may partially be due to a shift in government guidelines. In 2013, the US Departments of Justice and Education broadened the definition of sexual harassment from speech a "reasonable person" would find offensive to speech that is simply "unwelcome." Universities are now applying that standard to "unwelcome" speech around race and religion as well as gender, unwilling to favor the First Amendment over the slight possibility of a federal lawsuit. As Greg Lukianoff and Jonathan Haidt's widely circulated 2015 *Atlantic* piece on these issues put it, "Everyone is supposed to rely upon his or her own subjective feelings to decide whether a comment by a professor or a fellow student is unwelcome, and therefore grounds for a harassment claim. Emotional reasoning is now accepted as evidence."

When students disagree with a speaker invited to come to campus, they now would rather that the speaker not come at all. In the American Freshman Survey, support for banning extreme speakers reached an all-time high in 2015 (see Figure 9.14, page 250). Students at Smith College demanded the disinvitation of Christine Lagarde, the managing director of the International Monetary Fund; Rutgers protesters prompted Condoleezza Rice to cancel; and students at Brandeis blocked Ayaan Hirsi Ali, a women's rights champion who is also a staunch critic of Islam. A nonprofit organization that defends free speech found that disinvitations have quintupled since 2000, going from a rare event to a relatively common one. In 2016, the Foundation for Individual Rights in Education recorded forty-three disinvitation incidents, an all-time high (see Figure 9.15, next page).

President Obama weighed in on the disinvitation issue by saying "I think it's a healthy thing for young people to be engaged and to question authority and to ask why this instead of that, to ask tough questions about social justice. . . . Feel free to disagree with somebody, but don't try to just shut them up . . . What I don't want is a situation in which particular points of view that are presented respectfully and reasonably are shut down." In other words, protest, but let the other side speak, too.

The political scientist April Kelly-Woessner found that the rejection of free speech by social justice advocates is generationally new: social justice and free speech beliefs are unrelated among those over 40, but those under 40 who support social justice are less supportive of free speech. In a 2015 survey, 35% of college students believed that the First Amendment does not protect "hate speech" (it does) and 30% of liberal students believed that the

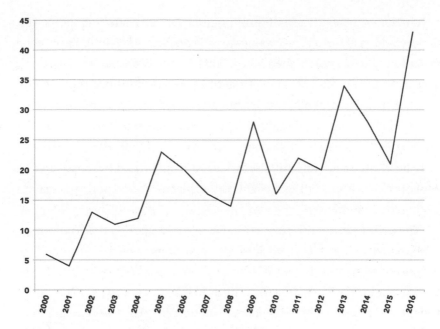

Figure 9.15. Number of speakers "disinvited" from speaking at US college campuses, 2000–2016. Foundation for Individual Rights in Education (FIRE).

First Amendment is "outdated." This echoes iGen's emphasis on safety featured in chapter 6—the extension of safety to include emotional safety and the belief in words as violence.

The fall 2015 protests at the University of Missouri were fueled by the Black Lives Matter protests in nearby Ferguson and by several incidents of racism on campus. The activism soon took a turn, however, when the protesters declared that they had the right to create a "safe space" on the public university campus and exclude the media. Several protestors got into a shoving match with a student photographer, and a faculty member yelled that they needed some "muscle" to get him out. The photographer stated (correctly) that he had a First Amendment right to be there.

When UC Irvine law professors Howard Gillman and Erwin Chemerinsky taught a college freshman seminar on freedom of speech, they were shocked by how often the students favored restricting speech protected by the First Amendment. It was a generational shift, they realized: the students had witnessed the harm of hateful speech but not the harm of censorship or punishment of dissent. The professors pointed out that restricting speech you dislike could easily lead to restricting speech you like. When officials have the power to regulate speech, they noted, "that power is inevitably abused. . . . Over the course of U.S. history, officials censored or punished those whose speech they disliked: abolitionists, labor activists, religious minorities, communists and socialists, cultural critics, gays and lesbians," they wrote in the *Los Angeles Times*. ". . . Our students came to realize that there was no way to create a 'safe space' on campuses where students could be free from one set of offenses without engaging in massive censorship, and perhaps creating another kind of offense."

The culture of speech restriction has created another victim: humor. Comedians such as Chris Rock say they no longer perform on college campuses because students are too easily offended. Writing in *The Atlantic* about campus comedy shows, Caitlin Flanagan concluded that college students preferred "comedy that was 100 percent risk-free, comedy that could not trigger or upset or mildly trouble a single student . . . thoroughly scrubbed of barb and aggression." At a convention where comics auditioned for campus gigs, campus representatives hesitated to book a gay comic who got huge laughs for his riff about having a "sassy black friend" because he was "perpetuating stereotypes." "We don't want to sponsor an event that would offend anyone," said Courtney Bennett, the president of the student activities board at Western Michigan University. This shows the two sides of campus tolerance: on the positive side, a kind inclusiveness, but on the negative side, a quick and brutal judgment of anyone who makes a comment deemed offensive, even if it's misinterpreted or meant as a joke.

Is This Just a Few Activists—or a New Norm?

I was curious if these views were just those of the extreme few. To find out, my graduate student and I surveyed two hundred introductory psychology students at San Diego State University (SDSU) in April 2016, asking them a wide array of questions on these topics. Although it is of course just one campus, SDSU has a diverse student body more representative of the average college student than the Ivy League universities often featured in stories about safe spaces.

The results were stunning: a massive three out of four SDSU students supported safe spaces for students who disagreed with controversial speakers, and three out of four also agreed that professors should be required to include trigger warnings if a course reading mentioned sexual assault.

The students' views provide a glimpse into why speech has become a hotly debated issue on college campuses recently. Nearly half of the SDSU students (48%) agreed that "A white person saying the 'n-word' (the racial epithet) is always offensive, even if it is being used as an example of historical discrimination and not as an insult toward a specific person." Fifty-two percent agreed that "People who are not black should never say the 'n-word,' no matter what."

The consequences of saying the wrong thing can be dire. More than one out of four students (28%) agreed that "A faculty member who, on a single occasion, says something racially insensitive in class should be fired." (We deliberately left the wording of the question vague, which makes this result even more chilling; what is "racially insensitive" could differ from one person to the next.) One out of four is more than enough for a critical mass to band together to report a faculty member to the administration, something that has occurred with increasing frequency. Students were slightly more forgiving toward their fellow students; 16% believed that "A student who, on a single occasion, says something racially insensitive in class should be expelled."

Most surprising to me was this: 38% of students believed that "Faculty members should not discuss average racial differences (in, for example, attitudes, traits, and IQ) in class." This is highly problematic, as classes in psychology, sociology, economics, public policy, political science, social work, and many other disciplines regularly present research on differences by racial group. According to this sizable minority of students, scientific research on race must not be discussed. This is especially shocking because these were students taking Introduction to Psychology, a class that covers both scientific methods and group differences. If that many students question the presentation of any material about racial differences, it is no wonder that many faculty are now afraid to teach any topic connected to race, effectively shutting down any discussion of ethnic and cultural differences—in theory, conversations that might lead to better understanding.

When I ask 20-year-old Georgia college student Darnell what he thinks about classes presenting material on racial differences, he says, "I can see why students would not like that, so I think it's best not to do that. Let's just stay away from that." Other students disagreed. "Testing of different racial groups, testing those hypotheses, is not necessarily bad," says James, a student at the same college. "Being easily offended by those types of things keeps you from learning. It keeps you from being able to keep an open mind and get to a truth, get to more knowledge."

Microaggressions: A Thousand Small Cuts

Then there are "microaggressions," usually defined as unintentionally hurtful things said to people of color. By definition, aggression is intentional, so the label itself is a misnomer. Nevertheless, many statements labeled as micro-aggressions are painful to hear. Buzzfeed posted a photo project of students at Fordham University in New York holding signs on which they'd written microaggressions directed at them. These included "You're pretty for a dark-skin girl," "So, what do you guys speak in Japan? Asian?" "So, like, what are you?" and "No, where are you *really* from?" (I'm struck by how socially inept these statements are—perhaps the product of a generation that has spent less time interacting with its peers face-to-face.) Clearly, hearing the same insensitive questions over and over is unpleasant and stressful for people of color. LGBT people also have to deal with this. Take this exchange posted on Twitter: "Cashier: So do you have a boyfriend? Me: I'm gay. Cashier: Oh! You don't look . . . you look good!"

In a 2014 MTV survey of 14- to 24-year-olds, 45% of people of color said they had personally been hurt by microaggressions, compared to 25% of whites. "What haunts me are the frequent, small actions that remind me I don't belong, that people look at me and see a black person before they see someone who's just a person," wrote Princess Ojiaku, a University of Wisconsin graduate student. "These reminders build into an invisible weight I carry. . . . They are the small and constant confirmations of your fear that people see you as a caricature rather than as an individual." Research finds that individuals who experience more microaggressions also report more anxiety and depression. (However, people who are higher in anxiety and depression might also be more likely to remember or perceive more micro-aggressions, or the link could be due to outside factors.)

Some statements labeled as microaggressions are more ambiguous, and that's where debates get started. The first statement listed on UCLA's guide to microaggressions is "Where are you from?" That's probably the most common question asked on a college campus during the first week of classes. Clearly it's not usually a microaggression. Other statements labeled as microaggressions include "I believe the most qualified person should get the job," "Everyone can succeed in this society, if they work hard enough," and "Where were you born?"

Are these statements offensive? That is in the eye of the beholder. The difficulty now is that if someone says he was offended, that is proof enough, even if the other person didn't mean to be offensive. This is one reason why iGen'ers have gained a reputation for oversensitivity, with their strong emphasis on people being offended by words. And there's little agreement on which words are offensive. Some Asian Americans are offended by being asked "Where are you from?" and some are not. One South Asian young man wrote, "I get asked 'Where are you from?'" on a weekly basis. . . . Victimhood culture tells me this is a 'microaggression' based on racism that should offend me. But it's not. We live in a multicultural society, and it's not always clear what someone's background is. I don't assume they're racist just because they're curious about my background. But victimhood culture tells me I should."

In the SDSU survey, only 18% agreed that "Where are you from?" is a microaggression. The vast majority also did not see "America is a land of opportunity" or "Gender plays no part in who we hire" as microaggressions. But more than 85% of students agreed that certain actions are microaggressions, including crossing the street to avoid a person of color, saying to an Asian person "You must be good in math, can you help me with this problem?" or saying "We are only women." Only 13% thought that a dorm cafeteria having a "Mexican night" was offensive, though 33% agreed that wearing a sombrero and poncho as a Halloween costume was offensive. With such a wide range of opinions, it's difficult to tell when a statement will offend most people—or just one person, which is enough to cause problems.

The Free and Open Discussion

iGen'ers are coming to adulthood in a confusing time for issues around group identity. In the MTV survey, 84% said their family had taught them that everyone should be treated the same no matter what their race. Yet only 37% said their families talked about race—only 30% among whites. Race is at once something that matters and doesn't matter, that is talked about and not talked about. iGen is color blind—but since racial bias still exists, that's not always a realistic position to take.

Then iGen'ers get to college, where they earnestly strive for equality but are so afraid of offending one another that they still don't talk about race. In the MTV survey, only 20% said they were comfortable having a conversation about bias. Forty-eight percent believe it's wrong to draw attention to someone's race even if you are being positive. But 73% think people should talk more openly about bias, and 69% would love the opportunity to have an open, respectful, and judgment-free conversation about bias. iGen'ers' bedrock sense of equality is a real opportunity for race relations in this country; the vast majority come to adulthood without the blatant prejudices of the past. But experiences do differ by race, due to prejudice and life experience, and as a result many students of color feel uncomfortable at predominantly white universities. iGen'ers want to talk about these issues—at least they say they do—but they also feel they can't. That's no wonder, given the culture of silence and recrimination around these topics. That, more than anything, is the reason the culture of offense needs to reconsider the best path for iGen and for us all.

iGen'ers' record levels of anxiety and depression, their slow path to adulthood, and their emphasis on inclusion have fused into the view that people need to be protected at all costs. Striking a balance between protection and free speech will continue to roil iGen and older generations well into the future.

Chapter 10

Independent: Politics

"I will be voting for Donald Trump," 20-year-old Mark tells me only a few minutes into our conversation on a Monday afternoon a few months before the 2016 election. Mark juggles community college, a job at an electronics store, and a steady girlfriend while living with his parents to save money. After graduating from high school, he tried living on his own for a year in his hometown near Fort Worth, Texas, but found that rent ate up most of his paycheck. His parents, a mechanic and a homemaker, told Mark he could live at home as long as he was going to college.

Mark doesn't care for all of Trump's statements, but after reading his and Hillary Clinton's platforms he decided that "out of the two poisons . . . Donald Trump is the least worse one." Like Trump, Mark believes that things are bad enough for Americans already without trying to help people from other countries. "With all of the immigrants coming in, not only will there be a shortage of jobs but a shortage of land to live in. The poverty level's going to skyrocket because there's not going to be enough resources to go around. I would much rather have a wall and keep our economy going than try to help people we can't help," he says, referring to Trump's campaign promise to build a wall along the US-Mexico border.

Nine months earlier and halfway across the country, I drove up the California coast to visit 18-year-old Cameron, at home on winter break from his freshman year at a private college. It's one of those rare days when traffic is relatively light on the 5 north, so I have the pleasure of not having to rush as I maneuver my minivan around the small winding streets of the gated beach community where Cameron's family lives. His house is just a few blocks from the ocean, in a development with a typical layout for a coastal neighborhood: large, beautiful homes on small lots. Cameron has bright blue eyes and a lean build honed by jogging and a vegan diet. He is majoring in math and strikes me as unusually focused for a college freshman, telling me all about the data analysis he's been doing for his internship with a tech company—which, despite my own affinity for statistics, I can barely follow.

Like many iGen'ers in early 2016, Cameron was feeling the Bern for Bernie Sanders, the politically independent socialist who mounted a strong challenge to Hillary Clinton during the 2016 Democratic presidential primaries. To Cameron, supporting Sanders wasn't about party politics—it was about his authenticity and moral message, especially around government funding for education. Cameron knows he has been given advantages that many other young people don't have, and he's not sure that's fair. "Nobody should be put at a significant disadvantage because of what they were born into," he says. He also strongly believes in equality and in legalizing certain choices: "Everybody should be afforded equal opportunity to live according to their own whims. For anything that doesn't affect other people—like drug issues—there shouldn't be control over that realm of someone's personal life."

Sanders was wildly popular with young voters. In a poll of Democratic voters entering the Iowa caucuses in February 2016, young adults were six times as likely to favor Sanders as Clinton (84% vs. 14%). As late as mid-July 2016, nearly half of Sanders's young supporters said they would vote for a third-party candidate instead of Clinton or Trump.

Trump did not begin as a youth favorite, but by November he managed to attract a large number of young voters. Among white voters 18 to 29 years of age, he won over Hillary Clinton 48% to 43%, a stunning result for a young generation often characterized as overwhelmingly liberal. Although Clinton won among young voters as a whole, a substantial 37% overall voted for Trump. That means nearly four out of ten iGen'ers and young Millennials voted for not just a Republican candidate but a candidate affiliated with a white nationalism many thought had died out long before iGen was born. Young Americans' votes helped sway the election in Trump's favor: 18- to 29-year-olds are now a larger percentage of voters than those over 65.

How did this happen? And what does it mean for US elections going forward that such a large percentage of young voters chose the Republican candidate even when he seemed like such a throwback?

Political Party Problems

Two months before the election, my colleagues and I published a paper with some glimmers of what was to come. For years, the assumption was that Millennials, and now iGen'ers, were overwhelmingly Democrats and would stay that way. In August 2016, *USA Today* predicted a "historic trouncing" of Trump among young voters. In 2014, the *Washington Post* announced that Republicans had a "young-people problem"—the party, it was assumed, just couldn't attract Millennials. Two years later, that was proven wrong. To figure out why, consider this question: What do Bernie Sanders and Donald Trump have in common?

The answer: both are political independents. Sanders is the longest-serving independent in the US Congress; his Senate web page mentions nothing about his being a Democrat. Before becoming president, Donald Trump had never held political office, and he battled with the Republican establishment throughout the primaries and general election campaign. In November 2016, the *Washington Post* called Trump "America's first independent president." Both Sanders and Trump were seen as free agents who spoke their minds and refused to bow to the party power brokers.

That's why young people liked them, despite the socialist Sanders and the nationalist Trump holding many views outside the political mainstream. In the most recent General Social Survey, an incredible 54% of 18- to 29-year-olds identified as independent, up from just a third in 1989 (see Figure 10.1, next page). That is one reason they flocked to Sanders and eventually to Trump. Just as iGen'ers and Millennials are avoiding institutions such as religion and marriage, more and more of them are refusing to identify with the major political parties.

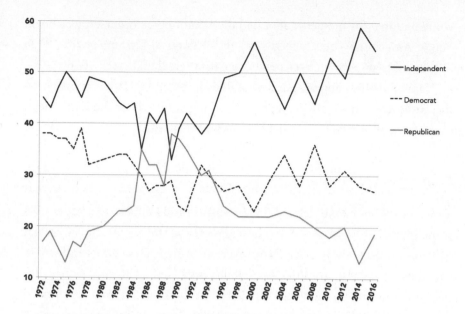

Figure 10.1. Political party identification, 18- to 29-year-olds (excludes "don't know" and "other party"). General Social Survey, 1972–2016.

Older generations are also now more likely to be political independents. Still, iGen'ers and Millennials are much more likely to be independent than Boomers and Silents in recent years. Thus, the growth of independents is both a time-period and a generational effect—adults of all ages have shifted away from the major parties, but Millennials and iGen'ers were even more likely to be Independent than everyone else in 2016.

That might be one reason why Hillary Clinton, heavily associated with the political establishment, didn't gather as many young voters as anticipated. When Clinton secured the Democratic nomination in June 2016 and became the first female US presidential nominee of a major party, Boomers were shocked when young people reacted with a collective yawn. Many just couldn't get on board with a candidate so identified with the political establishment, even if she did break a centuries-old glass ceiling for women. Eighteen-year-old Josephine Sicking, of Cleveland Heights, Ohio, told *Time* magazine in July 2016, "If Hillary wins, it's just the lesser of two evils. I know we could come up with a better system than what we have today." In contrast, Josephine's 78-year-old grandmother voted for Clinton in the primaries and was excited about the possibility of electing a female president, and her 49-year-old mother voted for Sanders but was "coming around." Josephine's mother told her, "We're going to talk you into voting." Josephine just shrugged.

The trend toward political independence may be another consequence of iGen'ers' individualism and reluctance to join groups and follow their rules. As Mike, 22, put it, "When people join political parties they take on some of their views and lose their originality." iGen'ers seem to take their views and decide where they fit, rather than joining a party based on the influence of family or religion and then deciding on their views. Here's how Rob, 19, explained how he decided how to label his political views: "In April, I heard two men at a soccer field discussing the intentions of Democrats and found out that I really didn't know where I stood politically. That night I went home and did a lot of research and took a lot of 'political quizzes' and mostly came out as a Libertarian Conservative."

The rise of political independents is not the only issue for Democrats. As Trump's win among young white voters helps demonstrate, the Democratic Party has been faltering among young people in the last few years. In the late-2000s Obama era, Democrats dominated Republicans among 18- to 29-year-olds by 16 percentage points. But since then, the number of young adult Democrats has dropped by 9 percentage points.

There's even worse news for Democrats among high school seniors, the 18-year-olds who are the potential harbingers of what young voters will look like during the next election cycle: the number of 12th graders identifying as Democrats is near an all-time low. Democrats are being siphoned off, with half of the shift coming from more identifying as Republicans and the other half from the growth of independents (see Figure 10.2, next page).

Maybe that's not bad news for the Democrats, if most of the independents are liberals. But they are not; nearly half of 12th-grade independents in 2015 described themselves as moderates. Still, liberals did substantially outnumber conservatives among young independents, 38% to 14%.

No matter what their party identification, iGen'ers often cite individualistic reasons for their choice. "I am a Republican and a conservative because

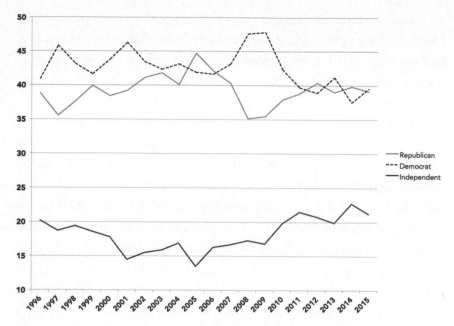

Figure 10.2. 12th graders' political party identification (excludes "don't know" and "other party"). Monitoring the Future, 1996–2015.

I value each individual taking care of themselves. I think that's absolutely the most fair way—everyone gets out of the system what they're willing to put into it," wrote Abby, 18. Even with beliefs at the other end of the political spectrum, Charlie, 21, used similarly individualistic language but toward different ends: "I am a proud liberal Democrat. I don't believe we should steer people into doing anything. We are free to be whoever we want to be as long as we are not hurting anyone in the process."

With party affiliations falling by the wayside, it's increasingly meaningful to look not at party affiliation but instead at whether young people describe themselves as liberal, moderate, or conservative. There is another surprise here: the number of 12th graders identifying as conservative has actually grown since the early 2000s, with more iGen conservatives than there were among Millennials when they were in high school (see Figure 10.2). There are just as many iGen conservatives now as at the height of the Ronald Reagan era, when young GenX conservatives shocked their elders (think Alex

P. Keaton on the 1980s TV classic *Family Ties*, continuously flummoxing his liberal Boomer parents with his support of Reagan's conservative ideals). In contrast, the number of high school seniors who describe themselves as liberal has barely budged since the early 1990s and even decreased slightly as iGen entered the scene in the 2010s (see Figure 10.3).

The definition of a conservative has also shifted, focusing more on economic issues and less on social ones. Mark, the community college student from Texas, describes himself as a conservative Republican. When I ask what that means to him, he says, "Being a conservative means you truly want to help the people, so they can sustain themselves. The welfare system allows people to be lazy and be supported by the government. I think there has to be a system where they eventually give back what they were given." He's skeptical of the Democrats' programs for "free college" because "someone is going to have to pay for that. Taxes are going to be so high that [wealthy people are] going to move out of the country."

So far, Mark is the picture of a classic conservative—and, as you might remember from chapter 5, a devout evangelical Christian. But when I ask

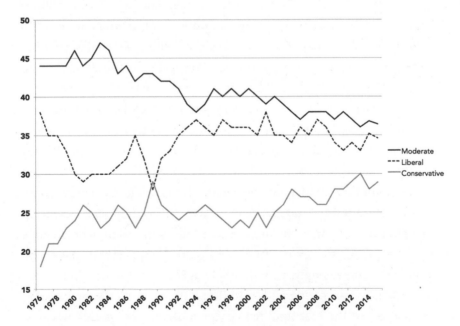

Figure 10.3. 12th graders' political views. Monitoring the Future, 1976–2015.

him about same-sex marriage, he says, "I try my best not to bring religion into it and just focus on the conservative viewpoint." He says same-sex marriage is fine as long as people don't "riot in the streets." He also favors legalizing marijuana: "I think it should be left up to the individuals themselves, instead of some state or the government saying it's legal or illegal." On gun control, he says, "You can justify either side. If you want to own a firearm, go out and buy a firearm. If you don't, then sit at home and don't. Don't try to force the world to respect your beliefs." Although his economic conservativism is clear, his stance on social issues would have been unrecognizable to most conservatives just ten years ago. Instead, it's an individualistic, libertarian view that government should stay out of people's private business.

Like many iGen'ers, Mark is also concerned about getting a good job in a still challenging economy. That's one reason why Trump's idea of keeping out immigrants appeals to him; he thinks the government needs to focus more on its own citizens. "When we have a poverty level of zero and a debt of zero and crime of zero, that's when I feel like we can go out and help all the other countries out there that need our help," he says. This is nationalism and isolationism born out of economic fears. In an October 2016 poll of 18- to 29-year-olds, those who believed whites were falling behind economically were more likely to vote for Trump. For all the attention paid to older white working-class voters, as we saw in chapter 7, it's the young ones who are not working and thus feel even more left behind in the new economy. iGen'ers' interest in safety and their heightened concerns about their economic prospects have combined to make them more politically conservative than most anticipated and more open to nationalist messages.

There's another trend afoot: the decline of the moderate. Among both high school and college students, fewer and fewer say they are moderate in their political views, with the number of moderates reaching an all-time low in the college survey in 2016 (see Figure 10.3, previous page, and Appendix I). Increasingly, young people agree with the old joke about what happens to someone with middle-of-the-road views: he gets run over. That is just the first sign that compromise, for all intents and purposes, is dead.

The Poles of Politics

How would you feel if you found out that your son or daughter was going to marry someone of the other political party? In 1960, just 5% of Republicans and 4% of Democrats said they would be upset. In 2010, 49% of Republicans and 33% of Democrats expressed displeasure. Few care anymore about cross-racial marriages; the new concern is cross-party marriages.

For all of iGen's lifetime, Democrats and Republicans have been deadlocked over issues from Bill Clinton's impeachment to war funding to health care. Everyone has retreated into their corners, and that is true of young people as well. Among high school seniors, those who described themselves as either "very" liberal or "very" conservative increased from 13% in 1976 to 20% in 2015, an all-time high. The number describing themselves as "very conservative" was the highest in the forty years of the survey—higher than in the Reagan-era 1980s and higher than in the post-9/11 George W. Bush 2000s (see Figure 10.4). Similar trends appear among entering

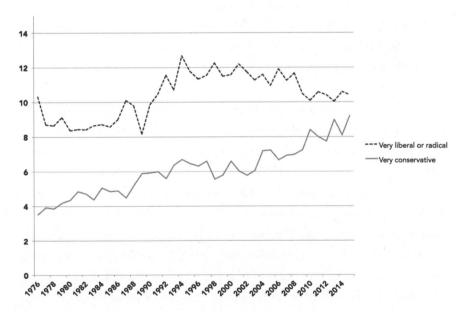

Figure 10.4. Extreme political views among 12th graders. Monitoring the Future, 1976–2015.

college students and young adults—the number of college students describing themselves as "far left" reached an all-time high in 2016. The numbers in both categories are very small in an absolute sense, but these are the students who get involved in politics on campus—who take part in demonstrations, advocate for change, and argue with fellow students over issues. With more students at the extremes, we can expect more divisiveness and more protests.

A few days before the 2016 election, CBS News gathered about twenty-five young voters for a group interview. One exchange in particular captured the deep divisions in the country's political and social beliefs. A young white woman, apparently responding to another voter's comment about race relations, spoke with barely controlled anger. "Trump hasn't been in the White House, so to say that Trump tore our country apart at the seams and created this racial divisiveness, no way," she said. "President Obama is the one who was in the White House for eight years, and race relations have been worse than ever in this country. Let's look at who was in office—an African American man who has torn apart this country." A young black man named Richard Lucas III spoke next. "To say that race relations have gotten as bad as they've ever been under President Obama shows a lack of historical depth. America is built on racial division, and Donald Trump's rhetoric, this other-ism built into that narrative—that has long been the narrative of American society," he said, his eyes moving to the side and his jaw set.

Those divisions only became more stark after the election, when many iGen'ers—especially racial minorities—felt betrayed by the white young voters who favored Trump. For some, his election was a body blow to their view of their generation as tolerant and welcoming of those who are different. Tiffany Onyejiaka, the daughter of African immigrants and an undergraduate at Johns Hopkins, wrote an open letter in the Huffington Post that began, "Dear White Millennials Who Voted for Trump . . . I wanted to thank you for voting for this monster. Not because I like him, but because you have helped reveal to me that I was so mistaken as to think the majority of white youth were socially progressive." She went on, ". . . In my naïve little brain, I never imagined that 48 percent of white people aged 18–29 would vote for a man who based his platform on racism, sexism, xenophobia, homophobia and so much more." She signed the letter "A black millennial who has to now be aware that nearly 50 percent of white people my age don't believe I deserve basic human rights."

The polarization goes beyond just the extremes: the political parties as a whole have become more ideologically split. While there were once conservatives and liberals in each party, now there are just conservative Republicans and liberal Democrats. Some have speculated that this was true only for "political elites"—elected politicians who have to toe the party line. But it's now true of a general sample of US adults (in the General Social Survey) and even of high school seniors, who might have less definite views. The correlation between political party choice and political ideology (liberal, conservative, moderate) has grown stronger with nearly every passing year, even among high school students (see Appendix I). Whereas the link between political party and political ideology was once weak, it's now strong. I remember hearing a joke in the 1980s: "A liberal Republican is like a unicorn: it doesn't exist." That wasn't entirely true then, but it is now.

In a 2016 poll, the Pew Research Center found that animosity between the political parties had reached unprecedented levels. Whereas only 21% of Republicans and 17% of Democrats had seen the other party as "very unfavorable" in 1994, 58% of Republicans and 55% viewed the other party with hatred in 2016. Seventy percent of Democrats describe Republicans as "close-minded," and 52% of Republicans say the same thing about Democrats. Nearly half of Republicans say that Democrats are "immoral." More than 40% of those in each party believe that the other party's policies "are so misguided that they threaten the nation's well-being." We are a nation divided, and iGen reaps what we sow.

Legal Marijuana, Legal Abortion, the Death Penalty, and Gun Control: Do What You Want, Libertarian

A few decades ago, the idea that drugs should be legal was often considered laughable. When I was a teen in the 1980s, TV ads showed frying eggs that proclaimed, "This is your brain on drugs," and Nancy Reagan advised us to "Just say no." Things are different now: recreational marijuana is legal in several states, including Massachusetts, Colorado, and California, and medical marijuana is legal in many others.

iGen'ers are a product of our modern and more pot-accepting high times. They are much more likely to believe that pot should be legal than GenX'ers when they were young—and support legal pot even more than the oft-stoned Boomers did in the 1970s. Nearly twice as many 12th graders in 2015 supported the legalization of pot than in the 1980s, as do three times as many iGen college students and young adults. By an October 2016 Gallup poll, 77% of 18- to 34-year-olds believed that pot should be legal.

At first, iGen'ers' support for legal marijuana may seem to contradict their interest in safety. But as we saw in chapter 6, iGen'ers are more likely to believe that marijuana is safe, and that belief in its safety has moved in lock-step with views on whether pot should be legal (see Figure 10.5).

iGen'ers also support legal pot partially because they believe that the government should stay out of personal decisions. One 18-year-old iGen'er told the Pew Research Center in 2015 that marijuana should be legal "because

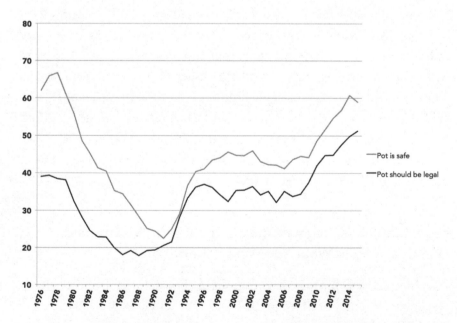

Figure 10.5. 12th graders' views on marijuana legality and safety. Monitoring the Future, 1976–2015.

people should be allowed to have control over their body and not have the government intervene in that." It's not just pot users who are driving this trend; recall from chapter 6 that fewer iGen'ers use pot than did Boomers at the same age. iGen'ers are willing to extend freedoms to others even if they don't want to experience those particular freedoms themselves. As the young Millennial singer Kacey Musgraves puts it in one of her songs, "Roll up a joint/Or don't."

The belief in personal choice may also be the reason behind the resurgence in support for legal abortion among young people. Half of 18- to 29-year-olds supported legal abortion if "the woman wants it for any reason" (sometimes called "abortion on demand") in 2014 and 2016, an all-time high. Support for abortion among college students has gradually increased over the last ten years, with iGen'ers more likely to be pro-choice than the Millennials just before them (see Figures 10.6 and 10.7, next page).

When I asked a few iGen'ers if they thought abortion should be legal and under what circumstances, all said "Under all circumstances," and all

Figure 10.6. Entering college students' views about abortion, legalizing marijuana, the death penalty, and gun control. American Freshman Survey, 1968–2015.

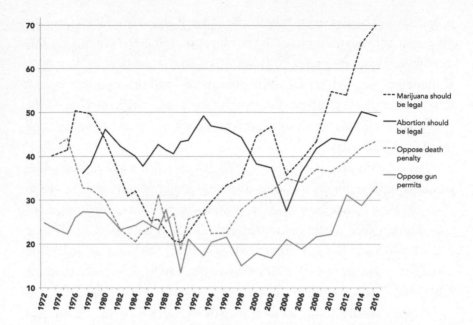

Figure 10.7. Views about abortion, legalizing marijuana, the death penalty, and gun control, 18- to 29-year-olds. General Social Survey, 1972–2016.

mentioned the rights of the individual. "I think abortions should be legal. Ultimately, I think it is all up to the choice of the woman," wrote Julianna, 21. "It is her life and her decision, and I don't think others should have a right to dictate her choices, since it is not hurting any of them." Some also mentioned safety. "Every pregnancy is a risk that no one should be forced to take," wrote Keely, 19. "It can be a massive financial, social and emotional burden, but it can also be a physical risk, and it's not anyone's place to tell someone they MUST endure it."

More iGen'ers also doubt the usefulness of the death penalty. Twice as many college students and young adults now than in the mid-1990s believe the death penalty should be abolished (see Figures 10.6, page 271, and 10.7). "It is a proven fact that the death penalty disproportionately affects poor minorities in this country," wrote Lilly, 20. "Some of the stories of injustice are shocking and sickening. Plus it is a proven fact that the death penalty is not a deterrent to crime."

So far, iGen'ers' beliefs seem like a liberal smorgasboard: legal marijuana, legal abortion, no more death penalty. But that's where it ends. iGen'ers are also more likely to oppose gun control, usually a conservative position. Among 18- to 29-year-olds in the General Social Survey, more than twice as many in 2016 than in 1998 opposed gun permits (see Figure 10.7, previous page). Twice as many college students in 2013 than in 1998 disagreed with the statement "The federal government should do more to control the sale of handguns" (see Figure 10.6, page 271). The Pew Research Center found an even larger shift over time in opposition to gun control, growing from 27% among Millennials in 2004 to 47% among Millennials and iGen in 2015.

Health care provides another surprise in iGen'ers' political beliefs: the average iGen'er is actually *less* likely to support national health care than Millennials were. In 2013, 39% of entering college students disagreed that "A national health care plan is needed to cover everybody's medical costs," up from 26% in 2007.

What about concern for the environment? Despite the common idea that iGen'ers are uniquely concerned about the environment, they are actually *less* likely to agree that the government should promote more environmental regulations. Boomers and GenX'ers were more likely to think that solving environmental problems was the government's job (agreeing that "Government should take action to solve our environmental problems even if it means that some of the products we now use would have to be changed or banned"), while iGen'ers are more likely to think it's the job of individual people ("People will have to change their buying habits and way of life to correct our environmental problems"; see Figure 10.8, next page).

Why would iGen'ers, so liberal on other issues, be more likely to oppose gun control, national health care, and government environmental regulation? Given iGen'ers' reputation as a liberal bunch, these seeming anomalies in their political views beg for an explanation. How can this set of beliefs coexist?

But they do: in the Libertarian Party. Libertarians put the individual first and are opposed to government regulation. Just like iGen'ers, Libertarians support equal rights for everyone. They support legal abortion and legal

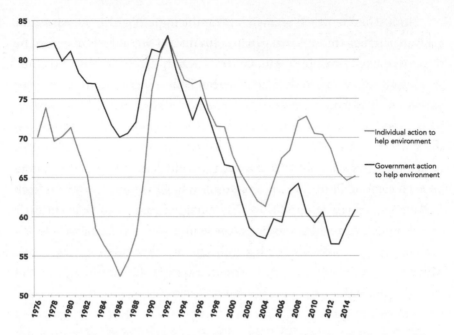

Figure 10.8. Percentage of 12th graders who agree that individuals or the government will need to take action to help the environment. Monitoring the Future, 1976–2015.

marijuana on the principle that government should not restrict individual rights. For the same reason, Libertarians also oppose restrictions on guns and government regulations on the environment. The idea is: get your laws off my body, my stuff, and my guns, and let me do what I please. Libertarians favor the free market over government programs, so they are also opposed to a national health care system (and they go even further in their 2016 party platform, calling for the elimination of the income tax and Social Security). Although Libertarians once took no position on the death penalty, they now oppose it as an instance of government overstepping its bounds.

So across six political issues—legalizing marijuana, abortion, the death penalty, gun control, national health care, and government environmental regulation—iGen'ers are more likely than previous generations to favor the liberal position on three and the conservative position on the other three. But they are more likely than their predecessors to favor the libertarian position on all six.

This makes perfect sense: iGen takes the individualistic mind-set for granted, and libertarianism is as close to cultural individualism as can be found in the political arena. Liberals tend to be individualistic about equal rights issues (say, same-sex marriage) but collectivistic about social programs (government-sponsored health care). Conservatives are individualistic about social programs (thinking people should help themselves) but collectivistic about equal rights issues (thinking traditional roles often work out better). But libertarians are individualistic about both. As the 2016 Libertarian Party platform preamble states, "As Libertarians, we seek a world of liberty; a world in which all individuals are sovereign over their own lives and no one is forced to sacrifice his or her values for the benefit of others. . . . The world we seek to build is one where individuals are free to follow their own dreams in their own ways, without interference from government or any authoritarian power." That's cultural individualism in a nutshell. In 2017, 24-year-old conservative firebrand Tomi Lahren found herself at odds with her antiabortion employer *The Blaze* after she said, "I can't sit here and be a hypocrite and say I'm for limited government, but I think the government should decide what women do with their bodies. Stay out of my guns, and you can stay out of my body as well." She responded to criticism of her seemingly contradictory views by tweeting, "I speak my truth . . . I will always be honest and stand in my truth. . . . I have moderate, conservative, and libertarian views. I'm human. I will never apologize, to anyone, for being an independent thinker." Lahren's views may not be consistent with either liberalism or conservatism, but they are completely consistent with individualism—and not particularly surprising for someone born in 1992.

There are two exceptions to iGen'ers' libertarian, small-government philosophy, and they're big ones: iGen'ers and the Millennials are more likely than older generations to want college education and child care to be funded by the government. Over-time data on this question are scant, so we have to rely on one-time polls that don't separate age from generation. Still, the numbers are striking: 43% more iGen'ers and Millennials support free universal child care and prekindergarten programs than do Boomers, and 70% more support free college tuition (see Figure 10.9, next page).

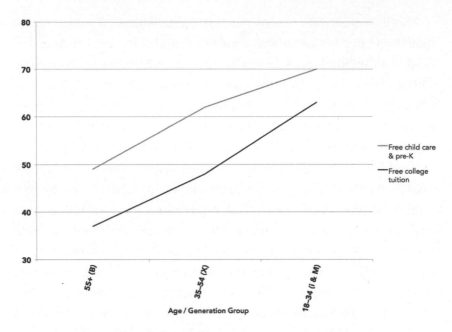

Figure 10.9. Percentage who agree that the government should fund education programs, by age group. Gallup Poll, April 2016.

When CNN interviewed college student body presidents in 2016, all said that tuition costs were students' primary political concerns. "The biggest issue students face today deals with college tuition and student loans—it becomes unaffordable for students," said Seth Ward, the student government president at the University of Maryland, Eastern Shore. "It keeps us from being able to continue college." Ward doesn't think college should be entirely free—"Students should have some money put into it, because when you put something into anything, you're more willing and more likely to work harder for it." Abraham Axler, student council president at the University of Virginia, said, "I think we need free education. Does that mean a four-year liberal arts college education for everybody? Probably not. [But] every student coming out of high school should be able to improve their skills past the age of 18."

Free college tuition at public universities was one of Bernie Sanders's main proposals during the 2016 Democratic primaries, likely a key reason for his strong support among young voters despite his own advanced age. There's also a generational irony here: when Boomers were in college, public universities (for example, in California) *were* tuition free for residents. California introduced tuition slowly, starting with the imposition of "fees" during the 1970s after persistent efforts by the governor at the time: Ronald Reagan. In virtually every state, tuition at public colleges has far outpaced inflation, and Millennials and iGen'ers face hefty student loan balances.

However, even some liberals are uncertain about this iGen and Millennial view of "free stuff" from the government. On his show *Real Time*, liberal boomer comedian Bill Maher pointed out that young people today have no memory of the former Soviet Union and instead associate socialism with "images of naked Danish people on a month-long paid vacation." He traces iGen's attraction to socialism to what he sees as handouts from their parents ("We've accepted that the new normal is people in their twenties and even thirties still on their parents' cell phone plans, health care plans, Mom and Dad still paying the car insurance") and the everything-is-free nature of the Internet ("If you add up all of the free things the under-40 crowd is used to getting, from the quick jerk at work to being able to sit in Starbucks all day for the price of a scone, from music, to Wi-Fi, to birth control, it's not such a jarring proposition that socialism comes along and says you are entitled to free stuff"). He ends with a variation on the classic grumpy-old-man "get a job" advice for young people: "I'm a baby boomer. I think the natural order of things is to pay for music I like. Not to do so doesn't make you a revolutionary—it makes you the person who goes to the bathroom when the check comes," he says. "That . . . must be why there's this proliferation of websites like Kickstarter and GoFundMe. Go fund me? Go fund yourself."

A headline-grabbing 2015 poll found that 18- to 24-year-olds were more likely to hold a favorable view of socialism than of capitalism (58% approved of socialism and 56% of capitalism). iGen'ers' and Millennials' support for Bernie Sanders, a self-described socialist, seems to confirm their comfort with the concept. Several observers theorized that this is because young people don't know what "socialism" means—when asked instead if they favor a "government managed economy" (a definition of socialism), only 32% said yes.

iGen'ers' and the Millennials' attraction to socialism might be based in their youth—young people rarely earn much—or in their perception that the economic system is rigged against them (as we saw in chapter 7). As iGen'ers grow older and start to earn more, it will be interesting to see whether their libertarianism or their socialism proves to be the stronger influence. Although libertarianism and socialism are opposing political philosophies— one wants small government and the other large government—they tap two of the forces shaping iGen'ers: their individualism and their economic fears. iGen'ers' financial fate may in the end determine their political views.

I Just Don't Trust You, and I Don't Want to Get Involved

College student Breeon Buchanan sits in a booth in a Philadelphia diner in July 2016, talking to a CBS News reporter. He's African American, wearing a red-and-navy-blue-striped polo shirt and sporting a beard. Like many iGen'ers, he has a lot of questions about the election. "What are we going to do to actually fix it?" he asks about the state of the country. "What will [the candidates] do by November that's actually going to motivate [young people] to vote—to get them ready and excited? What's going to push us? Because right now there's a lot of indifference."

Breeon is right—except that "indifference" might be an understatement. iGen is disconnected, dissatisfied, and distrustful of government and the political process—perhaps more than any other modern generation.

iGen is very dissatisfied with the state of the country. The percentage of 12th graders who say that institutions such as education, government, the news media, large corporations, and religious organizations are doing a good job reached an all-time low in 2014—lower than after Watergate, lower than at the peak of violent crime in the 1990s, and lower than during the Great Recession of 2007–2009 (see Figure 10.10, next page).

"I do not believe that the U.S. government is doing a good job—in fact I believe they are doing one of the worst jobs in history," wrote Antonio, 20. "I look at political debates and congressional hearings and all I can see is people who do not care about our country and who are willing to act like foolish teenagers throwing a fit in order to make sure that the other side does not

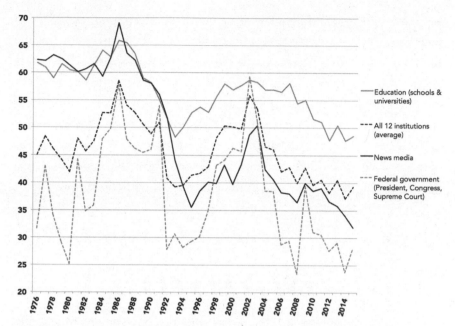

Figure 10.10. Percentage of 12th graders who believe that institutions are doing a good or very good job. Monitoring the Future, 1976–2015.

get what they want. It's like a war zone to see who can make sure the other party fails faster."

It's not just iGen'ers: the same trend appears among adults of all ages in the General Social Survey. There, the percentage who said they had "a great deal of confidence" in thirteen institutions (including the press, education, medicine, and government) averaged 21% in 2014, the lowest in the history of the survey, which goes back to 1972, and remained low in 2016. That explains something about the crazy election year of 2016, doesn't it?

iGen'ers don't just believe the government isn't working; many have also lost trust in government. High school seniors are less likely to say they trust the government, less likely to believe the government is run for the people (as opposed to the big interests), and less likely to believe that the people running the government are honest, with all three at all-time lows (see Figure 10.11, next page). Trust in the government has been sliding for a while, which should put to rest persistent rumors that Millennials trust government more than previous generations did.

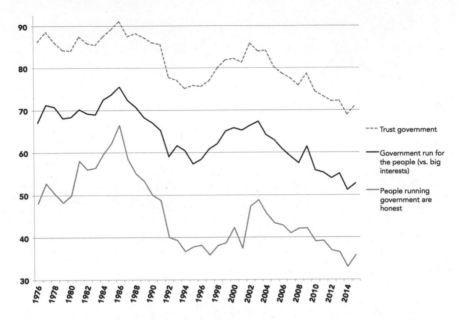

Figure 10.11. Percentage of 12th graders who trust government. Monitoring the Future, 1976–2015.

An October 2016 poll found that young people who agreed with statements similar to these were less likely to vote for Hillary Clinton, perhaps another reason young people's support for her was lower than anticipated. "I don't really trust anyone in the government because it's clear from even just this election cycle that pretty much every person who has any power or status at all in the government is bought and paid for already," wrote Logan, 20. "No way would I ever trust someone to do something in government that doesn't directly benefit them in some obvious way." Brianna, 19, agrees. "Most politicians are barely better than criminals. They are in the pockets of lobbyists for campaign donations and could not give a single fuck about their constituents," she wrote. "Just look at how many politicians become lobbyists themselves, using their connections to make more money! The fact that Donald Trump and Hillary Clinton are the nominees this year just goes to show how rotten the system is."

iGen'ers are also less interested in government than previous generations. That's especially intriguing because confidence and trust in the government were very low in the early 1990s, but interest in government was high. GenX'ers in the early 1990s distrusted the government and didn't think it was doing a good job but were interested in what was going on. iGen'ers' combination of low trust and low interest in government is unique (see Figure 10.12 and Figure 10.11, previous page). Perhaps iGen'ers are so distrustful of government that they don't see the point in being interested. Chandler, 21, feels that way. "I'm typically not interested in government affairs unless I have reason to believe it directly impacts my life," he wrote. "I find that the corruption of politicians negates any interest I would have in the issue."

Although iGen'ers are uninterested in government, they are a little more interested in social problems than early Millennials were. So iGen'ers have more interest in what's going on in the world but less interest in government. The two attitudes usually rise and fall in tandem, but for iGen'ers they have become disconnected (see Figure 10.12). It's yet another indication that they don't want to have much to do with government. For iGen, change will come from individuals, not from the government. There are also some signs of life

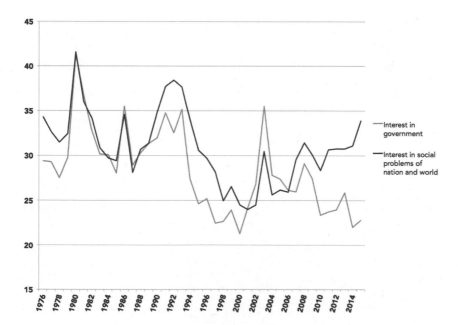

Figure 10.12. Percentage of 12th graders who are interested in government and in social problems. Monitoring the Future, 1976–2015.

in the college survey, where students in 2016 rated the importance of "keeping up with political affairs" at the highest level since 1992 (see Appendix I).

You might think that iGen'ers' heightened interest in social problems and political affairs would translate into action—writing to your representative to Congress, say, or participating in a demonstration. However, iGen'ers are actually *less* likely to take political action: political participation reached all-time lows in 2014 and 2015, with fewer saying they had written or would be willing to write to a public official, fewer saying they had participated in a demonstration, fewer who had worked for or donated to political campaigns (see Figure 10.13). Brianna says she does follow politics—but doesn't get involved. "I just find politics fascinating, the way some people enjoy sports," she wrote. "All the wheeling and dealing is fun for me. However, I don't translate my interest into anything more than reading about it or posting on Reddit. I don't protest or write my congressman and I don't get actively involved in campaigns. I'm just here to gawk and complain."

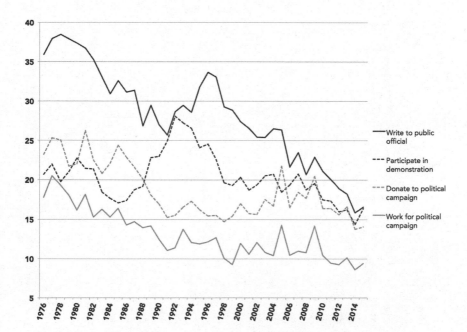

Figure 10.13. Percentage of 12th graders who have or probably will participate in political action. Monitoring the Future, 1976–2015.

Earlier, we heard from Charlie, who explained why he's a "proud liberal Democrat." Yet, he said, "I have never written to a politician or got involved in politics because it is all a dirty game. Even those claiming to be liberals and democrats, they have agendas and propagandas. I think politics is all about money. . . . Life is too short to spend it worrying about politics and politicians." Rob, the libertarian conservative who figured out his beliefs through online quizzes, mentioned another characteristically iGen reason for not getting involved: safety. "With all the crazy fighting in the streets of Bernie Sanders supporters and Trump supporters, I really didn't feel like going to any events or rallies," he wrote.

Many iGen'ers are deeply cynical about whether they can have any personal impact on politics and government—the political component of the more personal locus of control we discussed in chapter 7. The number of 12th graders who think that voting or citizen action groups can have any effect on government is near all-time lows. iGen'ers are more likely to think that nothing really helps, so there's no point in getting involved. "I do not participate [in politics] because it does not really make a change," wrote Justin, 21. "Look at how many people believed in Bernie Sanders. Mass amounts of people were out supporting him but Hillary still won the lead."

But do they vote? Voting is a small commitment compared to political activism, so perhaps the trends would be different. For a long time, it was rumored that Millennials—those immediately preceding iGen—would raise youth voter turnout to unprecedented levels and transform politics. That transformation didn't happen, though there was a slight uptick: the voter turnout of 18- to-24-year-olds was 2 percentage points higher in the presidential election years when Millennials dominated that age group compared to GenX. However, Millennial presidential election year turnout was still 3 percentage points less than that of Boomers at the same age (see Figure 10.14, next page).

More concerning, youth voter turnout in midterm election years has steadily declined. 2014 was the first midterm election year in which iGen'ers could vote, and youth voter turnout, like so many other things related to iGen and government, reached an all-time low: 33% fewer iGen'ers voted in the 2014 midterm election than did Boomers at the same age voting in mid-

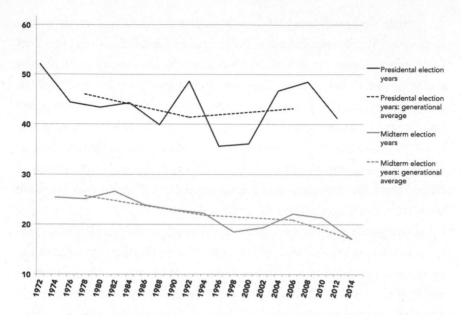

Figure 10.14. Voter turnout among 18- to 24-year-olds, presidential election years and midterm election years. Current Population Survey, 1972–2014.

term elections (22% fewer than GenX'ers and 18% fewer than Millennials). Voting has not suffered the steep declines of other types of political participation, but iGen's first outing at the voting booth in 2014 did not go well. Early results from 2016 suggest little change, with youth voter turnout about the same as in the previous presidential election year of 2012.

Not a Huge News Fan

So iGen'ers don't want to have much to do with government and politics and don't believe that getting involved will make a difference. Yet, as we saw in chapter 6, sometimes iGen'ers will at least talk the talk even if they don't walk the walk; they will consume information even if they don't act. After all, they have access to information from more sources than any previous generation, from the Internet to cable news channels to talk radio. Typically, "news junkies" get their news from more than one source: they'll watch TV news, read stories online, and listen to the radio to get different angles on a story. Those who are highly interested in the news will also consume it more often. By these measures—the frequency and diversity of sources of news consumption—iGen'ers are considerably less informed than their predecessors. As the generations turned from GenX to Millennials to iGen, the number of 8th and 10th graders who got the news often and from several sources fell from three out of four to barely one out of two (see Appendix I).

Of course, this might be because iGen'ers get all of their news online. However, the decline in news consumption among teens didn't begin with iGen; even before the Internet arrived, teens were less likely to pay attention to the news with each passing year. That suggests that Internet news consumption isn't the only social trend afoot. In addition, the decline in watching TV news is about twice the size as the decline in watching TV in general. For iGen'ers, online news is just about the only game in town. It can be a good one, if you go to the right places. The problem, as far as I could tell in the interviews and surveys I did with teens, is that few knew about those places.

Sofia, the 18-year-old college freshman from California we met in chapter 9, looks confused when I ask her if she reads news online. When I ask her if there are any national or world events she is interested in, she says, "Like, um, like what?" I ask what she might click on if she were browsing an online news site. "I don't know," she says and then begins telling me about a paper she wrote for a psychology class. Emily, the Minnesota high school freshman we met in chapters 1, 2, and 9, watches TV news in the morning with her family. But when I ask her about online news sites, she says, "I didn't even know that was a thing."

In the SDSU freshman survey, most students said they were "not interested" in the news. "I'm not a huge news fan," wrote Marisol, 19. "A lot of news is depressing." Another noted, "I don't have the patience for the news." When I asked the high school students I interviewed whether they kept up with current events, the most common response was "I look at that if I have to for a class." Ashley, the high school junior we met in chapter 7, was confused when I asked about what national or world events were interesting (saying "Hmm—I don't know. Like, what do you mean?"). She did say that Yahoo! News was her home page, but when I asked what stories she would click on, she said, "Usually my mom watches stuff, and she'll, like, tell me about something that happened—usually if there's, like, an accident or something major."

Political apathy and political polarization may have the same root cause: the Internet. Many hoped the Internet would usher in a new era of civic engagement, making it easier to gather information and organize protests and demonstrations. Writing to politicians has certainly become easier; most have a form on their website. Yet, compared to the days when writing to a public official involved looking up the address at the library, typing a letter, and mailing it, fewer young people contact their elected representatives. iGen'ers are finding new ways to move for social change, from changing their Facebook profile picture to an equality sign to hashtagging a tweet about a cause. It might not be marching in the streets, but—as the Supreme Court's ruling on same-sex marriage showed—such pervasive awareness can start to shift the opinions of average Americans and eventually the law. Much of the awareness of Black Lives Matter spread online. That is where iGen'ers shine—not in traditional political action but in spreading the word about a new issue. Sometimes that changes things (as in the case of same-sex marriage) and sometimes it doesn't (as with the "Kony 2012" video, which garnered millions of views but produced little action).

What types of political candidates will appeal to iGen? The Internet, and iGen's individualism, pulls for authenticity above all, that cardinal value of "being yourself." iGen'ers want someone who is seen as consistent in his or her views and does not change them for others. This was the key to Bernie Sanders's appeal to iGen'ers and the Millennials and likely to Donald Trump's appeal as well. "Although you may not agree with Bernie Sanders, at least respect him for his compassion and authenticity," wrote University of Massachusetts student Emilia Beuger in the *Massachusetts Daily Collegian*. ". . . He is authentic. He sticks to his beliefs and he is not afraid to express those beliefs. He is not going to let people tell him what to believe. . . . He does not let anyone tell him what to say or think." Similar words could be written about Donald Trump; many people liked that he seemed to say whatever he wanted. It's probably not a coincidence that Republican nominee Trump, seen as authentic, won in 2016, while Republican nominee Mitt Romney, seen as overly programmed, did not in 2012.

In the future, I can see a politician much like the presidential nominee Will Conway in the Netflix series *House of Cards* appealing to iGen voters: someone who is young, straightforward, and casual. In one episode, Conway live streams video from his house with his family, speaking without notes and seemingly completely relaxed. He turns out to not actually be that authentic, but his image is. iGen'ers, even more than the Millennials before them, have little patience for traditional political candidates, whom they see as dishonest, untrustworthy, and part of the large institutions they dislike.

Yet iGen'ers still have strong beliefs, mirroring the political polarization of the country as a whole. The downside of our online culture is that social media sites connect people to their personal cocoon of friends and family, allowing people to cluster with others who think as they do, further polarizing their views in an echo chamber. As a result, more young Americans hold strong political views, yet fewer are interested in staying informed or taking part in political life. We may see more candidates resort to the politics of celebrity to get iGen'ers' attention, with fame and bombastic proclamations the key to leading in the polls. Rising politicians trying to appeal to the next generation will not only have to accommodate iGen'ers' polarized views and libertarian values, they will also have to overcome their shrinking interest in politics overall—until a politician becomes a meme.

Understanding— and Saving—iGen

Thirteen-year-old Athena is on a roll, telling me about how she thinks technology has affected her generation. When she hangs out with her friends, she says, they are often looking at their phones instead of at her. "I'm trying to talk to them about something, and they don't actually look At. My. Face," she says, emphasizing every word in the last phrase. "They're looking at their phone, or they're looking at their Apple Watch."

"What does that feel like when you're trying to talk to somebody face-to-face and they're not looking at you?" I ask.

"It kind of hurts," she says. "It hurts. I know my parents' generation didn't do that. I could be talking about something superimportant to me, and they wouldn't even be listening."

Once, she says, a friend of hers was texting her boyfriend while they were hanging out in person together at her house. "I was trying to talk to her about my family, and what was going on, and she was like, 'Uh-huh, yeah, whatever,' so I took her phone out of her hands and I threw it at my wall."

I couldn't help laughing out loud. "You play volleyball," I said. "Do you have a pretty good arm on you?"

"Yep," she answered.

Athena's story intrigued me, not just because she actually did what many of us have fervently wanted to do (but lacked the gumption and the volleyball arm). At 13, Athena has not only never known a world without the Internet, but she can barely remember a time before smartphones. This is the only world she has ever known—yet she's not sure she wants to live in it.

In this chapter, I'll lay out some ways we can make things better for iGen. That necessitates striking a balance between solutions and acceptance. Cultural change is always a trade-off: with the good comes some bad. The trends that have shaped iGen are the usual mix of good and bad, with a healthy amount of "it depends" thrown in. Sometimes I wish we didn't have to label any generational trends as good or bad—they just are. Yet as a parent and educator, I also understand the urge to discuss "what we can do about it." For some trends, this arguably isn't necessary: with fewer teens drinking alcohol and having sex and fewer getting into car accidents, we can pat ourselves (and teens) on the back and call it a day. Teens are physically safer than ever and are making less risky choices than generations past. It's part of a larger picture of growing up more slowly rather than an overall shift toward responsibility, but it is still undeniably good that they are safer.

Other trends are more troubling: How can we protect our kids from anxiety, depression, and loneliness in our digital age? What can parents and colleges do to ease the transition from high school to college when fewer students have experienced independence? How can managers get the most out of the newest generation in the workforce?

In this last chapter, I'll discuss some possible ways forward. In many cases, I'll rely on the words of iGen'ers themselves to point the way. Like Athena, many iGen'ers are acutely aware of the downsides of their uniquely digital era. This is where the data give way to more subjective interpretation and opinion, so I'm grateful so many young people have made their views on these issues known.

Put Down the Phone

"Ever since my younger sister got her own Instagram and Twitter accounts, she has spent our car rides silently scrolling, head down, her face lit up with the blue-white of the 5.44 by 2.64-inch cellphone screen," wrote college student Rachel Walman in the *Massachusetts Daily Collegian*. "I try to engage in conversation with her, and she responds with absent-minded, one-word answers. I don't blame her for this, because I know I'm guilty of doing the same thing. Rather, I'm saddened by the fact that our online lives have become more important than our real ones."

iGen'ers are addicted to their phones, and they know it. Many also know it's not entirely a good thing. It's clear that most teens (and adults) would be better off if they spent less time with screens. "Social media is destroying our lives," one teen told Nancy Jo Sales in her book *American Girls*. "So why don't you go off it?" Sales asked. "Because then we would have no life," the girl said.

Based on the research presented here and plenty more, it's best to put off giving your child a cell phone as long as possible. There's really no reason for an elementary school child to have his own cell phone, so that's an easy one. By middle school, with kids in more activities and more likely to ride a bus, many parents buy phones for their kids for convenience and safety. However, that phone doesn't necessarily need to be a smartphone complete with Internet access and the ability to text. Instead, you can buy your child a phone with limited functions—for example, an old-school flip phone (also known as a "dumb phone") without Internet access or a touch screen (which means that texting involves hitting the same key several times to get different letters—remember that?). When my friend's son headed off to our local middle school recently, she bought him a flip phone. I plan to do the same in a few years when my oldest will be riding the bus to middle school as well—though I might not even go the flip-phone route until I see how the first few weeks go. After all, kids rode buses for decades before cell phones existed. We'll put off the phone for as long as possible.

Why wait, if "everyone else" has a smartphone, and your kid really wants one? Some people make the argument that teens will be on social media eventually, so you might as well get them a phone early. However, that ignores the collision between early-adolescent development and social media. Middle school has always been a fraught time for identity finding and bullying, and combining those with social media can create a tinderbox. That's why the links between social media use and depression are strongest among the youngest teens. Older teens, who are more certain of themselves, are less likely to be emotionally affected by social media. Given the emphasis on sexuality online—the butt selfies, the requests for nudes, and the likes on the sexually provocative Instagram posts—it makes sense to spare young teens that pressure for a few years. If they want to be on social media, there's an easy solution: sign them up, but from your computer. They can check in on their friends briefly and communicate about getting together, but it's not constantly in their pockets and hands like a smartphone. Sporadic use is unlikely to be harmful; electronic device use was linked to unhappiness and mental health issues only after more than two hours of use a day.

If these limits sound antediluvian, consider this: many tech CEOs strictly regulate their own children's technology use. When *New York Times* reporter Nick Bilton talked to Apple cofounder and CEO Steve Jobs in late 2010, he asked Jobs if his kids loved the iPad. "They haven't used it," Jobs said. "We limit how much technology our kids use at home." Bilton was shocked, but he later found that many other tech experts also limited their children's screen time, from the cofounder of Twitter to the former editor of *Wired* magazine. So even people who love technology—and make a living off it—are cautious about their kids using it too much. As Adam Alter put it in his book *Irresistible*, "It seemed as if the people producing tech products were following the cardinal rule of drug dealing: Never get high on your own supply."

Many parents wonder if we really need to worry about this stuff. Some argue that the flurry of concern over smartphones resembles the panic over previous advances in media, such as radio, music albums, TV, or even novels. That might be true, but it's not particularly relevant. Social media and electronic device use is linked to higher rates of loneliness, unhappiness, depression, and suicide risk, in both correlational and experimental data. Novels and music are not. TV watching is also linked to depression, and sure enough, more Boomers (the first TV generation) were depressed than previous generations that had grown up without TV. Just because an argument has been made before does not mean it's wrong; the "panic" over TV turned out to be somewhat justified. Thus an argument about whether a "panic" about media has happened before seems trivial—our kids need help now.

Another argument is that social media and texting are just teens interacting with one another just as they always have. Perhaps, but electronic communication is linked to poor mental health, whereas interacting in person is linked to good mental health. The two types of interaction are not the same.

Finally, there's the argument that people (including adults) like social media, so it can't be bad. That's clearly not true. Lots of people love junk food, too, but that doesn't mean it's good for our health. Keep in mind: social media companies are run by people looking to make a profit. Every time a new app catches on because teens stay up all night using it, those companies make money. It's just our kids who lose.

That might be especially true for girls, who are the primary consumers of social media and also the primary sufferers of the mental health issues they have wrought. Parents, teachers, and girls themselves have to do something, because social media companies are not going to. "The social media companies aren't going to do anything about it, as long as it's driving traffic," says Paul Roberts, the author of *The Impulse Society*. "Oh, your daughter's on Tinder? Well, she's just meeting friends. I don't think it's necessarily a cynical, let's destroy women thing—it's how can I get my next quarter's bonus?"

I am not suggesting that teens (or adults) give up smartphones (or even social media) entirely. If you or your teen limits your use to an hour a day, there may be no ill effects. In short doses, this is useful technology that enhances our lives. But things have clearly gone too far. Psychology journals are filled with articles on Internet addiction. Many teens communicate with their friends electronically far more than they do face-to-face, with as-yet-unknown consequences for their budding social skills. We already know that depression and anxiety have risen at an unprecedented rate and that twice as many young teens commit suicide as just a few years ago. It seems abundantly clear that screen time needs to be cut.

All of us, including adults, have to find a place of moderation for how much that phone is in our hands, how much our eyes are on that screen, and how much time we spend communicating digitally instead of in person. Melissa Nilles, a student at the University of California at Santa Barbara, captured this reality as only iGen can. "I had a terrible nightmare the other night," she wrote in the UCSB student newspaper. "Instead of meeting for a quick cup of coffee, my friend and I spent 30 minutes texting back and forth about our day. After that, instead of going in to talk to my professor during his office hours, I emailed him from home with my question. Because of this, he never got to know who I was, even though he would have been a great source for a letter of recommendation if he had. I ignored a cute guy at the bus stop asking me the time because I was busy responding to a text. And I spent far too much time on Facebook trying to catch up with my 1000+ 'friends,' most of whom I rarely see, and whose meaning sadly seems to dispel even more as the sheer number of 'connections' I've made grows. Oh wait, that wasn't a dream. This technological detachment is becoming today's reality." Technology, she writes, is "slowly ruining the quality of social interaction that we all need as human beings. So what are we doing with 3000 friends on the Internet? Why are we texting all the time? Seems like a big waste of time to me. Let's spend more time together with our friends. Let's make the relationships that count last, and not rely on technology to do the job for us." Life is better offline, and even iGen'ers know it.

Life Hacks for Smartphones

For parents, the specific choices around smartphones and social media can be overwhelming. Eventually, your teen is probably going to get a smartphone. But that doesn't have to mean it's all over. Before you even give your teen the phone, install an app that limits the amount of time he can spend on it. There are several apps that will do this, and the specific ones will probably change by the time you read this book; right now, there are several available, and most cost no more than a few dollars a month. Apps can limit time spent on certain sites, lock the phone after a certain amount of time, or even turn the phone off completely. It's tempting to give your teen the phone first and see if she is a responsible user, but it's better to install the controls first before she changes the passcode or becomes addicted to social media. It's just too easy for that to happen—just ask most adults, who are nearly as addicted to their phones as teens are. Setting limits is a nice solution, because then teens can still find out about events and communicate with their friends, but the phone doesn't become their central focus.

Another key rule: no one, adults included, should sleep within ten feet of his phone. Many iGen'ers and Millennials told me they almost always keep their phone on at night and are awakened by alerts and dings all night long. Many others told me they put their phones on silent but still end up grabbing it when they can't sleep, even in the middle of the night. This is not a formula for healthy sleep. It's not just the stimulation of the phone, but the light it emits: our caveman-evolved brains interpret it as sunlight, reducing our production of the sleep hormone melatonin and making it even harder to sleep.

What if you use your phone as your alarm clock, as every teen and young adult I talked to said they did? Simple: buy an inexpensive alarm clock. Then your phone, with its stimulating material and wake-inducing light, can be across the room from you as you go to sleep at night and wake up in the morning.

Let's say your teen wants to join a social media site. If you want to limit him to one, which one should he join? According to most experts, Snapchat. First, most teens share snaps with their friends that disappear after a few seconds. They share only with individual friends; they have to select exactly whom they send them to. Thus, what they are sharing isn't on display for a larger audience to comment on and "like" (or not like), which is the way Instagram, Twitter, and Facebook work. And if someone wants to share something with a larger audience, she can post it to her Snapstory. Even then, the Snapstory lasts only twenty-four hours.

Social media apps change quickly, so this advice might be outdated by the time you read it. But the general advice holds: favor platforms that allow brief and individual posts over those that encourage near-permanent and group posts. Posts meant to be seen by large audiences encourage the careful curating of an image—taking fifty pictures to get just the right selfie, obsessing over how to word something, posting something just for the "likes." This is problematic enough for adults and can be even worse for teens. Snapchat also doesn't allow users to search for content, meaning that teens are less likely to stumble upon inappropriate material. The new "live chilling" apps such as Houseparty are also useful—they are basically video chat for three or more and allow teens to see one another and talk. It's not quite face-to-face, but it's closer than most social media.

All of us, both teens and adults, can work on putting the phone away when we're with someone in person. Some friends have come up with a useful rule: when they have lunch or dinner together, everyone puts his phone facedown in the middle of the table, on silent. The first one who picks up his phone pays the bill. I think this might be a nice rule for adults as well.

One 18-year-old interviewed in *American Girls* had given up social media entirely—and, yes, she still has friends. "Sometimes there will be a 10-minute-long conversation where I can't participate because I didn't see that post or I didn't watch that video, but I'd rather not anyway. If I want to get to know someone, I don't want to know the version of themselves that they artificially created and posted online. . . . How important is it really to know what Mary posted yesterday on Instagram? If I want to know Mary, I'll call her up and ask her to hang out." She says she doesn't have any universal solutions, but concludes that "Social media . . . doesn't lead to a fulfilling life. People are not pursuing happiness with this. They are pursuing an attractive picture."

Our phones let us record our lives—but sometimes they can get in the way of living our lives. Will you remember everything through the lens of your smartphone or how you saw it with your own eyes? "You're surrounded by it no matter where you go," Alexandra Lee, a freshman at the University of Georgia, told the campus newspaper. "Nobody can just be present anymore. The second anything remotely fun happens, everyone takes out their phone and starts filming." The *Washington Post* recently profiled a family in which the youngest child, 4 years old, regularly discusses whether what they're doing should go on YouTube. That is not the way to be present in your own life.

Putting down the smartphone is also crucially important for studying or working. The human brain cannot multitask: we can focus our attention on only one cognitive task at a time. If we try to do two things that require our conscious attention at the same time, we have to switch our attention back and forth between them, which takes time and makes everything take longer. Mark, who's studying information technology at a community college, agrees that "to focus on college material, you can't multitask." His technique is to study intently for twenty minutes "and then, no matter what I'm doing I stop, and I take a five-minute break. I check my Facebook, check my Instagram, Twitter. Then my other alarm goes off saying, 'Hey, look, it's time to get back to work.'" I'd tweak Mark's plan a little—if you're on a roll studying or working, don't stop after twenty minutes. Wait until you feel distracted or fatigued, a maximum of forty-five minutes, and then take a break. But his five-minute rule for distractions is a good one. It should keep you from getting too far into the wilds of social media or clicking on multiple Internet slideshows of "Why Hollywood Won't Cast Brendan Fraser Anymore." The key point: if you're trying to work or study, put the phone away and stay off Google and email as much as possible. If you don't, you'll be interrupted by pings and alerts all the time and will constantly be switching your attention back and forth. It's the easiest way to have the whole day pass and realize you didn't get anything done.

Overall, the key to phones is moderation—for both teens and adults. Use your phone for all of the cool stuff it can do, but put it down and be present for the moment as much as possible. Use an app that cuts you off from social media if you have to. Carve out blocks of time to study or work when it doesn't intrude. Do not sleep with it or give it nude pictures of yourself. It is not your lover. Do not continuously turn your attention to it when you are talking with someone in person. It is not your best friend.

Noodz and Porn

For girls in particular, social media sites often exacerbate teens' already heightened emphasis on physical appearance—particularly a sexualized appearance. Many parents have no idea what their kids are posting online, so keeping an eye on their Instagram feed is a place to start. Parents need to have honest conversations with girls about the downsides of posting revealing pictures. They should never send nude photos, even on Snapchat. Although the app alerts users if someone else takes a screenshot, there's nothing to prevent it from happening. When someone receives a nude, whether through social media or texting, he can share it with whomever he likes. There are websites with galleries of nude teen girls, and those pictures often make their way around middle schools and high schools like wildfire. Parents need to make it very clear to teens, even younger teens, that it is never a good idea to send a nude picture of yourself. (Teens refer to this as "nudes" or use oh-so-creative misspellings such as "noodz.")

Thirteen-year-old Athena educated me about this. "Why don't you want them to take a screenshot?" I asked when she was telling me about Snapchat. "If it's a bad picture," she said. "Like a bad expression?" I ask. "No," she said quietly. "Nudes." If you send nudes, she says, "mean people" will show the photo to others and "they don't get caught" because they delete it from their phone. Nudes can spread through a middle school in a matter of minutes. Athena told me that two kids in her 7th-grade class were suspended for a week for sending nude pictures. And those were just the ones who got caught. So this is another piece of advice to convey to our teens: if someone asks for nudes, just say no. Or you can mimic the response of 16-year-old Reese Hebert. When she texted a boy that she was about to take a shower, he texted back, "Ooh I wanna see." So she sent him a picture of herself in the shower—from the neck up and wearing a multicolored umbrella hat.

Parents also need to prevent children and teens from seeing pornography. Due to its ubiquity online and the proliferation of electronic devices, kids are exposed to porn at younger and younger ages these days. Child filters on phones and tablets are far from foolproof—for elementary school–age kids, it's best to stick with devices such as Kindles that can be configured to not even include a web browser (they include ways to view videos and books, but within what some call a "walled garden"). Older teens also need restrictions, or at the very least an honest conversation about pornography. Like social media companies, pornography companies are in it to make money, and what makes them money is often degrading, aggressive sex. These are not videos of two people who love each other having hot sex—they are actors who participate in sex that is often brutal and almost always emotionally distant. Pornography does not portray normal adult sexuality. As a result, a generation of teens is getting a warped view of what sex is about; according to most pornography, it's about the man's pleasure only, often at the woman's expense.

The In-Person Deficit

Teens who spend more time with their friends in person are happier, less lonely, and less depressed, while those who spend more time on social media are less happy, lonelier, and more depressed. At the very least, online time does not protect against loneliness and depression, while in-person time does.

Given the benefits of in-person social interaction, parents might need to stop thinking that teens hanging out together are wasting their time. Teens are hanging out with their friends less, but they are not replacing that time with homework, extracurriculars, paid work, or housework; they are replacing it with screen time. Unfortunately, the time they spend communicating electronically is a poor substitute for the emotional connection and social skills gained in face-to-face communication—and it may be contributing to the alarming rise in teen depression and suicide.

Many parents see teens' in-person social activities as potentially unsafe. We all want to protect our kids, and we all need to have rules limiting what teens can do. The problem is that many parents have restricted an activity that has numerous benefits (in-person social interaction) while putting few limits on an activity devoid of most of those benefits (electronic communication). Teens may be physically safer with electronic communication, but that choice may come at the expense of their mental health. Parents are worried about the wrong thing.

A few studies have already shown that teens who communicate face-to-face, without electronic devices, have better social skills, such as reading emotion on others' faces. I suspect there will be more such studies in the future. iGen'ers are growing up in a world where more and more communication has moved online, but in-person social skills are always going to be useful. People still have to meet in person for dates, for job interviews, and for conversations. iGen'ers who hole up with their devices more and see their friends in person less will have more trouble with those social skills. As with everything, practice makes perfect. So parents: your teen going out with her friends is not a waste of time—it's an investment in her future.

Even though she's only 13, Athena already sees the consequences of the technology she has known all of her life. "We don't know how to communicate normally. We don't know how to communicate like normal people anymore," she says. "Do you think the way your generation is communicating will eventually become normal?" I ask. "Yep," she says. "And then there will be no reason to get off the couch."

iGen and everyone else: Let's get off the couch.

Beating Anxiety and Depression

"Sitting in a lecture hall that afternoon, I was focusing all of my energy on trying to slow my racing mind and calm myself. . . . All I could think about was the enormous amount of tasks I had to get done. Dozens of other minuscule thoughts took the opportunity to try and turn themselves into huge problems and blare inside my head. This is what anxiety is like, and when it begins it can be difficult to escape," wrote Kate Leddy in the *Massachusetts Daily Collegian*. ". . . I realized in the midst of all my internal debating about needing to just focus I'd hardly heard any of the lecture. So, I packed up and left. I went to the Recreation Center and ran for half an hour, and it was as though my body granted me an extra dose of endorphins that day when I finished. Almost immediately, I felt a wave of renewed energy, clarity and calm."

Kate discovered something that day that research confirms: exercise is a natural antidepressant. Stephen Ilardi, a clinical psychologist and professor at the University of Kansas, gave a TED talk titled "Depression Is a Disease of Civilization." He and others have found that mimicking the lifestyle of our caveman ancestors is one of the best ways to prevent and reduce anxiety and depression. The six-part program includes sunlight exposure, exercise, a diet high in omega-3 fatty acids, avoiding rumination, getting enough sleep, and engaging in in-person social interaction. His book *The Depression Cure* has specific suggestions for incorporating these lifestyle changes. Most of these techniques are free or low cost, though they do take time.

Where to get that time? Probably from that phone again. Look back at the graphs in chapter 3 showing the links between time use and psychological well-being. If an activity involves a screen, it's linked to less happiness and more depression. If it doesn't—particularly if it involves in-person social interaction or exercise—it's linked to more happiness and less depression.

Try an experiment on yourself (or on your teen, if you can): for a week, cut your phone, Internet, and social media time in half, and use that time to see friends and family in person and/or to exercise. More than likely, you'll end that week feeling happier.

Of course, lifestyle changes are not going to fix every case of anxiety and depression, especially if they are severe. The good news is that therapy works; a definitive study showed that depressed people who get therapy do get better faster than those who don't. Antidepressant medications can be very effective, especially for moderate to severe depression. Therapy and medication can allieviate suffering and save lives. The problem is that strapped budgets often make it difficult to find the resources for more mental health services. On college campuses, a few concrete steps seem logical, such as doing away with limits on the number of on-campus therapy sessions. Setting limits on therapy sessions is like telling students they can't go to the doctor if they feel sick too often. If campuses are going to stem the tide of mental health issues, students need to be able to get regular therapy throughout the school year. At residential colleges in particular, this needs to take place on campus. Resources also need to be available after hours: on many campuses, the counseling center closes at five, and there are few sources of help during the evening hours, which are often the most difficult for those with mental health issues.

Middle and high school students need more help as well, but the system of mental health care in the country is outstripped by the needs of young people and their families. With the rapidly rising rates of depression among 12- to 17-year-olds, this problem is only going to get worse. Parents should be aware that even very young teens (and children) can suffer from anxiety and depression, and take it seriously. Most will have to wade through the health care bureaucracy and wait overly long to get an appointment, perhaps one of the reasons why teen suicide remains unacceptably high. In general, getting help sooner rather than later is best. Therapists don't just help kids during sessions; they can give children and teens coping skills that will be useful for the rest of their lives.

At the very least, I hope that the data in chapter 4 help convince those who believe that there has not been any real change in mental health issues.

The data presented there compare young people now to those in the past using random sampling and anonymous reporting, a design that sidesteps criticisms of previous reports. The trends are also remarkably consistent: loneliness, depressive symptoms, major depressive episodes, anxiety, self-injury, and suicide are all on the rise, mostly since 2011. iGen is crying out for help, and we need to listen.

Growing Up Slowly

More and more teens are leaving high school never having had a paying job, driven a car by themselves, gone out on a date, had sex, or tried alcohol. These trends are an adaptation to the current cultural context; in other words, they are not inherently good or bad. They just are.

However, the implications are profound. Young people are entering college and the working world without as much experience with adult independence. For parents, this means more calls home about how to navigate adult responsibilities and more worries that young people are not prepared for college and the workplace. For student affairs professionals at colleges and universities, this means advising more students who don't know how to manage their lives by themselves. More students will have their first drink of alcohol on campus, and more will have their first sexual experience or adult relationship during college. So, compared to previous generations, they will be chronologically older when they have these adult experiences—in many ways a positive development. However, they may also be away from home and the support of their parents and longtime friends. This presents challenges for those who shepherd students' mental health and their lives on campus.

The decline in sexual experience also presents challenges for preventing sexual assault among young people on campus and elsewhere, as students with little experience may have more difficulty navigating the sexual fire hose that is college. The good news is that rates of sexual assault appear to be declining. However, they are still too high. Many incidents occur when students are taking those first steps into adulthood: college freshmen are two and a half times as likely as older students to be sexually assaulted.

We now live in a culture where teens watch more porn than ever and start asking each other for nude pictures at 11—yet they wait longer to have sex. This combination of considerable fantasy experience and little real-world experience may be problematic.

If you're the parent of a teen and want him to learn more independence before he goes to college, there are a few things you can do. First, relax curfews and rules about going out with friends; he will gain social skills and independence from these experiences. Second, insist he get a driver's license; stop driving him around. As much as possible, put aside your worries. Teens today are safer drivers than ever and are much less likely to get into accidents or even to get tickets.

Other adult activities are more of a gray area. The data on after-school jobs are complicated. Teens from disadvantaged backgrounds seem to gain key benefits from working, but benefits for kids from middle-class families are less clear. Many teen jobs are unskilled, rote positions. However, they do teach valuable lessons about time management, responsibility, and social skills. With the cost of college these days, the money teens earn from jobs might help them pay some of their tuition and ease their student debt burden later on.

Alcohol is an even more fraught issue, and there is no one solution. More young people are arriving at college without much experience with alcohol and then colliding with the college party culture of binge drinking. Should they have the experience of getting drunk at home while they are safe? Maybe, but it's not always the best idea to condone alcohol use among underage young people. An alternative is to have a realistic conversation about what many college parties are like and how to stay safe. For some students, not drinking might be the best choice. Many universities now have substance-free dorms, and I expect even more will offer this option in the future. iGen'ers are more accepting of other people's choices, so someone who chooses not to drink at college is not necessarily going to be ostracized. Sometimes "Just say no" really is the best advice, especially given the dangers of binge drinking.

Some have suggested that a "gap year" between high school and college might be one solution to the mental health issues and lack of adult experience among college students. A gap year provides time to work, travel, volunteer, and generally grow up. Gap years were brought to national attention recently when Malia Obama decided to take one before attending Harvard. At least by their own reports, students who take gap years believe that the time helped them; in one study, 73% of those who took a gap year said it had helped them prepare for college, and 57% said it had helped them decide what to study. Gap years aren't for everyone; they are most likely to benefit students who are already set on getting a college education but who need some time to grow up a little before hitting the semiadulthood of college (especially college away from home). Joe O'Shea and Nina Hoe, college administrators and researchers, examined the data on gap years and concluded that their benefits outweigh the risks for many students. "Expanding gap year education will help more high school graduates arrive at college equipped with skills they need to achieve both personal and academic success," they concluded on Quartz.

Safe but Not Unprepared

Our kids are safer than ever, which is the best news imaginable. Yet, as often happens, this cultural trend has been taken to an illogical extreme. Concerns about safety might be one of the reasons teens are seeing their friends in person less, with parents afraid of car accidents and other perils.

The word *safety* is now used to explain responses to incidents that don't actually involve anyone's safety. Last week, the principal of my children's elementary school sent an email informing parents that someone, rumored to be some middle school students, had drawn "profanity and the image of a swastika" on the school building. "The safety of our students, staff and families is a top priority and I appreciate all of your efforts to keep our school and community free of this inappropriate and offensive behavior," the principal concluded. Yes, it was completely unacceptable behavior, but framing it in terms of "safety" was pushing it. No one was threatened or hurt. Mentioning safety just inflamed the situation. The goal should instead be to educate those young people about what the symbol actually means and figure out why they would do something so stupid. Safety is cited as the reason for the most unlikely situations. When Bryce Maine wanted to bring his 69-year-old grandmother as his date to the prom at Eufaula High School in Alabama in spring 2017, the school principal said no, citing their rule that prom attendees must be 20 years old or younger. "Safety of students and staff is the first and most important of the many tasks of a school administrator," he said in a statement. "We do not chance leaving any stone unturned when it comes to safety." Bryce was told the rule was in place to prevent older people buying alcohol for underage students—an unlikely scenario in his grandmother's case. In the current climate, not even grandmothers are safe.

These are not isolated examples. Listen carefully, and you'll hear "safety" used as an explanation or excuse for just about everything—by both administrators and students. I think school administrators should think more carefully about using safety as a reason or explanation, given its potential to escalate tensions and reinforce the idea that our children shouldn't be let out of our sight. In such a climate, our kids will be terrified when they head to their first jobs or to college (and they often are). If we emphasize safety less, it might also make it less likely that students will flinch at the idea of talking to their peers about difficult issues. iGen'ers are so frightened of confrontation that they would rather tell an administrator that a fellow student said something that upset them than say a few words to that person themselves.

Concerns about safety now include not just physical safety but emotional safety. School programs now seek to protect kids from bullying—not just physical bullying but insults, taunting, and name-calling. Bullying has an undeniably negative effect—in fact, I coauthored some of the first controlled experiments on the effects of social rejection, a form of bullying.

Taking steps to protect children from bullying by peers is, in my view, long overdue. On the other hand, I also agree with critics that such programs sometimes take things too far, teaching children that the normal ins and outs of childhood friendships are bullying or equating hurt feelings with physical harm. Many antibullying policies are so broad and vague that they may make students afraid of any interaction. Aiken Elementary School in West Hartford, Connecticut, defines bullying as any communication or physical act that "causes physical or emotional harm" to a student. The policy carefully defines everything from who is a school employee to which things are considered "mobile electronic devices" but does not define "emotional harm." There is no denying that bullying causes emotional harm—but so do other, more ambiguous, childhood experiences, such as a friend deciding to play with someone else that day, common playground insults, or arguments over the rules of a game. The way the policy is written, any child who hurts another child's feelings, unintentionally or not, is a bully. This may create a situation in which children are constantly aware of negative interactions, afraid they are the victim of this terrible thing they've heard about called bullying. Antibullying programs may, as a side effect, have shaped iGen children into kids who are constantly on the lookout for being harmed.

As the psychologist Nick Haslam points out, the criteria for what is considered "trauma" now include just about anything bad that can happen to someone, creating a culture of victimhood that may exaggerate the emotions involved. As recently as 1980, psychiatrists used the word *trauma* to describe only events "outside the range of the usual human experience." Now, however, many more events are included in the official list, and laypeople use the word *trauma* to describe experiences such as a bad hair day and seeing chalked words supporting a presidential candidate (as happened at Emory when "Trump 2016" was written on sidewalks and students protested, yelling, "We are in pain!"). In the Google Books database, the use of the word *trauma* quadrupled between 1965 and 2005.

Many iGen'ers (and younger Millennials) appear deeply emotional when someone simply disagrees with them. Instead of treating such an experience as "trauma," a better approach to a controversial opinion might be to discuss it, ignore it, or develop logical arguments against it. That goes even for opinions that are racist, sexist, homophobic, or transphobic: there are logical arguments against racism, sexism, homophobia, and transphobia. If young people (and the rest of us) react to such opinions with tears and statements of feeling unsafe, things won't change much. If we instead argue against such views, we can destroy them. The tide of history is against prejudice; the battle is being waged, and usually won, every day.

iGen'ers in the Classroom

iGen'ers are different, and college faculty and staff are beginning to notice. Millennials marched onto college campuses with optimism, confidence, and a strong sense of entitlement. Faculty encountered students who expected A's just for showing up, who argued strenuously over grades, and who believed they deserved special treatment. The story is different for iGen'ers: growing up in the shadow of the Great Recession, iGen'ers expect less and display less narcissism and entitlement. iGen'ers are more pessimistic and less confident than Millennials, with students now more willing to work hard and less likely to vociferously question their grades. On the other hand, iGen'ers are more hesitant to talk in class and to ask questions—they are scared of saying the wrong thing and not as sure of their opinions. (When McGraw-Hill Education polled more than six hundred college faculty in 2017, 70% said students were less willing to ask questions and participate in class than they were five years ago.) It takes more reassurance and trust to get them to actively participate in class.

As the first completely post-Internet generation, iGen'ers are used to finding information by themselves. But that doesn't mean they won't listen to lectures, because they are also very anxious about doing well in their classes. When I've polled my students about how they'd prefer to spend class time, most have said they are fine with lectures as long as they convey information that is helpful to doing well on the exams. They like discussion but don't want it to take too much time away from learning the material they'll be tested on. With that said, it's important to keep class interesting. The videos iGen'ers watch online are rarely more than three minutes long, and i'Gen'ers skip between apps on their phones within seconds. Reaching them in the classroom often means catering to this short attention span, toggling among lecture, discussion, videos, and demonstrations. iGen'ers are more accepting of authority than Millennials but just as likely to fall asleep in class if they don't participate or at least get to watch a few short videos.

iGen'ers also come to college with much less experience reading books or even long magazine articles. To bridge the reading gap, publishers are turning to e-textbooks with videos, interactive figures, and built-in quizzes—excellent ways to reach iGen. I believe textbooks also need to stop covering so many topics in so much detail. My friend Kate Catanese, who teaches psychology at Cuyahoga Community College, has noticed this generation's reluctance to read. "I've had students complain that I'm making them read too much, that an eight-page popular press newspaper article is somehow too lengthy and can't keep their attention," she told me. I'm not suggesting that faculty give in to such complaints; students will need to learn to read long passages eventually. However, we also have to meet them where they are, and covering a little less is often the best compromise. Kate takes this approach in her classes. "I really go for depth over breadth, and I think the students are better off that way anyway. Cover the cool stuff and leave everything else out," she says. I think textbooks should take a similar approach, covering the most important topics in enough detail that students can understand the different sides of the issues, but without the lengthy list of topics and fine-grained detail that end up boring them to tears. It is also essential that the books be updated frequently, at least every three years. For example, high schools update their books only every ten years (if that), which leaves iGen'ers believing that books can't be trusted because they are so out of date. In many fields, ten years is enough for the whole field to change. That sends iGen'ers online, again, and they still don't learn how to read long passages of text. One solution to this is electronic textbooks, which can be updated more frequently.

Given how much iGen'ers learn online, one of the most important lessons is how to judge content. As the impact of "fake news" during the 2016 election showed, many people have a difficult time figuring out what's real online and what's not. iGen'ers need to be taught about sources and evaluating evidence. Many high schools are beginning to do that, but this type of critical thinking needs to be emphasized throughout iGen'ers' education and within specific areas. For example, students in the sciences and social sciences can be taught about the standard for publication in a peer-reviewed journal and how it differs from a publication by someone who does a few analyses in a blog post or polls a few hundred people. Students need to be taught about the importance of control groups and representative sampling, issues that arise in marketing, human resources, journalism, and politics, not just in academia.

iGen has continued the Millennial tendency to focus more on extrinsic values (the concrete outcome) and less on intrinsic values (the inherent pleasure in the activity) than previous generations. iGen students are afraid they will not make the cut in a competitive world and will end up on the "have-not" side of the increasing divide between the haves and have-nots. They are practical, serious, and anxious, focusing more on the exam grade and less on the joy of learning. They go to college to get a better job and make more money, not necessarily to improve their minds. This is a tough pill to swallow for many Boomer, GenX, and even Millennial faculty members, who love the material they teach and want their students to enjoy it as well. In my classroom, I try to balance this by devoting at least some class time to discussion—usually by asking students about their own experiences and how they relate to the material. Even though I know that many of them just want the grade, I'm hoping they will also see how the material can help them understand their world. Most students also recognize that the discussions help them remember the material—a win-win.

Hiring iGen'ers—and Getting Them to Stay

iGen'ers already dominate the cohort of students graduating from college. Businesses that were just coming to understand what Millennials want in the workplace now have to figure out iGen. Fortunately, the data in chapter 7 provide a good way forward to understanding iGen'ers—and in a much more conclusive way than the early one-time polls and confusing rumors did about Millennials fifteen years ago. This time, we know what this generation looks like, with definitive data from the beginning, as they're entering the door to their careers.

The first managers to hire iGen'ers were those in service industries such as restaurants and retail. Many quickly discovered that iGen'ers had no idea how to write a résumé—but were very good at making videos (which makes sense, given how little they read and how much they use social media). Some businesses use apps such as JobSnap, which ask potential iGen employees to make a brief video of themselves in lieu of submitting a résumé. Employers can then screen applicants based on the videos, which for many entry-level service jobs might better capture the attributes necessary for the position (such as good language and social skills). And since iGen'ers can apply using only their phones, managers should have more good applicants to choose from.

Overall, iGen is good news for managers: iGen'ers are more focused on work and more realistic about what that entails than the Millennials just before them. iGen'ers want good, stable jobs and are eager to prove themselves. Contrary to popular belief, they don't want to be entrepreneurs—in fact, they are *less* likely than previous generations to want to own their own business or be self-employed. That means iGen talent is ripe for the picking for the right businesses. iGen'ers are also less entitled and narcissistic than Millennials and have more moderate expectations. They are less likely than Millennials to expect to be CEO of the company in five years and less likely to expect more pay for less work. They are not as overconfident, and they have a stronger work ethic. The downside is that more young employees are anxious and uncertain; they are eager to do a good job but are scared of making mistakes. iGen'ers are more likely to put in extra work to get a presentation finished in time but less confident that it will be successful. Whereas Millennials needed praise, iGen'ers need reassurance. Given their slow upbringing, many are also less independent. Give them careful instructions for tasks, and expect that they will need more guidance. Managers who learned to be cheerleaders for Millennials will find they are more like therapists, life coaches, or parents for iGen'ers.

How do you sign them up? Compensation is key. Income inequality has ingrained iGen'ers with the fear of not making it, and they are even more likely than Millennials to say that "becoming well off financially" is important. They often carry staggering student loan debt. They are also interested in flexibility and vacation time, though not quite as much as Millennials were a few years ago.

Like Millennials, iGen'ers want to know that the job has a clear career path—that they can advance, preferably quickly. When considering the timeline of promotions, make them more numerous; instead of a big leap every two years, consider four smaller leaps every six months. To the Snapchat generation, six months feels like six years. Give feedback much more frequently than the annual review. With their short attention span and impatience, iGen'ers respond best to brief feedback on specific tasks, not lengthy reviews of performance over the long haul. Keep the feedback short and to the point. And although iGen'ers lack Millennials' outsize self-confidence, they are still a highly individualistic generation that respond to personal attention and customization. They want to make a personal impact, not be just a cog in the wheel. Some companies have started to allow employees to choose their own job title and customize their career paths. These are options attractive to both Millennials and iGen'ers, who share a common interest in being treated as unique individuals.

Use the word *safety* or refer to your "safe environment." iGen'ers have been taught to value safety more than any generation before them, and these words are not just comforting but expected. They want to know that they will feel safe and protected—not just physically but socially and emotionally. That doesn't mean you have to coddle them—they should be brought up to speed on the realities of business—but they do need a more gentle touch than the Millennials did. Always emphasize that you want to help them, that you're on their side and the feedback you're offering is to help them succeed. (Specifically say "I want you to succeed.") Frame criticism as the best path toward better performance.

Many businesses that recruit young college graduates have begun to involve their parents in the recruiting and orientation process. I expect that this trend will continue and even get stronger as iGen'ers enter the workforce. iGen'ers are becoming adults at a slower pace than Millennials did and are products of colleges that are increasingly focused on safety and protection. Do not be shocked when your young employees consult their parents when they need advice or when they seem more like 18-year-olds than 22-year-olds. By Boomer and GenX standards, they basically are.

iGen'ers bring new attitudes about communication. Many don't understand why anyone uses email when texting is so much faster. "For a while, I thought email was what people meant when they referred to 'snail mail,'" wrote 16-year-old Vivek Pandit in his book *We Are Generation Z*. "Eventually I realized that snail mail was the paper stuff that [takes] days to reach someone. I call that 'ancient mail.'" Even texting may be on its way out: with the popularity of Instagram and Snapchat, much of iGen's communication is visual rather than via words. iGen'ers speak in emojis, images, and video clips. Eventually organizations may adjust to the iGen way of communicating, but until then many iGen employees will need instruction about how to best communicate with older coworkers and clients; in other words, tell them to be careful with emojis, videos, and constant images. Many Boomers don't know what every emoji means, and not all GenX'ers appreciate being sent a video instead of an email. iGen'ers will also need to adjust their attention span. Reading long passages of text and writing long reports will tax iGen'ers more than it did Millennials and GenX'ers. For their entire lives, communication has meant dealing with short snippets of information, not pages and pages of pure text.

iGen'ers will also bring their attitudes about trigger warnings, safe spaces, and microaggressions into the workplace. If you have a (perhaps older) employee who's still a little clueless about race, gender, sexual orientation, or transgender issues, expect to get an earful from your new iGen employees about microaggressions. In the coming years, employees might begin requesting safe spaces at work. More and more will become emotional in meetings when they hear something they disagree with. iGen'ers will learn to adapt to the reality of the workplace as they age, but the workplace will also adapt to them—in still unknown ways.

What Lies Ahead for iGen?

In the three years I spent working on this book, making dozens of line graphs, reading campus newspapers, and listening to the stories and opinions of young people during in-depth interviews, I've realized this: iGen'ers are scared, maybe even terrified. Growing up slowly, raised to value safety, and frightened by the implications of income inequality, they have come to adolescence in a time when their primary social activity is staring at a small rectangular screen that can like them or reject them. The devices they hold in their hands have both extended their childhoods and isolated them from true human interaction. As a result, they are both the physically safest generation and the most mentally fragile. They are more focused on work and more realistic than Millennials, grasping the certainty that they'll need to fight hard to make it. They're exquisitely tolerant and have brought a new awareness of equality, mental health, and LGBT rights, leaving behind traditional structures such as religion. iGen'ers have a solid basis for success, with their practical nature and their inherent caution. If they can shake themselves free of the constant clutch of their phones and shrug off the heavy cloak of their fear, they can still fly. And the rest of us will be there, cheering them on.

To access the appendices, which include information
about this book's sources, methods, and additional data,
please visit simonandschuster.com/igen-index.

For more information on iGen and Jean's other projects,
visit jeantwenge.com.

Acknowledgments

Thanks go first to Jill Kneerim and Lucy Cleland, my agents and first readers, for your crucial and wise advice. I truly could not have done it without you.

Thanks to all of the great folks at Atria Books, especially Peter Borland, Milena Brown, Sean Delone, Tory Lowy, Leslie Meredith, and Daniella Wexler. You are my book-publishing home and thus my favorite place.

A special thanks to the teens and young adults who generously gave their time to answer my questions about your generation and tell me about your experiences. I am grateful for your honesty and your insight; you brought iGen to life. I'd also like to thank the friends, family, and high school teachers who introduced me to the teens I interviewed; your help must stay anonymous, but it was invaluable. Thanks as well to the online survey participants and SDSU students who told me more about iGen'ers' thoughts and opinions. I wish you success as you stride out into the world.

I'd also like to thank the dedicated, tireless people who administer the large over-time surveys I draw from in this book (Monitoring the Future, the American Freshman Survey, the General Social Survey, and the Youth Risk Behavior Surveillance System). Somehow, despite the sometimes insulated world of academia, I have yet to meet any of you personally, but I clearly owe you a drink. On behalf of many, please keep doing what you are doing. Your data sets are national treasures. Without them, people would still be stumbling around in the dark making wild guesses about generational differences.

With them, we are in the light, able to see clearly how the generations have changed. May your funding be perpetual.

Thanks to my good friend W. Keith Campbell, my partner in crime on many papers and two other books, for always helping me stay sane. Angela Beiler-May, Stacy Campbell, Nathan Carter, Malissa Clark, Kristin Donnelly, Julie Exline, Joshua Foster, Patricia Greenfield, Joshua Grubbs, Garrett Hisler, Nathan Honeycutt, Thomas Joiner, Sara Konrath, Zlatan Krizan, Sonja Lyubomirsky, Gabrielle Martin, Heejung Park, Radmila Prislin, Megan Rogers, Ramya Sastry, Samia Shaikh, Ryne Sherman, Brian Spitzberg, Yalda Uhls, Hannah VanLandingham, and Brooke Wells were outstanding collaborators on the journal articles based on this data, filling in gaps in my expertise and generally being cool, smart people. I count myself very lucky to know you. May your universities treat you well and give you raises.

Thanks to my friends and family who were nice enough and patient enough to listen when I talked about the book: Ken Bloom, Kate Catanese, Kim and Brian Chapeau, Lawrence Charap, Jenny Crowhurst, Jody Davis, Eli Finkel, Jeff Green, Nick Grossman, Curtis Hall, Chris Harris, Brandelyn Jarrett, Malhar Kale, Sarah and Dan Kilibarda, Marta Kolthoff, Ron Louden, Erin Mitchell, Bill and Joan Moening, Bud and Pat Moening, Darci and Brad Olsen, Shruti Patkar, Trinty Perry, Steven Siu, Marilyn Swenson, Drew Sword, Amy and Paul Tobia, Anna and Dusty Wetzel, Jud Wilson, May Yeh, Ashley and Mike Zahalan, Alice Zellmer, and Jennifer and Matt Zwolinski. Special thanks to my parents, Steve and JoAnn Twenge, for babysitting on those random nonschool days when I really needed to write, and the vacations when I really needed to not write.

Thanks to my husband, Craig, for all of the times when I talked about line graphs at dinner and the times when I stayed back from family fun to work on this book.

And finally, thanks to my three iGen daughters, Kate, Elizabeth, and Julia. You are the light of my life, my everything. I have just one question: If I name your generation, will you listen to me when I ask you to comb your hair? Thanks, girls. I love you.

Notes

The vast majority of the data used in *iGen* come from four national surveys: Monitoring the Future, the Youth Risk Behavior Surveillance System of the CDC, the American Freshman Survey, and the General Social Survey. These are referenced in the figure captions. All of these data sets are freely available online (the American Freshman Survey as aggregated data reported in PDFs, Mtf and GSS as data files, and the YRBSS as both a data file and an online tool that gives percentages by year).

This notes section includes the references for my own journal articles that report many of these analyses. Some of these were unpublished when *iGen* went to press—the peer-review process at journals can take years. However, they may be published in journals by the time you read this (a search for the title or my name may yield it, either via Google or a database such as PsycInfo). The notes below also include references to journal articles by others and media sources. For media sources, I include the author, title, publication, and date—though not the web link, as those can change.

Introduction

2 *"You have to have an iPhone"*: Sales, N. J. (2016). *American girls: Social media and the secret lives of teenagers.* New York: Knopf.

3 *how my own generation:* Twenge, J. M. (1997). Attitudes toward women, 1970–1995: A meta-analysis. *Psychology of Women Quarterly* 21, 35–51. Twenge, J. M. (1997). Changes in masculine and feminine traits over time: A meta-analysis. *Sex Roles* 36, 305–325. Twenge, J. M. (2000). The age of anxiety? Birth cohort change in anxiety and neuroticism, 1952–1993. *Journal of Personality and Social Psychology* 79, 1007–1021.

4 *That research culminated:* Twenge, J. M. (2006). *Generation Me: Why today's young Americans are more confident, assertive, entitled—and more miserable than ever before.* New York: Free Press. Twenge, J. M. (2014). *Generation Me: Why today's young Americans are more confident, assertive, entitled—and more miserable than ever before.* 2nd ed. New York: Atria Books.

5 *"I am not a true"*: Juliet Lapidos. Wait, what, I'm a Millennial? *New York Times*, February 4, 2015.

7 *"We think it's the name"*: Bruce Horovitz. After Gen X, Millennials, what should next generation be? *USA Today*, May 4, 2012.

7 *be called the* Homelanders: Neil Howe. Introducing the Homeland generation. *Forbes*, October 27, 2014.

8 *In 2015, teens polled by MTV*: Josh Sanburn. Here's what MTV is calling the generation after Millennials. *Time*, December 1, 2015.

8 *As far as I know*: Twenge. *Generation Me*. The term *iGen* is used on p. 6 in the April 2006 hardcover edition, as well as in the 2007 paperback edition. I also mentioned the term *iGen* in the Q&A on the Generation Me web page and named my consulting firm iGenConsulting.

10 *Using the birth years 1995 to 2012*: U.S. Census data, Current Population Survey.

Chapter 1: In No Hurry

18 *"Childhood is gone"*: Sales, N. J. (2016). *American girls: Social media and the secret lives of teenagers*. New York: Knopf.

19 *iGen teens are less likely*: Twenge, J. M., & Park, H. (in press). The decline in adult activities among U.S. adolescents: 1976–2016. *Child Development*.

20 *Bill Yates*: Brandon Griggs. "A real slice of time": Scenes from a 1970s roller rink. CNN.com, October 6, 2016.

24 *An approach called*: Ellis, B. J., Del Giudice, M., Dishion, T. J., Figuerdo, A. J., Gray, P., Griskevicius, V., Hawley, P. H., Jacobs, W. J., James, J., Volk, A. A., & Wilson, D. S. (2012). The evolutionary basis for risky adolescent behavior: Implications for science, policy, and practice. *Developmental Psychology* 48, 598–623. Mittal, C., & Griskevicius, V. (2014). Sense of control under uncertainty depends on people's childhood environment: A life history theory approach. *Journal of Personality and Social Psychology* 107, 621–637.

27 *As of 2016, forty-nine states*: Governors Highway Safety Association. Teen and novice drivers.

28 *Someone saw the children*: Kelly Wallace. Maryland family under investigation for letting their kids walk home alone. CNN.com, January 21, 2015.

28 *In a 2015 poll*: Peter Moore. Little interest in "free range" parenting. YouGov, April 20, 2015.

31 *Fewer teens work during the summer*: Catey Hill. American teens don't want to work. MarketWatch, August 4, 2014. Catey Hill. Sasha Obama aside, fewer than one in three American teens gets a summer job. MarketWatch, August 5, 2016.

37 *A study of this trend*: Jager, J., Schulenberg, J. E., O'Malley, P. M., & Bachman, J. G. (2013). Historical variation in drug use trajectories across the transition to adulthood: The trend toward lower intercepts and steeper, ascending slopes. *Development and Psychopathology* 25, 527–543.

38 *As one college student put it*: Schulenberg, J. E., & Maggs, J. L. (2002). A developmental perspective on alcohol use and heavy drinking during adolescence and the transition to young adulthood. *Journal of Studies on Alcohol*, suppl. 14, 54–70.

41 *In a 2014 op-ed:* David Finkelhor. Are kids getting more virtuous? *Washington Post*, November 26, 2014.

41 *A 2016* Post *article continued:* Christopher Ingraham. Today's teens are way better behaved than you were. *Washington Post*, December 13, 2016.

41 *Williams describes iGen as "boring":* Jess Williams. Are my generation really as boring as everyone says? *New Statesman*, September 19, 2014.

41 *One magazine agreed:* Rachael Dove. Charting the rise of Generation Yawn: 20 is the new 40. *Telegraph*, August 31, 2014.

42 *Around the world, young adults:* Twenge, J. M., & Campbell, W. K. (2017). Cultural individualism is linked to later onset of adult-role responsibilities across regions and time. Unpublished manuscript.

45 *A recent study found:* Smith, A., Bodell, L. P., Holm-Denoma, J., Joiner, T., Gordon, K., Perez, M., & Keel, P. (2017). "I don't want to grow up, I'm a [Gen X, Y, Me] kid": Increasing maturity fears across the decades. *International Journal of Behavioral Development*.

46 *A 2016 article in* Adweek: Christine Birkner. Brands are reaching out to Millennials who want a break from "adulting": Coloring books, summer camps, and nice, hot meals. *Adweek*, April 10, 2016.

46 *In a 2013 poll, 85%:* Emily Alpert. Kids like being kids, study finds, perhaps thanks to parenting. *Los Angeles Times*, July 21, 2013.

46 *When 7-year-old Hannah was asked:* Ibid.

47 *observed Julie Lythcott-Haims:* Julie Lythcott-Haims. The over-parenting trap: How to avoid "checklisted" childhoods and raise adults. *Time*, June 9, 2015.

47 *One safe space, for example:* Judith Shulevitz. In college and hiding from scary ideas. *New York Times*, March 21, 2015.

Chapter 2: Internet

49 *The New York Police Department's 33rd Precinct:* Ben Hooper. New York Police: Don't put charging phones under pillow. UPI, February 16, 2016.

49 *A similar incident :* Daniel Bean. Girl's Galaxy S4 smartphone burns under her pillow as she sleeps. Yahoo! Tech, July 28, 2014.

55 *The* Washington Post *recently profiled Katherine:* Jessica Contrera. 13, right now: What it's like to grow up in the age of likes, lols and longing. *Washington Post*, May 25, 2016.

57 *"You realize how insane":* Quoted in Sales, N. J. (2016). *American girls: Social media and the secret lives of teenagers.* New York: Knopf.

57 *In fall 2016:* Lauren Johnson. Snapchat beats Instagram and Facebook as the top social platform for teens: Study finds 80% use the app once a month. *Adweek*, October 14, 2016.

57 *by spring 2016:* Shannon Greenwood, Andrew Perrin, and Maeve Duggan. Social media update 2016. Pew Research Center, November 11, 2016.

60 *In the late 1970s:* Twenge, J. M., Martin, G. E., & Spitzberg, B. (2017). Trends in U.S. adolescents' media use, 1976–2015: The rise of the Internet, the decline of TV, and the (near) demise of print. Manuscript under review.

60 *a 2014 Pew Research Center study:* Kathryn Zickhur and Lee Rainie. Younger Americans and public libraries. Pew Research Center, September 10, 2014.

61 *Some researchers have argued:* Robinson, J. P. (2011). Arts and leisure participation among IT users: Further evidence of time enhancement over time displacement. *Social Science Computer Review* 29, 470–480.

62 *When NPR asked:* Jennifer Ludden. Why aren't teens reading like they used to? NPR, May 12, 2014.

63 *As one teen put it:* How the new generation of well-wired multitaskers is changing campus culture. *Chronicle of Higher Education*, January 5, 2007.

64 *One study installed a program:* Yeykelis, L., Cummings, J. J., & Reeves, B. (2014). Multitasking on a single device: Arousal and the frequency, anticipation, and prediction of switching between media content on a computer. *Journal of Communication* 64, 167–192.

Chapter 3: In Person No More

70 *iGen teens spend less time:* Twenge, J. M., & Uhls, Y. T. (2017). Less in-person social interaction among U.S. adolescents in the 21st century and links to loneliness. Unpublished manuscript.

74 *so many malls across the country have closed:* Aaron Smith. Once the world's biggest mall is being torn down today. CNN.com, December 30, 2014.

78 *One study asked college students:* Kross, E., Verduyn, P., Demiralp, E., Park, J., Lee, D. S., Lin, N., Shablack, H., Jonides, J., & Ybarra, O. (2013). Facebook use predicts declines in subjective well-being in young adults. PLOS ONE 8, e69841.

79 *Another study of adults:* Shakya, H. B., & Christakis, N. A. (2017). Association of Facebook use with compromised well-being: A longitudinal study. *American Journal of Epidemiology* 18, 203–211.

79 *A third study randomly assigned:* Tromholt, M. (2016). The Facebook experiment: Quitting Facebook leads to higher levels of well-being. *Cyberpsychology, Behavior, and Social Networking* 19, 661–666. The Facebook experiment: Does social media affect the quality of our lives? Happiness Research Institute, 2016.

86 *"They said, 'Nobody likes you'":* Sales, N. J. (2016). *American girls: Social media and the secret lives of teenagers.* New York: Knopf.

86 *David Molak was:* Madalyn Mendoza. Alamo Heights student was a victim of bullying before committing suicide, family says. *San Antonio Express-News*, January 8, 2016. Melissa Fletcher Stoeltje and John Tedesco. Who's to blame in David Molak's death? *San Antonio Express-News*, January 16, 2016.

87 *Gabby Douglas, the Olympic gymnast:* Lindsay Kimble. Gabby Douglas cried "gallons" after Olympics cyberbullying—and is now dedicated to helping fellow victims. *People*, December 22, 2016.

87 *One set of studies:* Justin W. Patchin and Sameer Hinduja. Summary of our cyberbullying research (2004–2016). Lifetime cyberbullying victimization rates, ten different studies 2007–2016 [graph]. Cyberbullying Research Center.

89 *We found that even a brief:* Twenge, J. M., Baumeister, R. F., Tice, D. M., & Stucke, T. S. (2001). If you can't join them, beat them: Effects of social exclusion on aggressive behavior. *Journal of Personality and Social Psychology* 81, 1058–1069. Twenge, J. M., Catanese, K. R., & Baumeister, R. F. (2002). Social exclusion causes self-defeating behavior. *Journal of Personality and Social Psychology* 83, 606–615. Twenge, J. M., Catanese, K. R., & Baumeister, R. F. (2003). Social exclusion and the deconstructed state: Time perception,

meaninglessness, lethargy, lack of emotion, and self-awareness. *Journal of Personality and Social Psychology* 85, 409–423.

89 *Neuroscientists have found:* Eisenberger, N. I., Lieberman, M. D., & Williams, K. D. (2003). Does rejection hurt? An fMRI study of social exclusion. *Science* 302, 290–292.

89 *One study had college students:* Sherman, L. E., Minas, M., & Greenfield, P. M. (2013). The effects of text, audio, video, and in-person communication on bonding between friends. *Cyberpsychology: Journal of Psychosocial Research on Cyberspace*, 7.

89 *"I find [social media] really stressful":* Kathy Evans. Are digital natives really just digital labourers? Teens turning off social media. *The Age*, May 15, 2016.

90 *In one study, 6th graders:* Uhls, Y. T., Michikyan, M., Morris, J., Garcia, D., Small, G. S., Zgourou, E., & Greenfeld, P. M. (2014). Five days at outdoor education camp without screens improves preteen skills with nonverbal emotion cues. *Computers in Human Behavior* 39, 387–392.

Chapter 4: Insecure

93   *UC Berkeley student Ilaf Esuf:* Ilaf Esuf. I'm fine, I promise. *Daily Californian*, July 29, 2016.

94   *As the tide of individualism rose:* Reynolds, J., Stewart, M., MacDonald, R., & Sischo, L. (2006). Have adolescents become too ambitious? High school seniors' educational and occupational plans, 1976 to 2000. *Social Problems* 53, 186–206. Twenge, J. M., Campbell, W. K., & Gentile, B. (2013). Changes in pronoun use in American books and the rise of individualism, 1960–2008. *Journal of Cross-Cultural Psychology* 44, 406–415. Twenge, J. M., Campbell, W. K., & Gentile, B. (2012). Increases in individualistic words and phrases in American books, 1960–2008. PLOS ONE 7, e40181. Twenge, J. M., Campbell, W. K., & Gentile, B. (2012). Generational increases in agentic self-evaluations among American college students, 1966–2009. *Self and Identity* 11, 409–427.

95   *Then iGen arrived, and happiness began to falter.* Twenge, J. M., & Martin, G. E., & Campbell, W. K. (2017). Decreases in psychological well-being among American adolescents since 2012 and the rise of smartphone technology. Manuscript under review.

96   *Thirteen-year-old Grace Nazarian:* Lisa A. Flam. Social media means kids are excluded in real time. *Today*, March 17, 2015.

100 *These administrators say:* College counseling centers face "perfect storm," expert says. CU-CitizenAccess.org, August 27, 2012. Novotney, A. (2014). Students under pressure: College and university counseling centers are examining how best to serve the growing number of students seeking their services. *Monitor on Psychology* 45, 36.

100 *teens' depressive symptoms have skyrocketed:* Twenge, J. M., Martin, G. E., & Campbell, W. K. (2017). Decreases in depressive symptoms, suicide-related outcomes, and suicide rates among U.S. adolescents after 2010 and links to increased new media screen time. Manuscript under review.

101 *Megan Armstrong:* Laura Heck. A generation on edge: A look at millennials and mental health. *Vox Magazine*, November 19, 2015.

102 *On Tumblr, a microblogging site:* Rebecca Ruiz. Teens are struggling with their mental health—and talking about it on social media. Mashable, May 3, 2017.

102 *"If you wanted to create":* Susanna Schrobsdorff. Anxiety, depression, and the modern adolescent. *Time*, November 7, 2016.

103 *"We're the first generation":* Ibid.

105 *An exchange among three 16-year-old girls:* Sales, N. J. (2016). *American girls: Social media and the secret lives of teenagers.* New York: Knopf.

106 *Nineteen-year-old Essena O'Neill:* Megan McCluskey. Instagram star Essena O'Neill breaks her silence on quitting social media. *Time,* January 5, 2016. Megan McClusky. Teen Instagram star speaks out about the ugly truth behind social media fame. *Time,* November 2, 2015.

107 *Madison Holleran was everything:* Kate Fagan. Split image. ESPN, May 7, 2015.

108 *The study is specifically designed:* Mojtabai, R., Olfson, M., & Han, B. (2016). National trends in the prevalence and treatment of depression in adolescents and young adults. *Pediatrics* 138.

109 *"Every single week we have a girl":* Schrobsdorff. Anxiety, depression, and the modern adolescent.

109 *one mother found that :* Ibid.

110 *A high school classmate once confided:* Whitney Howard. It's okay if you're struggling with mental health. *Utah Statesman,* March 20, 2016.

110 *After declining during the 1990s:* Curtin, S. C., Warner, M., & Hedegaard, H. Increase in suicide in the United States, 1999–2014. NCHS Data Brief no. 214, April 2016. Sabrina Tavernise. U.S. suicide rate surges to a 30-year high. *New York Times,* April 22, 2016.

111 *An article in* The Atlantic: Lucy Dwyer. When anxiety hits at school. *The Atlantic,* October 3, 2014.

112 *experiments that randomly assign:* Tromholt, M. (2016). The Facebook experiment: Quitting Facebook leads to higher levels of well-being. *Cyberpsychology, Behavior, and Social Networking* 19, 661–666. Sherman, L. E., Minas, M., & Greenfield, P. M. (2013). The effects of text, audio, video, and in-person communication on bonding between friends. *Cyberpsychology: Journal of Psychosocial Research on Cyberspace,* 7.

112 *One study asked college students:* LeMoyne, T., & Buchanan, T. (2011). Does "hovering" matter? Helicopter parenting and its effect on well-being. *Sociological Spectrum* 31, 399–418.

113 *As Asbury University student Alyssa Driscoll wrote:* Alyssa Driscoll. Twenty One Pilots' new song really GETS US. The Lala, April 24, 2015.

113 *"I stay up all night":* Sales (2016). *American girls.*

114 *More teens now sleep less than seven hours most nights:* Twenge, J. M., Krizan, Z., & Hisler, G. (2017). Decreases in sleep duration among U.S. adolescents 1991–2105 and links to screen time. Manuscript under review.

115 *An extensive meta-analysis:* Carter, B., Rees, P., Hale, L., Bhattacharjee, D., & Paradkar, M. S. (2016). Association between portable screen-based media device access or use and sleep outcomes: A systematic review and meta-analysis. *JAMA Pediatrics* 170, 1202–1208.

116 *Sleep deprivation is linked:* Altman, N. G., Izci-Balserak, B., Schopfer, E., et al. (2012). Sleep duration versus sleep insufficiency as predictors of cardiometabolic health outcomes. *Sleep Medicine* 13, 1261–1270. Meerlo, P., Sgoifo, A., & Suchecki, D. (2008). Restricted and disrupted sleep: Effects on autonomic function, neuroendocrine stress systems and stress responsivity. *Sleep Medicine Reviews* 12, 197–210. Owens, J. (2015). Insufficient sleep in adolescents and young adults: An update on causes and consequences. *Pediatrics* 134, e921–e932.

116 *people who don't sleep enough:* Ilardi, S. (2010). *The depression cure.* New York: Da Capo.

117 *Brian Go, a junior at Caltech:* Robin Wilson. An epidemic of anguish. *Chronicle of Higher Education,* September 4, 2015.

117 *After Shefali Arora ran through:* Ibid.

118 *"I worry about the lack":* Logan Jones. Mental health week only works if we let it. *Utah Statesman,* March 24, 2016.

118 *"If I thought I might":* Cooper Lund. Cooper Lund on the weight of depression, ending mental illness stigma. *Daily Oklahoman,* December 6, 2015.

Chapter 5: Irreligious

119 *Their skateboard park:* Naftali Bendavid. Europe's empty churches go on sale. *Wall Street Journal,* January 2, 2015.

120 *The few changes that did appear:* Smith, C., & Snell, P. (2009). *Souls in transition: The religious and spiritual lives of emerging adults.* New York: Oxford University Press.

120 *As studies by the Pew Research Center showed:* America's changing religious landscape. Pew Research Center, May 12, 2015.

121 *Beginning in the 1990s:* Twenge, J. M., Sherman, R. A., Exline, J. J., & Grubbs, J. B. (2016). Declines in American adults' religious participation and beliefs, 1972–2014. *Sage Open,* 6, 1–13. Twenge, J. M., Exline, J. J., Grubbs, J. B., Sastry, R., & Campbell, W. K. (2015). Generational and time period differences in American adolescents' religious orientation, 1966–2014. PLOS ONE 10, e0121454.

124 *In an interview on NPR:* Tom Gjelten. Causes and consequences of declining religious affiliation in the U.S. *Diane Rehm Show,* NPR, May 13, 2015.

130 *a recent study found:* Charles Tyler. (2011). True love isn't waiting. *Neue* 6, 32–36.

130 *the religious scholar Robert Fuller:* Fuller, Robert. (2001). *Spiritual but not religious: Understanding unchurched America.* New York: Oxford University Press.

131 *When sociologist Christian Smith interviewed:* Smith & Snell (2009). *Souls in transition.*

132 *For years, religious scholars:* Becka A. Alper. Millennials are less religious than older Americans, but just as spiritual. Pew Research Center, November 23, 2015. Berger, P. L. (2011). *The sacred canopy: Elements of a sociological theory of religion.* New York: Open Road Media. Berger, P. L., Davie, G., & Fokas, E. (2008). *Religious America, secular Europe? A theme and variation.* Burlington, VT: Ashgate. Finke, R., & Stark, R. (2005). *The churching of America, 1776–2005: Winners and losers in our religious economy.* New Brunswick, NJ: Rutgers University Press. Fuller. *Spiritual but not religious.* Religion among the Millennials. Pew Research Center, February 17, 2010. Putnam, R. D., & Campbell, D. E. (2012). *American grace: How religion divides us and unites us.* New York: Simon & Schuster. Smith & Snell (2009). *Souls in transition.* Smith, T. W. (2012). Beliefs about God across time and countries. NORC.org.

138 *To more precisely analyze:* Twenge et al. (2015). Generational and time period differences in American adolescents' religious orientation, 1966–2014.

138 *When Christian Smith interviewed:* Smith, C., & Denton, M. L. (2009). *Soul searching: The religious and spiritual lives of American teenagers.* London: Oxford University Press.

139 *For example, half:* Kinnaman, D. (2016). *You lost me: Why young Christians are leaving church . . . and rethinking faith.* Grand Rapids, MI: Baker Books.

139 *A 2012 survey of 18- to 24-year-olds:* Robert P. Jones. Why are Millennials leaving the church? Huffington Post, July 8, 2012.

140 *David Kinnaman's book* unChristian *reported:* Kinnaman, D., & Lyons, G. (2012). *unChristian: What a new generation really thinks about Christianity . . . and why it matters.* Grand Rapids, MI: Baker Books.

141 *one church in Oregon:* Ibid.

141 *"This is family":* Clarice Silber and Dan Reiner. As churches prepare to close, parishioners mourn. *Journal News*, July 7, 2015.

142 *"At the end of the day":* Gjelten. Causes and consequences of declining religious affiliation in the U.S.

142 *Others see positives:* Ibid.

Chapter 6: Insulated but Not Intrinsic

145 *A 2016 survey asked:* John Beltz Snyder. Millennials don't want cars, but Generation Z does. Autoblog, March 16, 2016.

150 *sexual assault is actually less common:* David Finkelhor and Lisa Jones. Have sexual abuse and physical abuse declined since the 1990s? Crimes Against Children Research Center, November 2012.

152 *Former* Village Voice *rock critic Richard Goldstein:* Richard Goldstein. Today's no-risk kids don't get the '60s. The Daily Beast, May 13, 2015.

153 *When the writer Claire Fox:* Fox, C. (2017). *"I find that offensive!"* London: Biteback Publishing. Claire Fox. Generation Snowflake: How we train our kids to be censorious cry-babies. *The Spectator*, June 4, 2016.

154 *Greg Lukianoff and Jonathan Haidt's much-discussed:* Greg Lukianoff and Jonathan Haidt. The coddling of the American mind. *The Atlantic*, September 2015.

154 *As Josh Zeitz put it:* Josh Zeitz. Campus protesters aren't reliving the 1960s. *Politico Magazine*, December 21, 2015.

156 *When Williams College "disinvited":* Jonathan H. Adler. Suzanne Venker is unwelcome at Williams College. *Washington Post*, October 22, 2015.

156 *In his piece "I'm a Liberal Professor":* Edward Schlosser. I'm a liberal professor, and my liberal students terrify me. Vox, June 3, 2015.

156 *As Northwestern University professor Laura Kipnis wrote:* Laura Kipnis. My Title IX Inquisition. *Chronicle of Higher Education*, May 31, 2015.

157 *Everett Piper:* Susan Svrluga. College president: "This is not a day care. This is a university!" *Washington Post*, November 30, 2015.

158 *In October 2015, the administration:* Email from Erika Christakis: "Dressing yourselves," email to Silliman College (Yale) students on Halloween costumes. The Fire, October 30, 2015.

158 *A group of protestors then confronted:* Conor Friedersdorf. The perils of writing a provocative email at Yale. *The Atlantic*, May 26, 2016.

159 *As Yale faculty wrote:* A. Douglas Stone and Mary Schwab-Stone. The sheltering campus: Why college is not home. *New York Times*, February 5, 2016.

159 *the sociologists Bradley Campbell and Jason Manning argued:* Campbell, B., & Manning, J. (2014). Microaggression and moral cultures. *Comparative Sociology* 13, 692–726.

161 *In* The Atlantic, *Conor Friedersdorf argued:* Conor Friedersdorf. The rise of victimhood culture. *The Atlantic*, September 11, 2015.

161 *protestors shouted at campus administrators:* Sam Budnyk. Emory students express discontent with administrative response to Trump chalkings. *Emory Wheel,* March 22, 2016.

161 *"I had no idea":* Matt Taibbi. College kids aren't the only ones demanding "safe spaces." *Rolling Stone,* April 6, 2016.

161 *Another incident occurred:* Jamie Ballard, Will Fritz, and Jacob Sisneros. Hundreds of students protest President Hirshman regarding BDS posters. *Daily Aztec,* April 27, 2016.

161 *Student protestors believed:* Ibid. Astrid Solorzano and Bree Steffen. SDSU students corner President Hirshman in car, demand response for anti-Islamic flyers. ABC 10 News, April 27, 2016.

162 *Lukianoff and Haidt argued:* Lukianoff and Haidt. The coddling of the American mind.

162 *In a* New York Times *op-ed:* Judith Shulevitz. In college and hiding from scary ideas. *New York Times,* March 21, 2015.

164 *As Hanna Rosin observed:* Hanna Rosin. The overprotected kid. *The Atlantic,* April 2014.

164 *In 1969, 48%:* How children get to school: School travel patterns from 1969 to 2009. National Center for Safe Routes to School, November 2011.

164 *An elementary school in Michigan:* Tim Cushing. Schools ban tag, cartwheels and "unstructured play": The inevitable outcome of unrealistic promises and expectations. Techdirt, October 10, 2013.

164 *Another school banned cartwheels:* Ibid.

164 *Many cities have banned street hockey:* Colin Horgan. Game off! Why the decline of street hockey is a crisis for our kids. *Guardian,* July 5, 2016.

164 *In a recent poll, 70%:* Peter Moore. Little interest in "free range" parenting. YouGov, April 20, 2015.

165 *Hanna Rosin argued in* The Atlantic: Rosin. The overprotected kid.

166 *In her book* A Nation of Wimps: Marano, H. E. (2008). A nation of wimps: The high cost of invasive parenting. New York: Crown Archetype.

166 *Lenore Skenazy made the case:* Skenazy, L. (2010). *Free-range kids: How to raise safe, self-reliant children (without going nuts with worry).* New York: Jossey-Bass.

166 *"Society has forced us":* Horgan. Game off! Why the decline of street hockey is a crisis for our kids.

167 *For example, a 2013* New York Times *op-ed:* Emily Esfahani Smith and Jennifer L. Aaker. Millennial searchers. *New York Times,* November 30, 2013.

167 *However, that survey queried:* The future of millennials' careers. Career Advisory Board and Harris Interactive, January 28, 2011.

Chapter 7: Income Insecurity

181 *slightly* fewer *iGen'ers and late Millennials:* Twenge, J. M., Campbell, S. M., Hoffman, B. R., & Lance, C. E. (2010). Generational differences in work values: Leisure and extrinsic values increasing, social and intrinsic values decreasing. *Journal of Management* 36, 1117–1142.

183 *In 2016, an article in* Forbes: Caroline Beaton. Science sets us straight on Yelp CEO letter scandal: The truth about the Millennial work ethic. *Forbes,* February 24, 2016.

185 *the wages of Americans:* The rising cost of not going to college. Pew Research Center, February 11, 2014.

185 *The average student graduating:* Aimee Picchi. Congrats, class of 2016: You're the most indebted yet. CBS MoneyWatch, May 4, 2016. Jillian Berman. Class of 2015 has the most student debt in U.S. history. MarketWatch, May 9, 2015.

186 *A report by the advertising firm:* Alex Williams. Move over, Millennials, here comes Generation Z. *New York Times,* September 18, 2015.

186 *"Millennials are realizing":* Rob Asghar. Study: Millennials are the true entrepreneur generation. *Forbes,* November 11, 2014.

186 *iGen'ers are actually* less *likely:* Campbell, S. M., Campbell, W. K., & Twenge, J. M. (in press). Bright and fuzzy lines: Making sense of the differences between generations. *Work, Aging, and Retirement.*

186 *A Wall Street Journal analysis:* Ruth Simon and Caelainn Barr. Endangered species: Young U.S. entrepreneurs. *Wall Street Journal,* January 2, 2015. Maria Hollenhorst. Millennials want to be entrepreneurs, but a tough economy stands in their way. NPR, September 26, 2016.

188 *"Every time I see it":* Erik Hurst. Video killed the radio star: How games, phones, and other tech innovations are changing the labor force. Chicago Booth Review, September 1, 2016. Derek Thompson. The free-time paradox in America. *The Atlantic,* September 13, 2016.

189 *Hurst found a simple answer:* Hurst. Video killed the radio star.

193 *However, as women make up 57%:* U.S. National Center for Education Statistics, Digest of Education Statistics.

193 *female physicians make $20,000 a year less:* Catherine Saint Louis. Dr. Paid Less: An old title still fits female physicians. *New York Times,* July 11, 2016.

195 *At 25% of the population:* Ninety-two percent of GenZ teens own or plan to own a vehicle, according to Autotrader, Kelley Blue Book study. Autotrader press release, March 16, 2016.

198 *A 2016 survey:* Ibid.

199 *In 2016,* Harper's Bazaar *ran an article:* Kerry Pieri. The jean scene: The 12 coolest trends in denim now. *Harper's Bazaar,* March 17, 2016.

199 *The British writer Rachael Dove:* Rachael Dove. Charting the rise of Generation Yawn: 20 is the new 40. *Telegraph,* August 31, 2014.

200 *Compared to Millennials recalling:* John Beltz Snyder. Millennials don't want cars, but Generation Z does. Autoblog, March 16, 2016.

200 *Of all the generations, Millennials:* Waggle Dance Marketing Research, Spring 2016 Snacking survey, waggledance-marketing.com.

Chapter 8: Indefinite

203 *"Our 20s are meant":* Leigh Taveroff. 8 reasons why relationships in your 20s just don't work. TodaysLifestyle.com, May 21, 2015.

204 *In 2015, a* Vanity Fair *article:* Nancy Jo Sales. Tinder and the dawn of the "dating apocalypse." *Vanity Fair,* September 2015.

205 *iGen'ers' and Millennials' attitudes toward sex:* Twenge, J. M., Sherman, R. A., & Wells, B. E. (2015). Changes in American adults' sexual behavior and attitudes. *Archives of Sexual Behavior* 44, 2273–2285.

206 *Boomer women born in the 1940s:* Wells, B. E., & Twenge, J. M. (2005). Changes in young people's sexual behavior and attitudes, 1943–1999: A cross-temporal meta-analysis. *Review of General Psychology* 9, 249–261.

206 *When Peggy Orenstein interviewed teens:* Orenstein, P. (2016). *Girls & sex: Navigating the new landscape.* New York: Harper.

207 *more young adults are not having sex at all:* Twenge, J. M., Sherman, R. A., & Wells, B. E. (in press). Sexual inactivity during young adulthood is more common among U.S. Millennials and iGen: Age, period, and cohort effects on having no sexual partners after age 18. *Archives of Sexual Behavior.*

207 *a* Los Angeles Times *news story:* Melissa Batchelor Warnke. Millennials are having less sex than any generation in 60 years: Here's why it matters. *Los Angeles Times*, August 3, 2016.

208 *"Sex . . . [is] not something":* Brogan Driscoll. Five "sexually inactive" Millennials on why they aren't having sex. Huffington Post, May 8, 2016.

209 *one study found that teen births:* Kearney, M. S., & Levine, P. B. (2014). Media influences on social outcomes: The impact of MTV's 16 and Pregnant on teen childbearing. NBER Working Paper No. 19795. Jacque Wilson. Study: MTV's "*16 and Pregnant*" led to fewer teen births. CNN.com, January 13, 2014.

209 *"There are just so many risks":* Driscoll. Five "sexually inactive" Millennials on why they aren't having sex.

210 *"I would do really graphic sexting":* Orenstein. *Girls & sex.*

210 *One study found that the teen birthrate:* Guldi, M., & Herbst, M. (2015). Offline effects of online connecting: The impact of broadband diffusion on teen fertility decisions. IZA Discussion Paper no. 9076. Internet access and the decline in teen childbearing. The National Campaign to Prevent Teen and Unplanned Pregnancy, September 9, 2015.

210 *As a* Washington Post *article:* Danielle Paquette and Weiyi Cai. Why American teenagers are having much less sex. *Washington Post*, July 22, 2015.

211 *Claudia, 19, told the* Washington Post: Tara Bahrampour. "There isn't really anything magical about it": Why more Millennials are avoiding sex. *Washington Post*, August 2, 2016.

211 *Indiana University Southeast student Jennifer:* Sales. Tinder and the dawn of the "dating apocalypse."

211 *"Maybe Netflix has replaced sex?":* Driscoll. Five "sexually inactive" Millennials on why they aren't having sex.

211 *when the sociologist Lisa Wade interviewed:* Wade, L. (2017). *American hookup: The new culture of sex on campus.* New York: W. W. Norton & Company.

212 *watching a porn video in the last year:* Price, J., Patterson, R., Regenerus, M., & Walley, J. (2016). How much more XXX is Generation X consuming? Evidence of changing attitudes and behaviors related to pornography since 1973. *Journal of Sex Research* 53, 12–20.

212 *As early as 2005:* Wolak, J., Mitchell, K., & Finkelhor, D. (2007). Unwanted and wanted exposure to online pornography in a national sample of youth Internet users. *Pediatrics* 119, 247–257.

212 *Noah Patterson, 18:* Bahrampour. "There isn't really anything magical about it." (Version on the Hartford Courant website.)

212 *A 2016* Time *magazine cover story:* Belinda Luscombe. Porn and the threat to virility. *Time,* March 31, 2016.

213 *As Wade told Minnesota Public Radio:* Sex? More millennials are saying "meh." Minnesota Public Radio, August 18, 2016.

214 *"I have students who say":* Orenstein. *Girls & sex.*

215 *"I question the assumption":* Flannery James. Love isn't always worth the risk (letter to the editor). *Columbia Spectator,* February 2, 2016.

215 *"There's this idea now":* Orenstein, *Girls & sex.*

215 *"Like your boyfriend could have been":* Sales, N. J. (2016). *American girls: Social media and the secret lives of teenagers.* New York: Knopf.

216 *"Being sober makes it seem":* Ibid.

216 *One study found that the average college hookup:* Ibid. Online College Social Life Survey, http://www.nyu.edu/projects/england/ocsls.

216 *In* American Hookup, *one college woman:* Wade. *American hookup.*

217 *One website offered "32 Signs":* Danielle Pryor. 32 signs you're catching feelings for your f*ck buddy. Pucker Mob.

217 *Another website for college students:* The relationship game: How to avoid catching feelings for someone. College Times.

217 *"The worst thing you can get called":* Sex? More millennials are saying "meh."

217 *Ghosting, wrote Columbia University:* Madison Ailts. The haunting reality of ghosting. *Columbia Spectator,* April 7, 2016.

218 *As Kate Hakala wrote on Mic.com:* Kate Hakala. 20-somethings have invented a new relationship status, and it's called "dating partner." Mic.com, February 20, 2015.

218 *Two recent surveys found:* Wade. *American hookup.*

218 *"There's this disconnect":* Sex? More millennials are saying "meh."

218 *As a 19-year-old put it:* Sales. *American girls.*

221 *when Barnard College student Melyssa Luxenberg:* Ariela Martin. Engaged at 20: Meet Melyssa, BC '18. *Columbia Spectrum,* December 1, 2015.

222 *US marriage rate:* Lois M. Collins. U.S. marriage rate hits new low and may continue to decline. *Deseret News,* May 20, 2015.

223 *Percentage of 18- to 29-year-olds:* Lydia Saad. Fewer young people say I do—to any relationship. Gallup, June 8, 2015.

224 *Take Louis Tomlinson:* Louis Tomlinson is going to be a dad! One Direction star expecting baby with Briana Jungwirth. *People,* July 14, 2015.

225 *Women's ages at reproductive milestones:* Finer, L. B., & Philbin, J. M. (2014). Trends in ages at key reproductive transitions in the United States, 1951–2010. *Women's Health Issues* 24, 271–279.

225 *by 2016, Tomlinson and Jungwirth:* Kathleen Harper. Louis Tomlinson & Briana Jungwirth custody battle: She doesn't want his GF near Freddie. Hollywood Life, June 30, 2016.

225 *after rising for decades:* Births: Final data for 2014. *National Vital Statistics Reports,* December 23, 2015.

Chapter 9: Inclusive

227 *Snickers tweeted a picture:* Jarry Lee. 32 of the best brand tweets celebrating marriage equality. Buzzfeed, June 26, 2015.

228 *As the country singer Kacey Musgraves:* Sam Lansky. Kacey Musgraves takes twang into the 21st century. *Time,* June 18, 2015.

228 *The 2000s and 2010s ushered in:* Twenge, J. M., Sherman, R. A., & Wells, B. E. (2015). Changes in American adults' sexual behavior and attitudes. *Archives of Sexual Behavior* 44, 2273–2285. Twenge, J. M., Carter, N. T., & Campbell, W. K. (2015). Time period, generational, and age differences in tolerance for controversial beliefs and lifestyles in the U.S., 1972–2012. *Social Forces* 94, 379–399.

229 *Anthony Liveris, the vice president:* Cody Permenter. Millennials react to same-sex marriage cases. *USA Today,* March 27, 2013.

232 *the number of young women:* Twenge, J. M., Sherman, R. A., & Wells, B. E. (2016). Changes in American adults' reported same-sex sexual experiences and attitudes. *Archives of Sexual Behavior* 45, 1713–1730.

233 *Raven-Symoné said:* Rachel McRady. Raven-Symone: I don't want to be labeled as gay or African American. *Us Weekly,* October 6, 2014.

233 *Miley Cyrus says she's had relationships:* Sierra Marquina. Miley Cyrus reveals she's had relationships that weren't "straight, heterosexual." *Us Weekly,* May 6, 2015.

234 *In January 2017,* National Geographic *featured Avery:* Susan Goldberg. Why we put a transgender girl on the cover of *National Geographic. National Geographic,* January 2017.

234 *Looking up the definition:* Michelle Ruiz. Jazz Jennings: The transgender teen and wannabe mermaid the Internet needs. *Cosmopolitan,* June 8, 2015.

235 *Will Smith's son Jaden:* Amy Zimmerman. Miley Cyrus and Jaden Smith's "gender fluid" revolution. Slate.com, June 18, 2015.

235 *College senior Justice Gaines:* Mei Novak. Schoolwork, advocacy place strain on student activists. *Brown Daily Herald,* February 18, 2016.

236 *Others prefer to use "they":* Zimmerman. Miley Cyrus and Jaden Smith's "gender fluid" revolution.

237 *more and more Americans agreed:* Donnelly, K., Twenge, J. M., Clark, M. A., Shaikh, S., Beiler-May, A., & Carter, N. T. (2016). Attitudes toward women's work and family roles in the United States, 1976–2013. *Psychology of Women Quarterly* 40, 41–54.

238 *sociologists David Cotter and Joanna Pepin:* Cotter, D., & Pepin, J. (2017) Trending towards traditionalism? Changes in youths' gender ideology. Council on Contemporary Families. https://contemporaryfamilies.org/2-pepin-cotter-traditionalism/.

241 *"All that crap about people's race":* Toni Monkovic. Lasting damage for G.O.P.? Young voters reject Donald Trump. *New York Times,* March 24, 2016.

241 *Men driving by:* Susan Svrluga. What the student body president did after he was called the N-word—again. *Washington Post,* September 16, 2015.

241 *At Clairmont McKenna College in California:* Julie Zellinger. These students were told they don't fit their college's "mold"—but they're fighting back. Mic.com, November 13, 2015.

241 *in a 2016 Pew Research Center poll:* Juliana Menasche Horowitz and Gretchen Livingston. How Americans view the Black Lives Matter movement. Pew Research Center, July 8, 2016.

248 *One University of Wisconsin student:* Daniel Kershner. Eneale shares "L.I.F.E." inspirations. *Daily Cardinal,* March 31, 2016.

248 *When Rutgers University student Yvanna Saint-Fort:* Yvanna Saint-Fort. Be unapologetic about who you are. *Daily Targum,* April 26, 2016.

248 *In a survey of 14- to 24-year-olds:* Jamelle Bouie. Why do millennials not understand racism? Slate.com, May 16, 2014. Links to 2014 MTV/David Binder Research Study. Sean McElwee. Millennials are more racist than they think. *Politico Magazine,* March 9, 2015.

250 *The Pew Research Center found that 40%:* Jacob Poushter. 40% of Millennials OK with limiting speech offensive to minorities. Pew Research Center, November 20, 2015.

251 *When two white fraternity brothers:* Allie Bidwell. Racist fraternity chant learned during leadership cruise. *U.S. News & World Report,* March 27, 2015. Eliott C. McLaughlin. "Disgraceful" University of Oklahoma fraternity shuttered after racist chant. CNN.com, March 10, 2015.

251 *"Speech is powerful":* Lee Ross. Westboro funeral pickets are protected speech, high court rules. Fox News, March 2, 2011.

251 *A Latino student was offended:* Campbell, B., & Manning, J. (2014). Microaggression and moral cultures. *Comparative Sociology* 13, 692–726.

251 *Students at Oberlin College complained:* Justin Wm. Moyer. Oberlin College sushi "disrespectful" to Japanese. *Washington Post,* December 21, 2015.

251 *A Colorado College student was suspended:* Katie Barrows. Colorado College suspends student for two years for six-word joke on Yik Yak. FIRE: Foundation for Individual Rights in Education, December 7, 2015. Courtney Such. College suspends student for six months for saying black women are "not hot." The College Fix, December 14, 2015.

251 *A faculty member at the University of Kansas:* Scott Jaschik. A class implodes over race. Inside Higher Ed, November 23, 2015.

251 *As sophomore Rachel Huebner wrote:* Rachel Huebner. A culture of sensitivity. *Harvard Crimson,* March 23, 2016.

251 *In 2013, the US Departments of Justice and Education:* Greg Lukianoff and Jonathan Haidt. The coddling of the American mind. *The Atlantic,* September 2015.

252 *As Greg Lukianoff and Jonathan Haidt's:* Ibid.

252 *Students at Smith College demanded:* Abby Phillip. One of the most powerful women in the world won't speak at Smith College after protests. *Washington Post,* May 12, 2014.

252 *Rutgers protesters prompted Condoleezza Rice to cancel:* Emma G. Fitzsimmons. Condoleezza Rice backs out of Rutgers speech after student protests. *New York Times,* May 3, 2014.

252 *students at Brandeis blocked Ayaan Hirsi Ali:* Brandeis withdraws honorary degree for Islam critic Ayaan Hirsi Ali. Associated Press, April 9, 2014.

252 *President Obama weighed in:* Sam Sanders. Obama warns campus protestors against urge to "shut up" opposition. NPR, December 21, 2015.

252 *The political scientist April Kelly-Woessner:* April Kelly-Woessner. How Marcuse made today's students less tolerant than their parents. Heterodox Academy, September 23, 2015.

252 *In a 2015 survey, 35%:* Michael McGough. Sorry, kids, the 1st amendment does protect "hate speech." *Los Angeles Times,* October 30, 2015.

253 *The activism soon took a turn:* Justin Wm. Moyer, Michael E. Miller, and Peter Holley. Mass media professor under fire for confronting video journalist at Mizzou. *Washington Post*, November 10, 2015.

253 *When UC Irvine law professors:* Howard Gillman and Erwin Chemerinsky. Don't mock or ignore students' lack of support for free speech. Teach them. *Los Angeles Times*, March 31, 2016.

254 *Comedians such as Chris Rock say:* Caitlin Flanagan. That's not funny! Today's college students can't seem to take a joke. *The Atlantic*, September 2015.

256 *Buzzfeed posted a photo project:* Heben Nigatu. 21 racial microaggressions you hear on a daily basis. Buzzfeed, December 9, 2013.

256 *"What haunts me":* Princess Ojiaku. All snowflakes look the same. *Pacific Standard*, February 28, 2015.

257 *individuals who experience more microaggressions:* D. W. Sue. (2010). *Microaggressions in everyday life: Race, gender, and sexual orientation.* New York: Wiley.

258 *In the MTV survey:* Bouie. Why do millennials not understand racism?

Chapter 10: Independent

260 *In a poll of Democratic voters:* Ronald Brownstein. The great Democratic age gap. *The Atlantic*, February 2, 2016.

260 *As late as mid-July 2016:* Rebecca Savransky. Poll: Nearly half of Sanders's millennial supporters would vote third-party. *The Hill*, July 14, 2016.

260 *Among white voters 18 to 29:* The 2016 youth vote: Youth vote choice by race & ethnicity. CIRCLE: The Center for Information & Research on Civic Learning and Engagement, http://civicyouth.org/quick-facts/youth-voting.

261 *Two months before the election:* Twenge, J. M., Honeycutt, N., Prislin, R., & Sherman, R. A. (2016). More polarized but more independent: Political party identification and ideological self-categorization among U.S. adults, college students, and late adolescents, 1970–2015. *Personality and Social Psychology Bulletin* 42, 1364–1383.

261 *In August 2016, USA Today predicted:* Susan Page and Fernanda Crescente. Young voters flee Donald Trump in what may be historic trouncing, poll shows. *USA Today*, August 14, 2016.

261 *In 2014, the Washington Post announced:* Chris Cillizza. Republicans' young-people problem. *Washington Post*, March 9, 2014.

262 *Boomers were shocked:* Molly Roberts. Why Millennials are yawning at the likely first female major-party nominee for president. *Washington Post*, June 7, 2016.

262 *Eighteen-year-old Josephine Sicking:* Charlotte Alter. Women support Hillary Clinton by large margins. But they're no monolith. *Time*, July 21, 2016.

266 *In an October 2016 poll:* Cohen, C. J., Luttig, M. D., & Rogowski, J. C. (2016). Understanding the Millennial vote in 2016: Findings from GenForward. A survey of the Black Youth Project with the AP-NORC Center for Public Affairs Research. PDF report available on the GenForward website.

267 *How would you feel:* Iyengar, S., Sood, G., & Lelkes, Y. (2012). Affect, not ideology: A social identity perspective on polarization. *Public Opinion Quarterly* 76, 405–431.

268 *"Dear White Millennials":* Tiffany Onyejiaka. To the white Millennials who voted for Donald Trump. Huffington Post, November 10, 2016.

269 *In a 2016 poll:* Partisanship and political animosity in 2016: Highly negative views of the opposing party—and its members. Pew Research Center, June 22, 2016.

270 *belief in its safety has moved in lockstep with views on whether pot should be legal:* Campbell, W. K., Twenge, J. M., & Carter, N. (2017). Support for marijuana (cannabis) legalization: Untangling age, period, and cohort effects. *Collabra: Psychology, 3,* 2.

270 *One 18-year-old iGen'er:* In debate over legalizing marijuana, disagreement over drug's dangers: In their own words: supporters and opponents of legalization. Pew Research Center, April 14, 2015.

276 *Percentage who agree:* Lydia Saad. Americans buy free pre-K; split on tuition-free college. Gallup Poll, May 2, 2016.

277 *A headline-grabbing 2015 poll:* Emily Ekins. Poll: Americans like free markets more than capitalism and socialism more than a govt managed economy. Reason.com. February 12, 2015.

286 *"Although you may not agree":* Emilia Beuger. Bernie Sanders shows compassion and authenticity. *Massachusetts Daily Collegian,* April 19, 2016.

Conclusion

290 *"Ever since my younger sister":* Rachel Walman. Keep your head up and put down your cellphone. *Massachusetts Daily Collegian,* April 6, 2016.

291 *"Social media is destroying our lives":* Nancy Jo Sales. (2016). *American Girls: Social media and the secret lives of teenagers.* New York: Knopf.

292 When New York Times *reporter Nick Bilton:* Alter, Adam. (2017). *Irresistible: The Rise of Addictive Technology and the Business of Keeping Us Hooked.* New York: Penguin Press.

293 *"The social media companies":* Ibid.

293 *Melissa Nilles:* Melissa Nilles. Technology is destroying the quality of human interaction. *Bottom Line,* January 24, 2012.

296 *One 18-year-old interviewed:* Sales. *American Girls.*

296 *"You're surrounded by it":* Rachel Grace. Do it for the 'gram, or don't do it at all. RedAndBlack.com, September 19, 2016.

296 *The* Washington Post *recently profiled:* Jessica Contrera. Their tube: When every moment of childhood can be recorded and shared, what happens to childhood? *Washington Post,* December 7, 2016.

298 *Or you can mimic the response:* Rachel Moss. Teen girl has genius response to guy who asked for shower selfie. Huffington Post, July 11, 2016.

300 *"Sitting in a lecture hall":* Kate Leddy. I skipped class to go to the gym and don't regret it. *Massachusetts Daily Collegian,* February 9, 2016.

304 *At least by their own reports:* Joe O'Shea and Nina Hoe. A gap year could be the answer to the student mental health crisis. Quartz, September 14, 2016.

305 *When Bryce Maine wanted to bring his 69-year-old grandmother:* Travis M. Andrews. A teen asked his grandmother to her first prom. Too old, said the school. *Washington Post,* April 4, 2017.

305 *in fact, I coauthored:* Twenge, J. M., Baumeister, R. F., Tice, D. M., & Stucke, T. S. (2001). If you can't join them, beat them: Effects of social exclusion on aggressive behavior. *Journal of Personality and Social Psychology* 81, 1058–1069. Twenge, J. M., Catanese, K. R., & Baumeister, R. F. (2002). Social exclusion causes self-defeating behavior. *Journal of*

Personality and Social Psychology 83, 606–615. Baumeister, R. F., Twenge, J. M., & Nuss, C. K. (2002). Effects of social exclusion on cognitive processes: Anticipated aloneness reduces intelligent thought. *Journal of Personality and Social Psychology* 83, 817–827.

305 *Aiken Elementary School in West Hartford:* Safe School Climate Plan—Anti-Bullying. Aiken Elementary School website, School Info page.

306 *As the psychologist Nick Haslam points out:* Nick Haslam. How we became a country where bad hair days and campaign signs cause "trauma." *Washington Post*, August 12, 2016. Haslam, N. (2016). Concept creep: Psychology's expanding concepts of harm and pathology. *Psychological Inquiry* 27, 1–17.

Index

Page numbers in *italics* refer to graphs.

A

abortion, 271–73, *271, 272,* 275
academic skills, 111
    SAT scores, 63, *64*
adolescence, 41, 42, 112
adulthood, 45–46, 113
advertisers, 195–97, *197,* 200–201
AdvertisingAge, 7
Adweek, 46
Age, 89
alcohol, *see* drinking
allowances, 34–35, *35*
Alter, Adam, 292
alone:
    feeling, *see* loneliness
    spending time, 28–29, 42, 74–75
American College Health Association (ACHA), *104*
American Freshman (AF) Survey, 9, 103, *105, 220, 250, 252, 271*
American Girls: Social Media and the Secret Lives of Teenagers (Sales), 2, 56, 86, 105, 106, 114, 215, 218, 291, 296
American Hookup (Wade), 211, 216
American Psychiatric Association, 108
Anosike, Chiamaka, 63
anxiety, 103, *104,* 105, 108, 111, 112, 116, 118, 163, 167, 192, 257, 293, 300–302
Arab Spring, 175
Armstrong, Megan, 101
Arora, Shefali, 117
Atlantic, 111, 154, 161, 162, 164, 165, 252, 254
Avenue Q, 212
averages, in data, 14–15
Axler, Abraham, 276

B

Baby Boomers, 3, *6,* 8, 9, 13, 149, 168, 169, 173–74, 196–98, 250, 273, 275, 277, 292
    college as viewed by, 172–73
    individualism and, 94
    LGBT issues and, 228, 229
    marijuana and, 148, 270, 271
    and marriage and raising a family, 218–21, 224
    politics and, 262, 283–84
    race and, 241
    reading and, 60
    religion and, 124, 132
    safety and, 28, 144, 152–53, 164, 165
    social activity and, 74
    and speed of growing up, 20, 24, 26, 28, 29, 40–41, 44
    work and, 182–83, 186–88, 194
bars and nightclubs, 74
Baumeister, Roy, 89
Bell, Leslie, 215
Bennett, Courtney, 254
Beuger, Emilia, 286
Bilton, Nick, 292
birth control, 210
birthrates, 224–26
    teen, 22–23, *23,* 41, 209, 210
    for unmarried mothers, 221, 225–26
Bishop, Faith Ann, 103
Bismire, Amy, 90
Black Lives Matter, 241, 253, 286
blame, for generational changes, 13–14
Blaze, 275
Blockbuster Video, 67
body image, 106, 297
books, 59–65, *61,* 68, 115, 307
    textbooks, 64–65, 171, 307–8
brain, 42–43, 88–89, 144, 295, 296
Bretzke, James, 124, 142
Brown, Michael, 241
Buchanan, Breeon, 278
bullying, 79, 85–88, *86,* 99, 305–6
Bureau of Labor Statistics, *189*
Bush, George W., 267

C

Campbell, Bradley, 159–60
capitalism, 277

Carmichael, Matt, 7
cars:
    driving, *see* driving
    owning, 197–98, 200
Castagnoli, Lorraine, 141
Catanese, Kate, 308
Center for Inquiry, 142
Centers for Disease Control and Prevention
        (CDC), 9, *23, 88, 111,* 151–52, *225*
    Youth Risk Behavior Surveillance System, 9,
        22, 37, 83, *84, 85, 86,* 99, *114, 115, 117,* 150,
        150, 210
charities, 174–75, *174*
Chemerinsky, Erwin, 253–54
child care, 275
children, having, 3, 40, 41, 214, 218–20, *220,*
        223–26
Christakis, Erika, 158
Christakis, Nicolas, 158–59
Church, Noah, 212–13
Church of St. Joseph, 119
CIRP Freshman Survey, *30, 32, 61, 122, 123,* 131,
        168, 172, 174
civic engagement, 173–77, *174, 176, 177,* 281–82,
        281, 286
    see also politics
Clark, Marcia, 193
Clinton, Bill, 228, 267
Clinton, Hillary, 259, 260, 262–63, 280, 283
clothes, 198–99
cognitive behavioral therapy, 162
college, college students, 31–34, 40, 47, 60, 63, 302,
        307–9
    appeals to authorities and, 159–62
    attitudes toward, 169–73, *170, 171, 172*
    costs and student loans, 185, 190, 277, 303, 310
    and degree as necessity, 185
    drinking and, 37–38, 302, 303
    employment and, 189
    gap year between high school and, 303–4
    gender discrimination and, 192, *192,* 193
    government funding of, 275–77, *276*
    mental health issues and, 103–4, *104, 105,* 117,
        301, 303–4
    politics and, 267–68
    race and, 246, 248, 249, 258
    relationships and, 204
    safe spaces and, 47, 153–64, 173, 249–58
    speech restrictions and, 249–58, *250, 253*
community, *see* civic engagement
Cotter, David, 238
Crimes Against Children Research Center, 152
cultural change, 13–15, 24, 290
Current Population Survey, *225, 284*
cutting (self-harm), 108–9, 302
cyberbullying, 79, 85–88, *86,* 99, 305–6
Cyberbulling Research Center, 87
Cyrus, Miley, 233, 236

D

Daily Californian, 93
Daily Oklahoman, 118
Daily Show, The, 246
data, 8–13, 15
dating, 20–22, *21,* 24, 39–41, *40,* 74, 204, 206, 218
death penalty, *271,* 272–73, *272*
DeGeneres, Ellen, 228
demographics, 10–12, 25
depression, 3, 79, 81–84, *82,* 87, 88, 93, 94, 99–113,
        118, 167, 192, 208, 257, 293, 300–302
    clinical-level, 107–10, *109,* 302
    in girls vs. boys, 102–3, *103*
    phones and social media and, 100, 101, 104,
        105, *106,* 111, 118, 291–92
    rise in, 100, 104–5, 108, 111, 293
    sleep and, 116, *117,* 118
    stigmatization of, 118
    suicide, *see* suicide
Depression Cure, The (Ilardi), 300
developmental speed, 24–25, 42
    in iGen, 3, 17–47, 112–13, 144, 159, 163–64,
        204, 302–4
Diagnostic and Statistical Manual (DSM), 108
Douglas, Gabby, 87
Dove, Rachael, 199
drinking, 35–41, *36, 38, 40,* 71, 74, 146–47, 303
    binge, 37–38, 146, 147, *147, 148,* 303
    college and, 37–38, 302, 303
    driving and, 37, 143, 145–46
    safety and, 143–44, 146, *147, 148,* 149
    sex and, 216
Driscoll, Alyssa, 113
driving, 25–28, *26,* 39–42, *40,* 112, 303
    drinking and, 37, 143, 145–46
    safety and, 144–46, *145,* 149, 165, 198
drugs, 38–39, *39,* 148, 269
    marijuana, *see* marijuana

E

emotional attachment, 216–17
emotional injury, 156–57, 167
emotional safety, 144, 153, 156, 157, 173, 253, 305–6
employment, *see* work
entrepreneurship, 186–87, 310
environmental regulations, 273–74, *274*
equality, 3, 227–28, 249–50, 258, 275
    income inequality, 3, 42, 195, 310
    race and, 241–49, *242, 243, 244, 245, 247, 248*
    sexism, 192–93, *192,* 250–51
    see also LGBT issues
Esuf, Ilaf, 93
exclusion, 96–99, *97*
    see also loneliness
exercise, 84, 112, 300, 301
expectations, 94
extracurricular activities, 31, 32, 62

F

Facebook, 5, 54, 57, 78–80, 83, 101, 109, 294
fashion, 198–99
fault, for generational changes, 13–14
FBI, 150, 151, *151*
Feldman, Corey, 27
fights, physical, 149–50
Finer & Philbin, 225
Finkelhor, David, 41
First Amendment, 250–53
Flanagan, Caitlin, 254
FOMO (Fear of Missing Out), 97
Forbes, 183, 186
Ford, Tyler, 236
Foundation for Individual Rights in Education
    (FIRE), 252, *253*
Founders, 8
Fox, Claire, 153–54
Free-Range Kids (Skenazy), 166
Friedersdorf, Conor, 161
Fuller, Robert, 130

G

Gaines, Justice, 235–36
Gallop, Cindy, 213
Gallup Poll, *223,* 242, *276*
gaming, 58–59, 73, 189–90
gays and lesbians, *see* LGBT issues
gender discrimination and sexism, 192–93, *192,*
    250–51
gender roles, 235–40, *236, 237, 239,* 240
General Social Survey (GSS), 9, *121, 124, 127, 131,*
    134, 137, 272, 279
  on gender roles, *236, 237, 239, 240*
  on gun control, *272,* 273
  on LGBT issues, 229, *229, 230, 232*
  on politics, 261, *262,* 269
  on race, *247, 248*
  on sex, 205, *205, 207, 209*
generational changes, 13–15, 25
Generation Me (Twenge), 4, 5, 8, 13
Generation X, 3–5, 6, 7–9, 13, 149, 168, 196, 250, 273
  college as viewed by, 172–73
  gender roles and, 240
  homework and leisure time of, 31, 33
  individualism and, 94
  LGBT issues and, 229–30
  and marriage and raising a family, 220, 221, 224
  media and, 57, 60
  politics and, 264–65, 281, 283–84
  race and, 241
  religion and, 124, 132
  safety and, 28, 144, 164, 165
  sex and, 206–8
  social activity and, 70, 71, 74
  and speed of growing up, 28, 29, 40–41, 44
  work and, 182, 184, 186

Generation Y, 7
Generation Z, 7
Gillman, Howard, 253–54
Girls & Sex (Orenstein), 206, 210, 216
Go, Brian, 117
Goldstein, Richard, 152–53
government, 273–74, *274,* 278–81, *279, 280, 281*
  education and, 275–77, *276*
  environment and, 273–74, *274*
  see also politics
Great Recession of 2007–2009, 4, 20, 30, 105, 168,
    173, 174, 182, 188, 189, 191, 278, 307
Grootswagers, Lilian, 119
Guardian, 166
gun control, 266, *271, 272,* 273–75

H

Haddad, Fadi, 108–9
Haidt, Jonathan, 154, 162, 252
Haim, Corey, 27
Hakala, Kate, 218
happiness and unhappiness, 77–79, *78, 80, 84, 85,*
    87, 94–95, *95,* 292, 300–301
Harper's Bazaar, 199
Harvard Crimson, 251
Haslam, Nick, 306
health care, 273–75
Hebert, Reese, 298
Herbenick, Debby, 214
Hirsi Ali, Ayaan, 252
Hoe, Nina, 304
Holleran, Madison, 107
Homelanders, 7
home ownership, 197
homework, 31–33, 62, 111, 112, 116
homicide, 87, *88,* 150
honor, culture of, 159
Houseparty, 57, 295
Howard, Whitney, 110
Howe, Neil, 7
Huebner, Rachel, 251
Huffington Post, 66, 208, 210, 211
Hurst, Erik, 188, 189, 190

I

iGen, iGen'ers, 1–16, *6*
  birth year cutoffs for, 5–7
  data on, 8–13, 15
  demographics and, 10–12, 25
  as growing up slowly, 3, 17–47, 112–13, 144,
    159, 163–64, 204, 302–4
  as label, 7–8
  trends shaping, 3
  understanding and saving, 289–313
Ilardi, Stephen, 300
Impulse Society, The: America in the Age of Instant
    Gratification (Roberts), 57, 293
inadequacy, feelings of, 100–102, *101*

income inequality, 3, 42, 195, 310
independence, 112–13, 303
individualism, 2–3, 42, 94, 138, 139, 175–76, *176,*
        177, 200, 201, 204, 214, 216, 266, 275, 286
in-person social interaction, 3, 69–77, *72, 75,*
        80–81, 88–91, 98–99, 101, 104, 112, 116,
        118, 210, 219, 256, 293, 299–301
Instagram, 2, 50, 53–57, 106–7, 109, 146, 292, 297, 312
Internet, 2–5, 7, 12, 50–52, *51, 52,* 63, 68, 75–76, *75,*
        94, 169, 173, 290, 291, 297, 301
    civic engagement and, 175–77, *176, 177,* 286
    news on, 285, 308
    politics and, 286
    pornography on, 206, 212–14, 298, 303
    see also phones; social media
iPhone:
    introduction of, 2, 5
    see also phones
Irresistible (Alter), 292

J
James, Flannery, 215
Jenner, Caitlyn, 233–34, 236
Jennings, Jazz, 234
jobs, *see* work
Jobs, Steve, 292
Jones, Logan, 118
Joseph, Tyler, 113
Jungwirth, Briana, 225

K
Kelly-Woessner, April, 252
Kinnaman, David, 138–39, 140, 141
Kipnis, Laura, 156

L
Lagarde, Christine, 252
Lahren, Tomi, 275
Lapidos, Juliet, 5
latchkey kids, 28–29, *29*
Lean In (Sandberg), 193
Leddy, Kate, 300
Lee, Alexandra, 296
left out, feeling, 96–99, *97*
    see also loneliness
Lego Movie, The, 94
LGBT (lesbian, gay, bisexual, and transgender)
        issues, 227–35, *229, 230, 232,* 240, 249, 256
    bisexuality, 233
    religion and, 125–26, 129, 138–40, 142, 231,
        234–35
    safe spaces and, 154
    same-sex marriage, 129, 142, 227–32, 266,
        275, 286
    same-sex sexual experiences, 232–33, *232*
    transgender individuals, 125, 228, 233–35
libertarianism, 263, 266, 273–75, 278
License to Drive, 27

life goals, 167–68, *168*
life history theory, 24, 27, 42
life satisfaction, 95–96, *96*
life strategies, fast and slow, 24, 42
    see also developmental speed
Lindsay, Ronald, 142
Liveris, Anthony, 229
locus of control, 191–92, *191*
loneliness, 79–81, *81,* 83, 96–99, *97,* 102, 108, 112,
        208, 292, 302
Los Angeles Times, 207, 254
Lucas, Richard, III, 268
Lukianoff, Greg, 154, 162, 252
Lund, Cooper, 118
Luxenberg, Melyssa, 221
Lythcott-Haims, Julie, 47

M
magazines, 60–65, *61, 62,* 115, 307
Maher, Bill, 277
Maine, Bryce, 305
malls, 73–74, *73,* 75
Manning, Jason, 159–60
Marano, Hara Estroff, 166
marijuana, 147–49, *148, 149*
    legalization of, 39, 266, 269–71, *270, 271, 272,*
        273–74
marketing, 195–97, *197,* 200–201
marriage, 40, 41, 214, 218–22, *219, 220, 223, 224,*
        225, 226, 261
    age at, 23, 40, 203, 205–6, 211, 221–22
    having children, 3, 40, 41, 214, 218–20, *220,*
        223–26
    interracial, 246–47
    politics and, 267
    same-sex, 129, 142, 227–32, 266, 275, 286
    sex before, 130, 140–42, 205–6
Masback, Grace, 66
Massachusetts Daily Collegian, 286, 291, 300
material goods, *196, 197, 198,* 199–200, *199*
maturity fears, 45–46, 113
McGraw Hill Education, 307
media, 49–68, 292
    books, *see* books
    magazines, 60–65, *61, 62,* 115, 307
    television, 51, *51,* 66, *66,* 68, 112, 115, 169,
        285, 292
    see also Internet; social media
Mendes, Shawn, 156–57
mental health issues, 3, 81, 93–118, 293
    anxiety, 103, *104,* 105, 108, 111, 112, 116, 118,
        163, 167, 192, 257, 293, 300–302
    college students and, 103–4, *104, 105,* 117, 301,
        303–4
    depression, *see* depression
    feelings of inadequacy, 100–102, *101*
    happiness and unhappiness, 77–79, *78, 80,* 84,
        85, 87, 94–95, *95,* 292, 300–301

inadequate resources for, 117–18, 301
loneliness, 79–81, *81,* 83, 96–99, *97,* 102, 108,
    112, 208, 292, 302
rise in, 100, 111–13, 118
safe spaces and, 163
self-harm, 108–9, 302
sleep and, 116
social media and, 77–89, 106
suicide, *see* suicide
microaggressions, 161, 162, 256–58, 312
"Microaggressions and Changing Moral Cultures"
    (Campbell and Manning), 159–60
Millennials, 4–5, *6,* 7, 9, 13, 15, 39, 41, 57, 60,
    63, 95, 147, 157, 168, 169, 173, 196–97,
    200–201, 250, 273, 275, 281, 309
college as viewed by, 172–73
gender roles and, 240
individualism and, 94
LGBT issues and, 228–30
and marriage and raising a family, 220–24
politics and, 261, 262, 264, 277–79, 283, 287
race and, 241, 247–48
relationships and, 218, 219, 222
religion and, 120, 124–25, 127, 128, 130, 139,
    142
safety and, 145
sex and, 205–8, 210, 218, 224
social activity and, 71, 74
work and, 180–87, 193–95, 310
Molak, Cliff, 86–87
Molak, David, 86
money, 42, 112, 167–69, 200, 309
allowances, 34–35, *35*
financial success, 195–96, *196*
from teen jobs, 29–34, *30, 32, 35,* 39–40, *40,* 42
Monitoring the Future (MtF) surveys, 9, 118
on civic and caring attitudes, *174, 176, 177*
on depressive symptoms, 100, *101, 103, 106,*
    117
on drinking, *36, 38, 40, 147, 148*
on driving, *26, 40, 145*
on drug use, *39*
on environmental action, *274*
on gender discrimination, *192*
on gender roles in work, *236, 237, 239*
on going out on dates, *21, 40*
on going out to the movies, *67*
on going out without parents, *19*
on government, *279, 280, 281*
on happiness, 77, *78, 80,* 81–82, *81, 82, 95, 96*
on institutions, *279*
on locus of control, *191*
on loneliness, *97*
on marijuana, *148, 149, 270*
on marriage and family, *219, 220*
on material expectations and attitudes, *196,*
    197, 198, 199
on money, *35*

on new media and screen time, *51, 52,* 54, *54,*
    75, 78, 80, 81, 82
on parental supervision, *44*
on politics, *264, 265, 267, 282*
on race, *242, 243, 244, 245*
on reading, *61, 62*
on religion, *121, 123, 133,* 135–36, *135, 136*
on risk taking, *153*
on running away, *45*
on school, *170, 171*
on sleep, *114, 115, 117*
on socializing, *70, 72, 75*
on social problems, *281*
on spending time at home alone, *29*
on television, *66*
on work, *30, 32, 40, 181, 183, 184, 187, 194*
movies, going out to, 67–68, *67,* 74, 75
MTV, 8, 209, 248, 256, 258
Musgraves, Kacey, 228, 271
MySpace, 54

N

narcissism, 94, 169, 310
National Crime Victimization Survey (NCVS),
    151, *151*
National Geographic, 234
National Survey on Drug Use and Health
    (NSDUH), 108, *109*
Nation of Wimps, A (Marano), 166
Nazarian, Grace, 96
Netflix, 67, 71
news, 284–86, 308
newspapers, 60, 61, *62,* 63, 64, 68
New York Times, 5, 74, 123, 159, 162, 167, 241, 292
nightclubs and bars, 74
Nilles, Melissa, 293–94
Noah, Trevor, 246
NPR, 62, 124
nude photos, 292, 297–98, 303

O

Obama, Barack, 122, 252, 263, 268
Obama, Malia, 304
Ojiaku, Princess, 256–57
O'Neill, Essena, 106–7
Onyejiaka, Tiffany, 268–69
Orenstein, Peggy, 206, 210, 216
O'Shea, Joe, 304

P

Pandit, Vivek, 311
parents:
    fighting with, 44
    going out with or without, 18–20, *19,* 72
    living with, 222
    supervision by, 43–44, *44,* 47, 112–13, 144,
        164–66
parties, 69–71, *70, 75*

Patterson, Noah, 212
People, 87, 225
Pepin, Joanna, 238
Pew Research Center, 57, 60, 120, 142, 250, 269,
　　270–71, 273
phones, 1–7, 12, 13, 15, 49–53, 72–74, 76, 289–94,
　　301
　　catching fire, 49
　　depression and, 100, 101, 104, 105, *106,* 111,
　　　　118, 291–92
　　flip, 291
　　life hacks for, 294–97
　　loneliness and, 98–99
　　not getting replies on, 105–6, 217
　　sleep and, 49–50, 113–16, 295, 297
　　texting on, 50–53, *51, 52,* 64, 69, 76–77, 89,
　　　　293, 294, 311–12
　　see also social media
Piper, Everett, 157–58
Politico Magazine, 154
politics, 3, 259–87, *262, 264, 265, 267, 282, 284*
　　college and, 267–68
　　Internet and, 286
　　libertarianism, 263, 266, 273–75, 278
　　marriage and, 267
　　moderates and, 266
　　presidential election of 2016, 259–61, 268, 279
　　racial issues and, 268–69
　　socialism, 277–78
　　voting, 283–84, *284*
pornography, 206, 212–14, 298, 303
pregnancy, 22–23, *23,* 41, 209, 210
　　abortion and, 271–73, *271, 272,* 275
　　see also birthrates
Psychology Today, 166
PTSD, 163

R

race, 241–49, *242, 243, 244, 245, 247, 248,* 255–56,
　　258
　　affirmative action and, 248–49
　　marriage and, 246–47
　　politics and, 268–69
　　religion and, 132–37, *133, 134*
　　speech restrictions and, 250–517
rape, 150–52, *151*
reading, 59–65, 115, 307–8, 312
Reagan, Nancy, 269
Reagan, Ronald, 264–65, 267, 277
Real Time, 277
recession of 2007–2009, *see* Great Recession of
　　2007–2009
rejection, 89
relationships, 3, 144, 203–4, 207–8, 211, 214–18,
　　224–26, 238, 302
　　cheating in, 215
　　dating, 20–22, *21,* 24, 39–41, *40,* 74, 204, 206,
　　　　218

emotional attachment in, 216–17
　　ending, 217–18
　　live-in, 222, *223*
　　marriage, *see* marriage
　　safety and, 204, 216
　　sex and, *see* sex
religion, 3, 8, 119–42, 261
　　affiliation with and public participation in,
　　　　120–25, *121, 122, 123, 124, 133,* 135–36,
　　　　135, 136, 138
　　future of, 141–42
　　individualism and, 138, 139
　　LGBT issues and, 125–26, 129, 138–40, 142,
　　　　231, 234–35
　　polarization by race, socioeconomic status, and
　　　　region, 132–37, *133, 134, 135, 136, 137*
　　private beliefs and, 126–29, *127*
　　reasons for decline in, 137–41
　　science and, 139
　　sexuality and, 138–41
　　spirituality and, 130–32, *131*
responsibility, 33, 41–42, 47, 302
Rice, Condoleezza, 252
risk taking, 146, 149, 152–53, *153,* 187
　　see also safety
Roberts, John, 251
Roberts, Paul, 57, 293
Rock, Chris, 254
Romney, Mitt, 286
Rosin, Hanna, 164, 165–66
running away, 44, *45*

S

safety, 3, 143–67, 177, 201, 253, 266, 304–6, 311
　　drinking and, 143–44, 146, *147, 148,* 149
　　driving and, 144–46, *145,* 149, 165, 198
　　emotional, 144, 153, 156, 157, 173, 253, 305–6
　　fighting and, 149–50
　　parental supervision and, 28, 144, 164–66
　　relationships and, 204, 216
　　risk taking and, 146, 149, 152–53, *153,* 187
　　safe spaces and, 47, 153–64, 173, 249–58
　　sex and, 208–10
　　sexual assault and, 150–52, *151,* 209–10, 302
　　sports and games and, 164
　　upsides and downsides of protection, 165–67
Said, Edward, 156
Saint-Fort, Yvanna, 248
Sales, Nancy Jo, 56, 291
Sandberg, Sheryl, 193
Sanders, Bernie, 260, 261, 263, 276–77, 283, 286
SAT scores, 63, *64*
Sawyer, Diane, 236
Schlosser, Edward, 156
school:
　　academic pressure and, 111
　　attitudes toward, 169–73, *170, 171, 172*
　　college, *see* college, college students

homework, 31–33, 62, 111, 112, 116
   SAT scores, 63, *64*
   technology in, 170–71
science, 139
SDSU (San Diego State University), 33, 70, 90, 155, 161–62, 185, 254–55, 257, 285
self-harm, 108–9, 302
selfies, 106–7, 215
   nude, 292, 297–98, 303
sex, 3, 22–23, *22,* 25, 39–41, 144, 203–18, *205, 207, 209,* 224, 226, 292, 297, 302–3
   birth control and, 210
   bisexuality, 233
   double standards and, 107
   drinking and, 216
   hookup culture and, 204, 208, 210–11, 213–14, 216–18
   LGBT issues and, *see* LGBT issues
   nude photos, 292, 297–98, 303
   oral, 206
   pornography, 206, 212–14, 298, 303
   pregnancy and, *see* pregnancy
   premarital, 130, 140–42, 205–6
   religion and, 138–41
   safety and, 208–10
   same-sex experiences, 232–33, *232*
   sexting, 210
sexism, 192–93, *192,* 250–51
sexual assault, 150–52, *151,* 193, 209–10, 255, 302
sexual harassment, 251–52
sexually transmitted diseases (STDs), 206, 209
Sheller, Brian, 123
shopping, 195–201
shopping malls, 73–74, *73,* 75
Shulevitz, Judith, 162
Sicking, Josephine, 262–63
Silent generation, 229, 240, 250, 262
16 and Pregnant, 209
Skenazy, Lenore, 166
slactivism, 175
sleep, 33, 51, 113–16, *114, 115*
   consequences of lack of, 116
   depression and, 116, *117,* 118
   phones and, 49–50, 113–16, 295, 297
slut shaming, 107
smartphones, *see* phones
Smith, Christian, 131, 138
Smith, Jaden, 235
Snapchat, 1–2, 50, 53, 56–60, 71, 295, 297, 298, 312
socialism, 277–78
socializing in person, *see* in-person social interaction
social media, 5, 49–50, *52,* 53–59, *54,* 71, 73, 76–77, 292–97
   bullying on, 79, 85–88, *86,* 99, 305–6
   causes and, 175–77, *176, 177*
   depression and, 100, 101, 104, 105, *106,* 111, 118, 291–92

   drinking and, 146
   Facebook, 5, 54, 57, 78–80, 83, 101, 109, 294
   and feelings of inadequacy, 101
   happiness and, 77–79, *78, 80,* 84, *85,* 87, 94, 292, 300–301
   Instagram, 2, 50, 53–57, 106–7, 109, 146, 292, 297, 312
   loneliness and, 98–99
   mental health and, 77–89, 106
   not getting responses to messages on, 105–6
   sex and, 215
   sleep and, 113–16
   Snapchat, 1–2, 50, 53, 56–60, 71, 295, 297, 298, 312
   see also phones
social problems and civic engagement, 173–77, *174, 176, 177,* 281–82, *281,* 286
social rejection, 89
social skills, 90–91, 218
socioeconomic status (SES), 134
Soul Searching (Smith), 138
South Park, 154
Sparks & Honey, 186
speech restrictions, 249–58, *250, 253*
Spiritual But Not Religious (Fuller), 130
spirituality, 130–32, *131*
   see also religion
standard of living, 195–96, *196*
Stojic, Sofia, 89–90
Strauss, William, 7
suicide, 3, 83–88, *84, 85, 86, 88,* 107–8, 110, 111, *111,* 117, 167, 292, 293, 302
   in girls vs. boys, 110, *111*
   sleep and, 116, 117
Sydnor, Jamahri, 62–63

T
Taveroff, Leigh, 203, 214
television, 51, *51, 66, 66,* 68, 112, 115, 169, 285, 292
texting, 50–53, *51, 52,* 64, 69, 76–77, 89, 293, 294, 311–12
Time, 103, 108, 173, 212, 262
time-period differences, 15
Tinder, 204, 206, 210
Today, 96
Today's Lifestyle, 203
Tomlinson, Louis, 224–25
transgender individuals, 125, 228, 233–35
   see also LGBT issues
trauma, use of word, 306
trigger warnings, 47, 162–63, 255
Trump, Donald, 161, 175, 259–61, 263, 266, 268, 280, 286, 306
Tuffile, Fred, 186
Tumblr, 102
Twain, Mark, 156
Twenty One Pilots, 113
Twitter, 53, 65–66

U

UnChristian (Kinnaman), 140
USA Today, 7, 261

V

Vanity Fair, 204, 211, 236
VanLandingham, Hannah, 155
victimhood culture, 159, 257, 306
video chat, 51, *51*
video games, 58–59, 73, 189–90
videos, 65–68
volunteering, 31, 32

W

Wade, Lisa, 211, 213, 216, 217
Wall Street Journal, 119, 186
Walman, Rachel, 291
Ward, Seth, 276
Washington Post, 41, 55–56, 210, 211, 212, 261, 296
We Are Generation Z (Pandit), 311
Whitlock, Janis, 102
Williams, Jess, 41
Wilmore, Larry, 161
work, 3, 8, 169, 179–95, 302, 309
    attitudes toward, 182–83, *183*
    barriers to, 192–93
    career, 40, 41, 167, 172–73, 180, 310
    employment rates, 188–90, *189*
    entrepreneurship, 186–87, 310
    expectations for, 193–95, *194*
    hiring iGen'ers, 309–12
    sexism and, 192–93, *192*
    social aspects of, 182
    teen jobs, 29–34, *30, 32, 35,* 39–40, *40,* 42, 112, 116, 303
    unemployment, 105, *106,* 188
    work ethic, 183–85, *184,* 310
working mothers, *236,* 237–40, *237*

Y

Yates, Bill, 20
You Lost Me: Why Young Christians Are Leaving Church . . . and Rethinking Faith (Kinnaman), 138–39
Youth Risk Behavior Surveillance System (YRBSS), 9, *22,* 37, 83, *84, 85, 86,* 99, *114, 115, 117,* 150, *150,* 210
YouTube, 65, 106

Z

Zeitz, Josh, 154

About the Author

Jean M. Twenge, professor of psychology at San Diego State University, is the author of more than 120 scientific publications, the books *Generation Me: Why Today's Young Americans Are More Confident, Assertive, Entitled—and More Miserable than Ever Before*, *The Narcissism Epidemic: Living in the Age of Entitlement* (coauthored with W. Keith Campbell), *The Impatient Woman's Guide to Getting Pregnant*, and the textbooks *Social Psychology* (coauthored with David G. Myers) and *Personality Psychology: Understanding Yourself and Others* (coauthored with W. Keith Campbell). Her research has been covered in *Time*, *Newsweek*, the *New York Times*, *USA Today*, *U.S. News & World Report*, and the *Washington Post*, and she has been featured on *Today*, *Good Morning America*, *CBS This Morning*, *Fox & Friends*, *NBC Nightly News*, *Dateline NBC*, and National Public Radio. She holds a BA and MA from the University of Chicago and a PhD from the University of Michigan. She lives in San Diego, California, with her husband and three daughters.